Saving
Gracie

Saving Gracie

how one dog escaped
the shadowy world of
american puppy mills

Carol Bradley

Wiley Publishing, Inc.

Copyright © 2010, 2011 by Carol Bradley. All rights reserved.

Howell Book House

Published by Wiley Publishing, Inc., Hoboken, New Jersey

Credits appear on page 233 and constitute an extension of the copyright page.

For general information on our other products and services or to obtain technical support please contact our Customer Care Department within the U.S. at (877) 762-2974, outside the U.S. at (317) 572-3993 or fax (317) 572-4002.

Wiley also publishes its books in a variety of electronic formats. Some content that appears in print may not be available in electronic books. For more information about Wiley products, please visit our web site at www.wiley.com.

Library of Congress Cataloging-in-Publication Data

Bradley, Carol, date.
   Saving Gracie : how one dog escaped the shadowy world of American puppy mills / Carol Bradley. — 1st ed.
     p. cm.
   Includes bibliographical references and index.
   ISBN 978-0-470-44758-1 (cloth : alk. paper); ISBN 978-1-118-01227-7 (paper : alk. paper); ISBN 978-0-470-63397-7 (ebk.); ISBN 978-1-118-01935-1 (ebk.); ISBN 978-1-118-01985-6 (ebk.)
   1. Cavalier King Charles spaniel—Pennsylvania—Chester County—Anecdotes. 2. Animal welfare—Pennsylvania—Chester County. 3. Animal rights—Pennsylvania—Chester County. I. Title.
   SF429.C36B73 2010
   636.7'08320974813—dc22
                                   2010002932

Printed in the United States of America

First Edition

10 9 8 7 6 5 4 3 2 1

Edited by Beth Adelman

Book design by Lissa Auciello-Brogan

Book production by Wiley Publishing, Inc. Composition Services

For Steve
and for Gracie, who finally got the life
she deserved.

Contents

Preface   ix

1   Caged for Life   1

2   "Check Out That Place"   7

3   A Breeder's Rise and Fall   14

4   Orchestrating the Raid   25

5   Filth and Fear   37

6   Sorting the Dogs   46

7   A Safe Place for Dog 132   54

8   The Case Goes to Court   68

9   Proving Cruelty   80

10   The Breeder Appeals   92

11   The Soft, Cool Feel of Grass   99

12   Deciding on a Dog   105

13   Overwhelmed   115

14 Too Scared to Play   120

15 Learning to Trust   129

16 Tackling the Puppy Mills   145

17 A Bond Develops   162

18 The Crackdown Begins   172

19 Elsewhere, Suffering   188

20 Two Lives Changed   206

    Epilogue   216

Acknowledgments   221

Appendix: Finding the Right Dog   225

Notes   231

Photo Credits   233

Index   235

Preface

The north side of Great Falls, Montana, where I live, is ideal for dog-walking. Craftsman bungalows and 1940s-era houses line the residential streets, and the sidewalks are shaded by towering ash and elm trees. I head out each morning with Chachi, my Husky-Golden mix; my Border Collie, Jillie; and a pocketful of treats to dole out to canine friends along the way. Among the dogs we stop to visit are Bear, a shaggy German Shepherd with kind blue eyes; Jocko, a red-haired mutt who waits eagerly for his prize; and Cody, an Akita whose enormous nose peeks out from under a vinyl fence, quietly passing the time until a biscuit skitters her way.

Every now and then, on a less familiar block, I stumble across a dog confined to a small run, excrement piling up inside, obviously ignored by its family. These animals usually sit too far back from the street to toss a treat to—they would set off an alarming racket if I tried—yet I can see the yearning in their eyes as my own dogs trot by. The sight of a lonely, cooped-up dog is distressing. But then I remind myself that even these dogs live like kings compared to dogs confined in puppy mills.

It's one of America's most shameful secrets: the hidden world of substandard kennels, where dogs are caged like chickens and forced to produce puppies over and over, until they can produce no more. For all the attention we bestow upon man's best friend, all the designer collars we fasten around their necks, the doggy day care programs we enroll them in, and the organic wheat-free premium biscuits we feed them, you'd think we would be more curious about where dogs come from—that we'd be more knowledgeable about the bad breeders in our midst and more willing to blow the whistle on them.

In fact, many people are incensed. Do an Internet search on the phrase "puppy mills" and up pop 1.5 million results. Despite the plethora of information, I am continually surprised at how many of my friends and acquaintances haven't a clue that hundreds of thousands of companion animals in this country are living out their lives in barbaric conditions.

I didn't know puppy mills existed either until the fall of 2002, when Collie breeder Athena Lethcoe-Harman and her husband, Jon, tried to relocate their kennel from Alaska to Arizona. To make the 2,240-mile journey, the couple crammed 180 Collies into a tractor trailer, in cages stacked three high, and hit the road without stopping for food or water. By the time their rig crossed into Montana from Canada late on Halloween night, the dogs were wet, shivering, hungry, and yelping loudly enough to alert the customs inspector. He, in turn, contacted law enforcers for rural Toole County. Sheriff Donna Matoon could have taken the easy way out and let the Harmans pass through. Instead, she did the right thing: She ordered a deputy to arrest the couple and charge them with multiple counts of animal cruelty.

The case dragged on for nine months. For much of that time, residents of Shelby, Montana, were left to care for the dogs. They housed them in a barn at the local fairgrounds and devised a complicated schedule for feeding them, walking them, and working to dismantle their fear of human beings. As autumn turned to winter and then to spring, the workload required to operate "Camp Collie" was nothing short of staggering.

It took two trials to convict the Harmans and free the dogs up for adoption. Before the trials were over, dozens of animal lovers from Florida to California flew in to donate their time on the Collies' behalf. When Shelby-area residents became overwhelmed with the task, the dogs were moved to Great Falls, where another army of generous souls stepped forward to do their part.

I covered the case for the *Great Falls Tribune*, and it opened my eyes to the widespread existence of puppy mills and to the cost, both in real dollars and in human effort, required to salvage their victims. Years later, I still see survivors of Camp Collie around town. Adopted by loving families, most of these beautiful dogs have overcome their past abuse, but some never will forget. They are so scarred by their experience that they still hide in a corner or flinch at the sight of a belt.

I began to track puppy mill busts in other communities across the United States, places where animal shelters and volunteers suddenly find themselves caring for 50, 100, 300 dogs. The problem, I realized, was immense—a national disgrace. That's when the idea for this book began to take shape.

Pennsylvania isn't the worst puppy mill state, but it is home to a large number of dog breeders as well as a cluster of activists—veteran investigator Bob Baker, consumer advocate Libby Williams, vocal opponent Bill Smith, and even Governor Ed Rendell among them—who are determined to clamp down on the bad operators. The influences at work there created a perfect storm of events needed to tell this story.

It is in Pennsylvania, too, that I found Gracie, a Cavalier King Charles Spaniel whose breed was developed to be companion dogs but who instead seemed destined to spend her life in a cage. *Saving Gracie* traces this resilient dog's journey out of a puppy mill and tells the stories of the people who helped her along the way: from Cheryl Shaw, the humane society police officer who raided her kennel; to Lori Finnegan, the prosecutor who took Gracie's breeder to court; to Pam Bair, who cared for Gracie in a shelter; and finally to Linda Jackson, the woman who gave Gracie a permanent home. How Linda saved Gracie and Gracie, in turn, unlocked Linda's heart is a story that is replayed thousands of times over in this country each year as families rescue puppy mill survivors, realize for themselves the awful truth about the dark side of dog breeding, and begin spreading the word, one person at a time, that recklessly run kennels need to be shuttered for good.

1

Caged for Life

THE PUPPY BEGAN LIFE blind, deaf, and quivering with energy. The warm, pulsating shapes of her littermates surrounded her, and with every breath she inhaled the sweet scent of her mother's milk. The fragrance of the milk was overpowering. The puppy pushed her way toward the mother dog's belly, nuzzled against it, suckled until she was full, and then slept.

For this Cavalier King Charles Spaniel, the earliest chapter of life unfolded much the way it does for all puppies. Ninety percent of the day she slumbered; she nursed the other 10 percent. Satiating her hunger was foremost on her mind. Eyes shut, she squirmed under and around the other puppies to latch hold of a swollen nipple. She wedged as close to her mother as she could, dropping back only when a heavier puppy nudged her out of the way.

Two weeks of nursing and sleeping, and then one day her eyes opened. She could see—blurrily at first, faint blobs of light and then distinct shapes. In the darkened room she could make out her mother's pink stomach, puffed out with sustenance. She could see her peach-fuzzed littermates lined up beside her. She could detect the crisscross pattern of the metal cage she was housed in. And on the other side of the wire, she could glimpse the silhouettes of the people who came and went.

Once or twice a day, without warning, the door to the room swung open, the lights were flipped on, and the large shapes appeared. The people shuffled about silently. Hands reached into the crates to set down a pan of water or pour some food, then the people moved on.

At three weeks of age the puppy's ears began working, and suddenly her universe reverberated with noise. When the lights were on she could see rows of cages filled with dogs who yelped frantically whenever the big door opened and the people stepped inside. The dogs slammed against the cages hungrily, only to shrink back when footsteps neared. The clamor lasted as long as the people made their rounds. When the voices and the footsteps were gone, darkness filled the room and the barking subsided. Once again it was quiet enough for the puppy to hear the squirming grunts of her littermates and the comforting sound of her mother's rough tongue licking her coat.

In a loving environment, the black-and-white dog with the feathery ears would just be starting to sample life's mysteries. At two and a half weeks she would have been walking. At three weeks she would have learned to run. Loping, trotting, sprinting, she would have spent her days discovering the soft feel of carpet, the firmness of sidewalk, the coolness of grass. The people in her life would have held and played with her, dangled toys in front of her, and encouraged her to explore.

By week four the Cavalier would have begun eating food. She would be wagging her tail, baring her teeth, biting, growling, barking, and chasing. By week five she would be playing with the rest of her litter as a group. By week seven her sense of curiosity would be insatiable. She would be eager—no, anxious—to investigate everything she could see, taste, or smell. By week eight she would begin to respond to her name.

But this was not a loving home. There would be no running for this dog, no joyful discoveries, no toys. The Cavalier was born into a large-scale and shoddily run commercial kennel—a puppy mill. She shared a crate with her mother and the rest of the pups in her litter, but there was no room to frolic; there was barely any room to walk. The darkness of the room left little to see. She smelled plenty of scents, but they were disagreeable odors: the stench of feces, the caustic vapors of urine. Her eyes stung from the fumes.

No dog born into a puppy mill is lucky, but if fortune had shone on this Cavalier, she would have escaped the wretchedness. In a matter of weeks, the breeder might have sold her to a distributor for anywhere from $100 to $200. She would then be loaded onto a truck and shipped hundreds of miles away to the distributor's own facility, where she would be held for forty-eight hours, bathed, and given her "puppy shots." Next, she would be crated up and trucked again, this time to a pet store, which would pay the distributor anywhere from $200 to $300. Store employees would give her another quick bath, inject her with a new round of vaccinations, and offer her for sale. After a few days, maybe weeks in a pet store cage, she would be sold for $1,600 or more, the going rate for Cavaliers. In the fickle dog industry, Cavaliers were currently a popular breed.

The journey would not be pleasant. On the contrary, it would be fraught with risks. Had she been sold this way, the Cavalier likely would have been weaned early—a stressful occurrence that could instill in her a permanent sense of fearfulness and insecurity, made worse after being transported in a dark vehicle crammed with other unfamiliar dogs. The round of shots could overwhelm her immune system, exposing her to the very diseases the vaccines were supposed to prevent. The trip to the pet store might subject her to any number of illnesses—from kennel cough to diarrhea to intestinal parasites, eye and ear infections, even mange. That was scenario one.

In scenario two, the Cavalier might be sold directly over the Internet. That would be the most lucrative route for the breeder—no distributors and pet store owners looking for their own markup on the pup's price. If her new owners weren't able to pick her up at the kennel themselves, she would be flown to them in a crate. Her family would have no inkling of the conditions she was born into and no opportunity to meet the puppy's mother. By purchasing her, her family would be investing in a product of unsound breeding practices that increase the likelihood she would be predisposed to heart problems, neurological disease, hip and kneecap abnormalities, cataracts, and a host of other hereditary problems. The Cavalier's new owners might be willing to spend hundreds, possibly thousands of dollars to make her well. She might or might not overcome her lack of socialization, but at least she would have the chance to lead a happy, though compromised, life.

The worst fate of all was scenario three: to be kept behind, turned into breeding stock, forced to produce litter after litter and doomed to confinement for the rest of her life. If that were to happen, the Cavalier could look forward to a diet of substandard food and stagnant water. She would become covered in her own excrement, causing her skin to itch and her eyes to sting. The wire bottoms of her crate would produce sores on the bottoms of her paws, and her toenails might grow so long that she would have difficulty standing. There would be little to no veterinary care and almost no social interaction, and the psychological damage could be substantial. The little dog would learn to trust no one and nothing. She would live out her life in a state of uncertainty, fear, and tedium. The lack of socialization—no toys, no blankets, and little if any interaction with humans—could drive her insane: Like many puppy

mill dogs, she might begin to circle her cage endlessly and obses-
sively to stave off boredom.

Becoming a breeding dog in a puppy mill would subject this
Cavalier to the most brutally mundane life imaginable, a life far
worse than other victims of factory farming are forced to tolerate.
Veal calves are confined to wooden crates so small they can't turn
around, but they are slaughtered—spared further agony—at eighteen to twenty weeks. Pigs live in overcrowded concrete pens,
breathing dusty, noxious air, until they balloon up to 250 pounds;
but after six months, their brutal lives are ended. Chickens are
crammed four to a cage, beaks clipped, for just six weeks before they
are killed. But breeding dogs in puppy mills languish five to ten
years or more in a cage before they are finally put out of their misery. Even death, when it mercifully comes, can be painful. The last
thing many worn out, vacant-eyed puppy mill dogs experience is a
bullet to the head.

What would become of this Cavalier puppy? She had an eye-
catching coat—swaths of black hair sliced through with splashes of
white on her legs and chest. Her front left leg was distinguished by a
striking black mark, an inch-long checkmark swoosh. And she possessed the soulful brown eyes Cavaliers were known for. She was a
beauty, and that was a bad thing; it meant the breeder would keep
his eye on her. In time, he knew, her coat would grow long and silky,
with tiny feathers of hair adorning her front legs. And the appealing
roundness of her head and face could yield promising offspring.

He'd keep this one, the breeder decided. Turn her into a breeding machine. She would live out her days in his overheated kennel,
in the same cage where she had been born. The other puppies in
her litter would be shipped out in another couple of weeks, but this
dog would stay behind, forced to reproduce until she was worn out.

She would deliver her first litter while she was still a puppy herself, then every six months after that. With each new litter, she

would need to provide near-constant care: stimulating the puppies' bottoms when they were too young to eliminate on their own, nursing them, providing emotional stability as her offspring began to feel their way. But as her delivery dates grew near, there was no calm and quiet place to retreat to, no blanket in a whelping box to help her feel safe and secure. If she were to die while giving birth, it would be written off as the cost of doing business. As the saying goes, "With livestock comes deadstock."

The Cavalier would never get to experience the companionship she was bred to provide. She would learn quickly that each new day wasn't something to savor, but something to endure.

2

"Check Out That Place"

I T STARTED WITH a tip. On the afternoon of February 6, 2006, a
woman phoned the Chester County Society for the Prevention of
Cruelty to Animals (SPCA) in Pennsylvania to report problems at a
kennel in Lower Oxford, a small community twenty-three miles
away. She had visited the kennel in hopes of buying a puppy, the
caller said. To her horror, the breeder had emerged with a young
dog covered in dried feces and stale urine. The puppy reeked, and
the breeder didn't even seem to notice.

Something about the kennel wasn't right, the woman said. It
was unsanitary and smelled atrocious. In a back room, she could
hear lots of dogs barking. She declined the puppy, made some
excuses, drove away, and promptly phoned the SPCA. "You guys
need to check out that place," she told the receptionist. If the breeder tried to sell her a filthy puppy, there was no telling what shape the
rest of his dogs were in.

The caller didn't leave her name, but she did have the name of the kennel: Mike-Mar. The name of the breeder was Michael Wolf.

The SPCA assigned the case to Cheryl Shaw, one of its humane society police officers. Shaw had inspected the kennel once, years ago, and hadn't found anything. But this complaint definitely needed to be pursued.

She discussed the case with her supervisor, Becky Turnbull, and then phoned the state dog warden for Chester County, Maureen Siddons. Siddons agreed to accompany Shaw on an unannounced visit to Wolf's compound.

Mike-Mar Kennel was located at 1746 Baltimore Pike, in a dip off a two-lane highway between Lincoln University and the Strike 'N Spare bowling alley. The property was protected by a row of bushes and trees so thick that the driveway was nearly invisible. Anyone who wasn't looking for it carefully might miss it entirely. A breeding operation with lots of dogs to sell presumably would want to call attention to its wares, but there was no sign advertising Mike-Mar—no indication that beyond the foliage was a flourishing business.

Past the shrubbery, the driveway widened into the shape of an L, an area big enough to accommodate several vehicles. On the afternoon of February 8, Shaw and Siddons pulled in, parked their car and immediately saw Wolf on the porch of a house on the right side of the property. They were curious to see how he would react to their arrival. Wolf wasn't required to allow Siddons onto his property without a warrant. Since he was no longer licensed by the state to breed dogs, he could argue that there was no kennel to inspect. He could have told both women to take a hike, and they would have had no choice but to do so.

Instead, Wolf came forward and, to their surprise, greeted them cordially. When Siddons explained why they were there—"We want to see the dogs," she told him—he agreed to let them in.

Wolf knew Siddons. She'd inspected his kennel many times before. If he recognized Shaw, he didn't say so. But nothing about her seemed threatening. The brown-haired mother of two had a self-effacing, easygoing manner about her.

Right away, Wolf acted sheepish. He knew he had too many dogs, he said. He asked Shaw and Siddons to wait a moment and then he stepped inside the kennel.

Outside in the cold, Shaw stood with a clipboard in one hand and the other hand plunged inside a pocket of her fleece-lined jacket. She glanced about. In the middle of the property, several dozen yards to the rear of Wolf's house, was the kennel building. To the left of it sat a modular structure that appeared to be a second home. It had decks on the front and back. All three buildings were surrounded by a solidly built wooden fence, inside of which Shaw could see dogs trotting about. More dogs were in the side yard. Still more paced about in front of the modular home.

Minutes later, Wolf reappeared. He invited the inspectors inside the kennel. Shaw and Siddons stepped from bright sunlight into a dimly lit front room that smelled rank and felt like a furnace. The

Michael Wolf, in the center with a pole in his hand, makes his way across a deck covered with feces as a couple dozen of his dogs mill about.

Cavalier King Charles Spaniels stared silently
from inside filthy crates at Michael Wolf's kennel
in southeastern Pennsylvania.

temperature outside was 33 degrees Fahrenheit, but inside it had to
be 80 degrees, Shaw thought.

Squinting her eyes, she could make out cages lining the walls in
two rooms. The crates were stacked atop one another, three and
four rows high, and they were full of dogs. Feces and urine littered
the sides of the cages as well as the floor, and soiled newspaper overflowed from industrial-size garbage cans. Shaw could distinguish
Havanese, English Bulldogs, and Cavalier King Charles Spaniels,
dozens of them, crammed five and six to a crate the size of a large
television set. She was horrified, but kept her mouth shut.

From there, Wolf led the officers to his residence. There, too,
crates stacked with dogs lined the perimeter of what should have
been the living room, dining room, and kitchen. In one corner was
a playpen filled with puppies.

The noise was deafening. Dogs barked constantly—hoarse,
raspy yelps. Excited by the visitors, the animals rushed to the front
of their cages, only to cringe with anxiety as Shaw and Siddons
approached. "Hi, puppy puppy puppy," Shaw called out, but she
was standing too close. The dogs refused to come forward. The very
presence of human beings unnerved them.

As bad as the noise was, the smell was worse. It was a festering odor, a bottomless stink that permeated the inspectors' clothes and hair and stung their eyes. Wolf seemed oblivious to it. He walked the inspectors through the rooms, with Siddons following behind him and Shaw bringing up the rear. She couldn't believe what she was seeing. The cages were lined with paper soggy with waste, and they were so cramped the dogs barely had room to turn around. Bowls of food sat in one corner alongside slimy water bowls, many of which were empty. The animals' coats were stained with excrement.

Shaw had spent years doing criminal welfare work on behalf of animals. She thought she'd encountered every possible form of abuse. But she'd never seen this many suffering dogs in one place.

She peered inside the crates. Dozens of frightened eyes stared back. "I can't leave these guys here," she blurted out. Wolf was only a few feet ahead of her, but if he heard her, he didn't act like it. Minutes later, Shaw pulled out her camera and announced, "I'm taking pictures." Wolf turned to her and wanted to know why. She told him she needed to document the rooms for her report. To her surprise, he didn't try to stop her.

While Shaw snapped photos, Siddons went from room to room counting the dogs out loud and jotting down a tally. Adding together the number of dogs she saw outside with the puppies in the playpen and the dozens and dozens of dogs confined to crates, she came up with 136 dogs in all. "That's it," Wolf agreed. He knew he was over the limit, he said, but he loved his dogs too much. He had such a hard time letting go of his older breeding dogs that he'd finally stopped trying. He just kept them.

"You've got to lower your numbers," Siddons told him. Wolf didn't argue. The dogs needed to be groomed, Shaw added. "We can do that," Wolf replied. He showed the women how he would sit on his couch with the dogs and clip their nails.

In the warning she wrote up, Shaw focused on the lack of vaccinations: Wolf was unable to produce paperwork proving the dogs had had their shots. The squalid conditions were more disturbing, but Shaw played down her concern. The last thing she needed was for Wolf to panic and take matters into his own hands once she and Siddons left.

Wolf agreed to set up an appointment with his veterinarian, Tom Stevenson, who operated the Twin Valley Veterinary Clinic in Honey Brook, Pennsylvania. Stevenson's name sounded familiar: Among local animal welfare advocates, he was infamous for being the veterinarian on record for some of the largest puppy mills in the state.

Before leaving, the inspectors got a glimpse of Wolf's two partners. Gordon Trottier, a menacing-looking man with an unkempt beard, appeared briefly during the tour and then left just as quickly. Wolf's other partner, Margaret Hills, a woman in her sixties, was in the kennel building, removing soiled newspaper and putting new paper down. At one point Shaw also spied a young boy she later learned was one of Wolf's sons.

The visit lasted two and a half hours and ended on friendly enough terms. Just before the officers left, Wolf even turned over to them an English Bulldog who was visibly ill. The women crated the dog, put him in the back of the van, said goodbye, and pulled out onto the highway.

Shaw tried to act calm, but her pulse was racing.

She hadn't started out to be a humane society police officer. She'd studied graphic design, but abandoned that idea and instead she underwent officer training in the early 1990s. For several years she worked at an animal shelter in Montgomery County. After that, she juggled a couple of part-time jobs. But she missed helping needy dogs and cats. Animal work was what she'd been put on Earth to do, apparently—she couldn't imagine doing anything else.

So she'd started over, this time one county to the south. In the beginning, she commuted thirty miles from her home in Schwenksville to West Chester on Sundays to handle stray animals. Eventually, she got promoted to humane society investigations officer. Now 35, she had worked for the SPCA for six years. Her days were filled with grim cases of abuse and neglect—everything from starving and mistreated dogs to cat hoarders to victims of ritual sacrifice. Despite the grim nature of her work, she savored every aspect of it, the happy endings most of all—the days when she could rescue dogs and cats who were helpless to save themselves. The good outweighed the bad. She honestly believed that.

Now, though, she was driving away from the largest case of animal cruelty she'd ever witnessed. If these dogs were to have any chance at better lives, she needed to act fast.

She and Siddons were barely out of the driveway when Shaw pulled out her cell phone and called her supervisor, Turnbull. Quickly, she described the rancid, unhealthy conditions she and Siddons had observed. Filthy dogs were crammed into tiny crates, so many they were hard to count. There was no question what had to be done, as far as Shaw was concerned.

"We can't leave these guys there," she told Turnbull over the phone. She turned to Siddons and asked, "Do you agree with that?"

Yes, Siddons replied, she did.

3

A Breeder's Rise and Fall

C ONDITIONS AT MICHAEL WOLF'S kennel had been out of control for some time, but the public had no idea. For decades, Wolf had been a fixture in the dog show world, a crown prince in a sometimes surreal galaxy where dogs bore long and whimsical names, were groomed to perfection, and were pampered like royalty. He'd built a reputation for walking off with Best in Show trophies at some of the most prestigious dog shows in the country. A dog owned and handled by Wolf was very nearly impossible to beat in the ring.

Wolf began showing dogs in the mid-1960s and quickly made a name for himself. A bachelor in his late twenties, he was believed to be independently wealthy. There was nothing to interfere with his obsession with top show dogs.

He dabbled with several breeds, first Italian Greyhounds and Maltese, later Afghan Hounds, Löwchen, Boston Terriers, Poodles, and Chihuahuas. By the early 1970s, he was hooked on Pekingese.

The luxuriously long, thick coats and exotic, flat faces of the petulant-looking dogs captivated Wolf.

He kept an eye out for would-be champions, and when he discovered a Pekingese in California who showed particular promise, Wolf had to have him. He purchased the dog, brought him back east, and began entering him in all the major shows. In one single year alone, Champion Dan Lee Dragonseed won twenty-eight Toy Dog Group trophies. In 1969, he took Best in Show at the National Capital Kennel Club Show in Washington, D.C., and at the Boardwalk Kennel Club Show in Atlantic City.

Wolf had not just one prize-winning dog, but two. Champion High Swinger of Brown's Dean captured the top prize at the Pekingese Club of America's specialty show (a show just for Pekes). Wolf had also found Swinger in California; he'd acquired him after discovering that the dog had won five Group prizes. The day after Swinger claimed the Pekingese club title, the *New York Times* ran a photo of the little dog peering out of the cup of a huge silver trophy.

Kay Jeffords was equally passionate about dogs. Jeffords was a wealthy New Yorker. Her husband, Walter, was president of the Brooklyn Union Gas Company and a familiar figure in horse-racing circles. Walter Jeffords owned a number of race horses. He later acquired the first Thoroughbred foal sired by Secretariat, the magnificent Thoroughbred who captured the Triple Crown in 1973.

Walter Jeffords could have his horses; Kay Jeffords was head over heels about dogs. And, like Wolf, she had a habit of snapping up any contender who caught her eye. Buying up the competition was a surefire way to eliminate it. In 1972, Jeffords tried her best to acquire Wolf's latest obsession, Champion Dagbury of Calartha, a red Pekingese he'd imported from Britain the year before. Dagbury had been in the United States only a month, and had already won the Toy Group at the Bronx County Kennel Club Show, the

Kennel Club of Northern New Jersey, and the Queensboro Kennel
Club Show.

Wolf had no intention of selling Dagbury, to a rival fancier. To
avoid a stalemate, Wolf and Jeffords decided to form a partnership.
They would co-own Dagbury, and Wolf would handle him in the
ring.

Jeffords was wealthier by far, but Wolf brought his own cachet
to the table. He was known for his excellent manners: The man with
the muttonchop sideburns, brightly patterned plaid sports jackets,
and thick, gold chain around his neck always stood for the ladies.
More important, he knew dogs. He had a gift for spotting dogs who
represented the best of their breed—specimens with just the right
shape of nose, sweep of hindquarters, and ability to stand like a
champion.

Wolf's partnership with Jeffords lasted eight years. They col-
laborated so closely that, for a time, Wolf even moved into Jeffords's
home. By any measure, their joint venture was a glittering success.
A year after Wolf and Jeffords joined forces, Dagbury won his
fourth Best in Show at the Longshore-Southport Kennel Club
Show—his thirty-sixth first-place showing. The little dog captured
the title the same year Secretariat took the horse-racing world by
storm. "He's my Secretariat," Jeffords crowed about Dagbury the
night she hosted the Belmont Ball, the annual black-tie fund-raiser
sponsored by the New York Racing Association.

Other Pekingese owned by Wolf and Jeffords swept their fields.
Champion Dragon Hai Fanfare won three Bests in Show and nine
Toy Groups. Champion Quilkin the Stringman racked up eleven
Bests in Show, fifty-four Toy Groups, and three top prizes at the
Pekingese Club of America specialty shows. Champion Masterpiece
Zodiac of Dud Lee's captured eight Bests in Show and fifty-three
Groups.

Wolf had catapulted to the top of the dog show world. Together
with Jeffords, he traveled annually to the prestigious Crufts dog

show in England to search for up-and-coming Pekingese. On one trip alone they bought ten dogs who looked to be future show winners.

In the mid-1970s, Wolf immersed himself even further into the world of purebreds. He moved to Christiana, Pennsylvania, a rural village in the heart of Amish country, where two-lane roads connected one far-flung farm to another. His choice of location was no accident; the Jeffordses had a country retreat near Christiana. From his rural outpost, Wolf continued to import dogs. He also began to breed some of his own.

The dog show circuit took notice. "Mrs. Walter M. Jeffords Jr. of New York and Michael Wolf of Christiana, Pa., have owned some very good Pekingese over the last few years," the *New York Times* reported on March 21, 1976. "Now they have another one. He is a 4-year-old Scottish import, Ch. Yang Kee Bernard." Bernard had just won top prize out of 1,639 dogs at the Bronx County Kennel Club's fifty-fourth show, where he was deemed "an exceptional specimen of the breed." He went on to win seventeen Bests in Show and fifty-two Toy Groups, and walked off with the Pekingese Club of America specialty trophy. In 1976, he captured the Toy Group at Westminster, the pinnacle of dog shows.

Top show dogs are extremely healthy and well socialized. They cannot win a show if they have temperament problems, if they are underfed or underexercised, are poorly groomed, or walk in a way that suggests poor structure. His raft of awards demonstrated that at that point in his career, Wolf knew how to take proper care of his dogs.

Once his partnership with Jeffords ended, Wolf moved slightly closer to Philadelphia. He purchased three acres a few miles northeast of nearby Lower Oxford, a community on the fringes of the Brandywine Valley, where he continued to breed dogs. Wolf couldn't have picked a more bucolic spot to establish Mike-Mar Kennel. Chester County was centrally located—forty-five miles southwest of Philadelphia—and drenched in history. Just over the border in Delaware was the site where the paper used to print the Declaration of Independence and the country's first dollar bills was milled. A short drive away was the legendary Longwood Gardens, the landscaping extravaganza that attracted more than a million visitors a year.

Not only was the area historically prominent, it was prosperous—Chester County has the highest median income level in Pennsylvania—and influential. Less than a mile from Wolf's property was Lincoln University, the nation's first college for African Americans. Among its graduates were Thurgood Marshall, the first black justice to sit on the U.S. Supreme Court, poet Langston Hughes, and acclaimed actor Roscoe Lee Browne.

Yet in the picturesque hills that stretched for miles, agriculture still ruled. It wasn't unusual—in fact, it was quite common—to see black-clothed Amish farmers clop-clopping down the two-lane roads in their horse-drawn buggies on their way to and from their immaculate farms.

Along with its other amenities, southeastern Pennsylvania offered Wolf a less tangible but equally important amenity: privacy. In the 1700s, the gently sloping landscape had attracted Quakers, German peasants, Welsh farmers, and the Pennsylvania Dutch—people who prided themselves on their ability to tolerate diversity. Likewise, the biggest ethnic group to settle around Lower Oxford, the Scotch-Irish, had come to America to escape religious persecution. Their descendants had no interest in delving into the business of others.

In dog show circles, though, stories began to circulate about the questionable conditions at Mike-Mar Kennel. Wolf himself acknowledged he had a problem. In a 1983 interview published in *Kennel Review* magazine, he said he was reluctant to let his dogs go. "My kennel is past 100 dogs now, because I'm not very sensible," he told the magazine (which has since folded). "I have a lot of old friends in the kennel. They've given me a lot of joy as show dogs and breeding, so I keep them."

He went on to say, "A lot of people discipline themselves and place their bitches at five years old, and I think that's a great idea, but it's very hard for me to do."

By the late 1980s, Wolf's dogs were still winning trophies but Wolf himself had lost his own personal panache. One breeder who got to know him around that time said that, unlike other handlers who donned tailor-made suits for their moment in the spotlight, Wolf "always looked like he just got out of bed. His big belly was hanging over his pants." Not that it mattered. "At that time," the breeder said, "given his reputation . . . he could have taken in a hamster and he'd win."

Wolf entertained dog show judges with elaborate dinners at his home, but he began to step back from the rigors of the show circuit. By the 1990s, he was spending more time breeding dogs than showing them. He took on a new partner, Gordon Trottier, a reclusive man whose mother, Wendy, raised Papillons—small, graceful little spaniels best known for having enormous ears shaped like butterflies. Wendy Trottier had encountered problems of her own with the Pennsylvania Bureau of Dog Law Enforcement. Inspectors noted problems with ventilation, unclean bedding, and excrement in the Donwen Kennel she operated in Christiana. Also working with Wolf—the "Mar" in Mike-Mar Kennel—was Margaret Hills, a woman who was believed to have a master's degree in education but about whom little else was known.

In the early 1990s, Wolf adopted two young boys, Chad and Michael Jr. The boys reportedly were home schooled by Hills and were seldom seen publicly in town. The five of them—Wolf, Trottier, Hills, and the two boys—all lived at Wolf's compound.

As the years passed, the once-dapper Wolf became overweight, reclusive, and depressed. He developed asthma and diabetes and wrestled with high blood pressure. As his health spiraled downward, his dog-breeding standards plummeted, too. By the mid-2000s, a breeder interested in working with Wolf spent the night at Mike-Mar Kennel, and in a phone call to her husband she described seeing huge numbers of dogs. "The man's living in his kennel with his dogs because he can't stand to be 200 feet away from them," she reported in disbelief.

For most of this time, Mike-Mar Kennel managed to operate under the radar. Wolf wasn't raising any official red flags. But by 2000, conditions had deteriorated so badly that people began to take notice. The Chester County SPCA received its first anonymous call about Wolf that year from a concerned party who reported seeing dogs suffering from mangy skin conditions milling about his property. Humane society police officer Cheryl Shaw drove to Oxford to investigate, but found no violations. She noticed several large breeds in the yard, but the dogs appeared to be in good shape. They had shelter, which was important, especially given Pennsylvania's damp and freezing winters.

Many more dogs appeared to be housed inside, but Wolf refused to let Shaw in to see them. He was polite about it; he stood on the porch of his house and chatted at length with her. Even when Hills stepped outside and declared, in a loud voice, that Shaw didn't need to see anything, Wolf waved his partner away and kept talking. He acted as though he had nothing to hide. Before Shaw left, he showed her some of his birds—large, colorfully feathered macaws.

Two years later, during a routine inspection, a warden for the state Dog Law Bureau cited Wolf with two counts of failure to maintain his kennel in a sanitary and humane manner. Wolf pleaded guilty and paid an $87.50 fine. The state revoked his kennel license.

Two more years passed. Then, in 2004, the American Kennel Club (AKC) stepped in.

Puppy mill dogs are able to fetch high prices, in part, because they are registered as purebreds with the AKC, the country's pre-eminent dog registry. A certificate of registration looks impressive.

It suggests that a puppy has achieved certain standards of the breed and is known to have come from good stock. The AKC itself, though, acknowledges that registration papers guarantee only a dog's parentage and purebred status. The AKC website states that the registry "cannot guarantee the quality or health of dogs in its registry."

When it comes to parentage, the AKC has long relied on an honor system. It takes breeders' word for it that the puppies they've produced came from the parents listed on the registration certificate. In 2004, the year the Mike-Mar Kennel was inspected, the AKC registered 958,272 dogs born into 437,437 litters. Many of the registrations were done online. With that volume of registrations, critics say, the registry can't begin to verify the genealogy of every litter. As a result, critics claim, AKC papers don't really guarantee anything.

The organization currently charges breeders $25 to register each litter, plus an additional $2 for each puppy. The puppy's eventual owner must then pay an additional $20 to register the individual dog. Registration fees keep the AKC afloat.

The AKC also operates an inspection program aimed at high-volume breeders who sell AKC-registered puppies. But in 2004— the same year Wolf lost his kennel license with the state—an AKC inspector reported finding no problems with conditions at his kennel. Wolf claimed to have just forty-five dogs and eight puppies on his property, and the inspector, apparently unaware that the state had revoked Wolf's license, determined that living conditions were acceptable.

Five months later, the AKC did sanction Wolf on another count. The organization said he knew, or should have known, that registration applications he'd submitted contained false information about the puppies' pedigrees—their family tree. After simple DNA tests turned up incorrect or faulty record-keeping, the organization suspended Wolf for six months and fined him $500.

A suspension by the AKC means a person cannot compete in AKC sports or register any dogs. But it doesn't prevent a breeder from producing dogs. What happens inside a breeder's dark barn or basement is anybody's guess. Moreover, Wolf's suspension made no mention of his partner, Trottier. In reality, Wolf could continue to breed dogs in Trottier's name and face no repercussions whatsoever.

After serving his suspension, Wolf registered only a few litters with the AKC. From 2002 to 2004, he'd registered ninety-four litters with the organization. After 2004, he registered just three. Since he didn't appear to be breeding much anymore, the AKC removed Wolf from its list of high-volume breeders. He was no longer being watched. The state of Pennsylvania had stopped tracking him as well. Without a state license, Wolf technically was forbidden to have more than twenty-six dogs on his property over a year's time. But the absence of a license really meant that he could now go about his business without the aggravation of an unannounced inspection. If a dog warden did come knocking, Wolf had the legal right to turn him or her away.

In truth, he was conducting more business than ever—and conditions at Mike-Mar Kennel were worsening to the point that his neighbors were starting to object. In 2003, a year after the state revoked Wolf's kennel license, Crystal Messaros complained about the smell to Lower Oxford Township officials. Messaros's house sat on a hill directly behind Wolf's property. The township secretary told a newspaper she'd approached Wolf about the matter and assumed the problem was resolved. It wasn't. Messaros later said that her family was unable to sit out by their pool for three years because of the stench.

She knew Wolf had dogs, but she had no clue how many. There were so many dogs that Wolf and Trottier sold them via several websites. Not just puppies, either, but adult dogs, too.

One of the sites was called "Lightnings's Papillons." "Puppies available now!" the site announced. "Healthy and well socialized. Teens and adults occasionally. All colors available. Shots and worming up to date."

The site featured several photos of dogs for sale. In one, three Papillon puppies lay together, so young that their eyes were barely open. In another, a dog with humongous ears stared solemnly at the camera. A third photo depicted a lighter-colored Papillon posing out of doors, his front legs perched on a log, surrounded by grass. Two more shots showed dogs lounging in fluffy beds.

The Cavalier King Charles Spaniels were featured on another website, pets4you.com. Accompanying the text were two pictures of Blenheim (chestnut and white) and tricolor (black, white, and tan) puppies with chin-length ears adorned with wavy hair. Other photos showed a puppy posed inside a mailbox covered with flowers, a handful of pups sitting amid plush toys on a plaid bed, and a Cavalier dressed in a frilly outfit. The site touted Mike-Mar Kennel as "home of many A.K.C. champions," where the goal was to raise "top quality dogs."

"My puppies are home raised," the site said. "All hearts, eyes and hips are checked yearly. I can offer a very healthy, well bred cheerful puppy. To excellent pet homes only."

Wolf and Trottier also sold Papillons and Cavaliers on anypet. com, abcpets.com, and on breeders.net. Their ads were full of half-sentences and grammatical errors. On breeders.net they wrote that "our Havanese are wonderful they are extremely smart with a cheerful disposition. It's great they are non-shedding. All my dogs eyes Cerf'd there Patella's are checked yearly."

The site included a link to more information and photos. "I have been involved with Havanese for several years," the breeders. net site went on to say. "My first one became a champion from the puppy classes. It was so exciting because Trina was a very special pet. I sell my puppies to pet homes only the dogs are really the happiest being a loved family pet. My puppies are raised in my home. I have all my dogs eyes Cert'd yearly also there Patella's."

The "I" in the description apparently referred to Wolf, but it wasn't clear.

The page advertising his English Bulldogs stated that "Health is a very important factor they must breath easy is a number 1 concern. They need good hips and knees to carry the weight of a Bulldog. If they are constructed right you will have a happy wonderful friend." The site offered some advice for prospective customers. "Remember that Bulldog is called a 'head breed' because 39 points is a head and face," it said. "A compact package is what you are wanting. As far as color is concerned no good dog is a bad color. I can offer puppies that are healthy and close to the breed standard."

The accompanying photos showed one Bulldog wearing a straw hat and a pair of Bulldogs staring pugnaciously from their seat on a low-slung chair. To a would-be customer, the dogs looked precisely the way Wolf wanted them to look—like much-loved pets.

4

Orchestrating the Raid

A s soon as shaw got off the phone with her supervisor, she and Siddons sped back to Chester County SPCA headquarters. An hour later, they gathered in the office of executive director Susie Spackman. Joining them were Becky Turnbull, coordinator of animal protective services; operations manager Dennis McMichael; office coordinator Jill Green; and spokesman Chuck McDevitt. Shaw described in detail the conditions at Mike-Mar Kennel: the crates full of dogs, the reeking ammonia smell, the overall filth. Filing a report wasn't going to fix the problem, she told her bosses. The dogs needed to be removed, and the sooner the better.

Shaw was known for bringing passion to her work. Of all the officers employed by the SPCA, Spackman knew, Shaw was most apt to have a gung-ho, leap-into-action attitude. She was no less enthusiastic in this case, but Spackman could tell Shaw was also a little overwhelmed at the prospect of raiding a kennel. The SPCA would be committing itself to caring for 136 animals for who knew how long—the case could drag on for years. The financial implications could be crippling.

Staffers ran through the obstacles they might encounter trying to remove the dogs. For starters, it was impossible to guess how Wolf and his partners would react to a raid. The breeder had permitted Shaw onto his property this time; he might not do so again. The ramifications of bringing this many dogs into the shelter would be huge. The SPCA handled nearly 400 animals a year, but never anything of this magnitude all at once.

The final decision to go forward with the raid rested with Spackman, and once she heard the details, she was convinced that Shaw was right. The dogs had to be rescued. They were vulnerable and in a desperate situation. Morally, it was the right thing to do. Knowing what they knew, how could the SPCA even think of turning its back on these animals?

The group agreed to meet again the next morning to hash out the logistics.

Shaw's nerves were ready to explode. She wanted nothing more than to race back down to Lower Oxford, load up Wolf's dogs, and take them away for good. Instead, she drove home, an hour-long commute. Over dinner she filled her husband, Bobby, and their children, 15-year-old Chauna and Kevin, 10, in on the day's events. The fact that their mother spent her days trying to save animals struck both kids as exceptionally cool.

Later, Shaw cuddled with the family's German Shepherd, three Pugs, and four cats. Before turning in, she curled up on one end of the couch and watched a rerun of her favorite sitcom, *Reba*. But all night long she fought to fall asleep, struggling to rid her mind of the frightened brown eyes that had stared out at her from inside the wire crates. The thought of all those dogs enduring another day in such squalor gnawed at her.

She was back at work early Thursday, and by midmorning the SPCA brass had worked up a to-do list in anticipation of the raid. The shelter could accommodate Wolf's dogs, but it would require considerable effort. Staffers needed to line up transportation for the dogs, round up crates to carry them in, and arrange space to house them once they arrived. It was a good thing Wolf's dogs were small breeds, McDevitt pointed out. Half a dozen Cavaliers would fit inside a single cinderblock run.

On a typical day, the SPCA housed 100 or so dogs and cats who were available for adoption. Another 100 or so animals were kept in isolation—dogs and cats who were ill or injured or considered too aggressive to house in the main wing. The inn was nearly always full.

Chester County SPCA humane society police officer Cheryl Shaw. It was her job to orchestrate the raid on Michael Wolf's puppy mill.

To clear out space, the office staff went to work phoning breed rescue groups—organizations that take in and seek new homes for dogs of a specific breed—to see if they could handle some of the dogs currently housed at the shelter. Workers unearthed extra cages and carriers; they found a couple dozen in a barn adjacent to the main shelter. Humane officers cleaned the crates and got them ready for use. To augment the SPCA's own two vans, McMichael rented two more.

More important than the physical logistics was the search warrant Shaw needed to have in hand before she could legally cart off Wolf's dogs. The warrant needed to detail the conditions she and Siddons had uncovered the day before and outline the reasons they believed the dogs should be removed. Two signatures were required: one from the Chester County district attorney's office and one from a local district judge. Shaw worked into the evening Thursday to draft the warrant. On her way home, she stopped at the animal shelter in neighboring Montgomery County to borrow still more crates.

In addition to their normal caseload, assistant district attorneys took turns being on call twenty-four hours a day for a week at a time. The assistant D.A. on call that week happened to be Lori Finnegan, a ten-year veteran regarded as thorough and tenacious. Shaw phoned Finnegan first thing Friday morning to let her know the SPCA was planning to raid a large-volume dog breeder in Lower Oxford the next day. Finnegan told her to fax over the search warrant.

Shaw sent off what she had. In stilted legalese, she'd written, "Your affiant's visual observations of the animals lead your affiant to conclude that the strong ammonia type smell and the unsanitary conditions would be detrimental to the well-being of the animals if the situation is not rectified, for being kept in this situation could be a threat to the health and safety of the animals."

Under items to be searched for and seized, she wrote simply, "Any and all animals, living or dead, and any evidence of animal cruelty." The violation she cited was Pennsylvania state law 18, 5511, c, Cruelty to Animals.

Finnegan read over the search warrant and then phoned Shaw. "We need more detail," she said. Shaw faxed a second version to Finnegan at 11:45 a.m., fifteen minutes before Finnegan's on-call shift was scheduled to end. In a single-spaced page and a half, Shaw elaborated on the circumstances behind her request. She detailed the "overabundance" of dogs of various sizes and ages inside and outside Wolf's residence at 1746 Baltimore Pike. She recounted the excessive heat and overwhelming ammonia-type odor "commonly associated with animal urine" that permeated the premises. She cited the confinement of dozens of dogs in rusty, unsafe crates two, three, and four high, covered in what appeared to be feces and urine. And she described the water bowls that were green and dirty, the green mucus that dribbled from the eyes of some of the dogs, and their scabby skin conditions.

The fleshed-out version of the search warrant passed muster. Finnegan signed the document and faxed it back. It still needed the signature of a district judge, but Shaw would get that on her way to Wolf's kennel. When that was done, the SPCA would have the authorization it needed to carry out the raid.

On the way down, Shaw tried to phone dog warden Siddons to let her know a raid was imminent. Shaw had deliberately waited until the last minute to phone Siddons; the humane officer was mindful that the more people who knew about the raid, the greater the possibility the plans could be leaked. A few months earlier, according to Shaw, a raid on another puppy mill, Puppy Love Kennel in neighboring Lancaster County, was foiled when someone tipped off the breeder, Joyce Stoltzfus. Puppy Love was a notoriously derelict kennel but, forewarned, Shaw believed Stoltzfus had gone to work, scrubbing her kennel just enough to pass the inspection. As a result, the raid was a failure; inspectors were unable to gather the evidence necessary to seize her dogs.

The Chester County SPCA was determined not to let the same thing happen in Wolf's case, so on the day of the biggest operation in the organization's history, only a handful of people knew the raid was about to take place. The shelter's rank-and-file staff had no idea.

Shaw was unable to reach Siddons. The dog warden had taken the day off. When her work phone went unanswered, Shaw punched in the number for her cell phone and left a message: "Please call me back as soon as possible. I need to talk to you." Siddons never returned Shaw's call. The raid would go forward without her.

Shaw and Green left ahead of time to stop by the office of Harry Farmer Jr., the magisterial district judge in Oxford who would be handling the case. Shortly before 1 p.m., they met up with the rest of the troops in the parking lot of the bowling alley, a couple hundred yards down the road from Wolf's property. McMichael and humane society police officer Michele "Mike" Beswick rode together. Animal protective services officer Craig Baxter and kennel technician Liz Murray took a van. SPCA spokesman McDevitt drove himself.

Moments later, a highway patrolman pulled up alongside them. In Pennsylvania it was standard procedure for a highway patrol officer to be on hand to help execute a warrant. Shaw gave the officer a rundown of everything he could expect to encounter at Mike-Mar Kennel. She didn't expect Wolf to be violent, she told him, and she didn't think he'd interfere with the operation. But the trooper needed to brace himself for the foul condition of the property.

The convoy now consisted of half a dozen vehicles. Shaw followed the patrolman's car, and the others fell in line behind her. "Oh God, here we go," Shaw thought as they drove slowly down Baltimore Pike and, one by one, turned into the driveway of

Mike-Mar Kennel. This was a big-time breeder she was dealing with. Wolf knew all the right people, and he knew how the game was played. Everything about the raid had to go perfectly because of who he was and who he had once been. Shaw's heart was clutched with anxiety.

As soon as the vehicles pulled into the driveway, she spied Wolf in the doorway of the kennel. Immediately, she and the state trooper stepped out of their vehicles and climbed the stairs of the deck. The SPCA had a warrant, the trooper informed Wolf. "We're here to remove your dogs," Shaw said.

Wolf looked stunned. "You're taking all my dogs? Why?" he asked. Nevertheless, he stepped outside, came down the steps, and escorted Shaw and the trooper to his residence. McDevitt and Beswick got out of their vehicles and joined them.

Inside the house, Wolf protested. They'd had an agreement, he said, and he was taking the steps Shaw had asked him to take. Across the room she could see a couple of Cavaliers who appeared to be newly shaved, and Wolf hastily produced a sheaf of papers. The day before, just as she had requested, he said, a veterinarian had visited the kennel and vaccinated one hundred dogs. Shaw glanced at the paperwork. It was disorganized and incomplete; it was impossible to tell which dogs had gotten shots. Besides, she wasn't there to debate trivial improvements.

The conditions at Mike-Mar Kennel were unacceptable, she told Wolf. "You can't have these guys living this way."

The breeder shifted his argument. "Let me keep some of the dogs," he said. But Shaw wasn't interested in leaving any dog behind in this mess.

The game plan was straightforward. First, Shaw needed to inspect the perimeter of the compound and then every inch of the buildings' interiors. She wasn't expecting to find any more dogs, but she didn't want any surprises. She needed to videotape everything she saw. It was important to capture on film the deplorable conditions the dogs were living in, including the dirty water buckets, the lack of food, and the dogs' matted hair. She also wanted to show any diseases, infections, or injuries visible on the animals. The videotape would tell the tale in court.

Once that was done, workers would go room by room, starting with Wolf's residence, removing the dogs from their crates. They would assign each dog a number and write down the breed, gender, approximate age, and physical condition. Rescuers would photograph each dog, then place the animal inside a portable crate and carry the dog out to a van. As soon as a van was full, Craig Baxter or one of the other animal protective services officers, Dave Harper or Gene Brooks, would drive it back to West Chester. It would be dirty, disturbing work, but in a matter of hours all 136 dogs would be accounted for and on their way to new lives. If everyone worked with assembly-line efficiency, they should be wrapped up by supper time.

The sun shone high above the trees, but inside Wolf's house it was dark and nearly impossible to see. Rescuers opened the door to a bedroom and shone flashlights inside. Panicky eyes stared back— dozens of pairs of eyes, from every corner of the room, just as Shaw had described. The room reverberated with yelps. The rescuers peered inside a second room. Dogs lined the walls there, too.

Shaw was about to begin canvassing the grounds when the trooper approached her. He'd just finished circling the property on his own, and he'd discovered something.

"Did you know there are more dogs in the back of the kennel?" the patrolman asked Shaw.

"Are you sure?" she said.

Two days earlier, while examining the two front rooms of the kennel, she'd spied a door to the rear. The door was locked, and when Wolf told her there was nothing behind it—that he had shown them all there was to see—she'd believed him. Now, though, the officer was telling her that behind the door was a room with a window, and on the other side of the window were more dogs, dozens of them.

Shaw and Beswick jogged down the steps of Wolf's residence, across the yard, and up the steps to the kennel. They brushed past Hills, who was inside cleaning. "We've got a warrant," Shaw told her. "You need to get out." The officer walked through the front room and opened the door on the far side, into the hidden room where Wolf had insisted there were no dogs.

Shaw's heart pounded. Before her were dozens of crates lined up in rows, full of dogs. On the left were Cavaliers, four to six to a crate. On the right, English Bulldogs, in cages stacked two high. This couldn't be happening. She had orchestrated the rescue on the assumption that Wolf had 136 dogs, no more. Now it looked as if there could be 200.

At the sight of Shaw, the dogs hopped up on their hind legs, wagged their tails, and erupted into a frantic chorus. Her blood pressure rising, Shaw shut the door and strode back to Wolf's house.

"Look, I need to know," she said to him. "Do you have any more dogs on this property?"

A room at the rear of Mike-Mar Kennel revealed dozens more dogs confined to crates, along with an overpowering stench of ammonia.

"No," Wolf told her flatly.

This time, she knew better than to believe him. He'd lied to her before, and her instincts told her he was lying now. With a feeling of dread, she stepped back outside and walked in the direction of the third building, Trottier's house. Beswick fell in line behind her and Hills followed them. "Don't just stand there staring," Shaw told herself. "Check out the back." At the rear of the building was a deck, and beside the deck was a basement door. Next to the door she noticed a small window completely covered, except for a sliver of light along the bottom edge. A poop scooper rested beside the door. "What's that doing there?" Shaw wondered.

She turned to Hills and said, "You need to show me the basement. Right now." Wordlessly, Hills unlocked the door. "Watch your step," she warned as Shaw stepped inside, Beswick and Hills close behind her. They entered a room inhabited by three cats and a Mastiff. "Thank goodness that's all there is," Shaw thought. She was ready to turn around and leave the basement when she noticed a doorway blocked off by a baby gate, a sheet tacked up over it to hide the view. Behind the sheet came a muffled yelp.

Shaw whipped around to face Hills.

Crates stacked three high were covered with dried feces, despite Wolf's claims that his kennel was cleaned daily.

"What was that?" she demanded.

Hills shook her head. She hadn't heard anything.

Shaw turned to Beswick. "You hear that?"

"Yeah," Beswick replied.

The gate was there for a reason—but surely not to fence off more dogs. Shaw hesitated, then stepped forward and drew back the sheet. The room was filled with dogs—butterfly-eared Papillons—packed into crates, running loose on the floor, and clambering on top of a futon. There had to be dozens of them. In the middle of the room stood Trottier, glowering.

Shaw turned to Beswick. "Go get Dennis," she said.

Beswick hurried past Hills. Shaw turned back to Trottier. "You need to leave," she told him. Trottier punched the ceiling defiantly, then reached down and swept up a disheveled and sickly looking Papillon. "You're not taking my f——dogs!" he yelled.

Within seconds, Beswick and McMichael returned with a police officer. Trottier was now standing outside the baby gate. "Give me the dog," Shaw told him. He refused. The officer reached forward to take the dog out of Trottier's hands. Trottier threw a punch. A scuffle ensued, spilling from the hallway outside. The next thing anyone knew, Trottier was on the ground with the trooper, Shaw, Beswick, and McDevitt pinning him down. As blows were exchanged, the trooper somehow managed to hold the Papillon away from the line of fire.

A second police officer had arrived. He called for backup. Within minutes, fifteen marked and unmarked state police cars barreled onto the scene, lights flashing and sirens blaring. Officers arrested Trottier, charged him with assault, resisting arrest, and obstructing the administration of law, and took him away.

Shaw had no right to enter his house, Trottier shouted as he was trundled off—the search warrant she'd obtained was for Wolf's house, not his. With a start, Shaw realized that Trottier could very well be correct. The warrant authorized her to raid 1746 Baltimore Pike;

the street address for Trottier's residence was 1748 Baltimore Pike. This was a major snafu. If the paperwork was not in order, a judge might disregard any evidence gathered at Trottier's address. By calling Shaw's attention to her mistake in time to correct it, Trottier had done her a favor.

She used her cell phone to call Finnegan and explain the situation. "What do we do now?" Shaw asked.

"Come back to West Chester, type up another warrant, and send it over to me," Finnegan said.

Shaw fought back a surge of panic as she climbed into one of the vans and floored it onto the highway. Here she was in charge of this raid, and she was leaving the scene just as rescuers were beginning to comprehend the enormity of the problem. Wolf had many, *many* more dogs than anyone had suspected.

She made it to West Chester in record time. Hastily, she drew up a new warrant and faxed it to Finnegan. It was 5:15 p.m., past quitting time. Finnegan called in a favor from district judge James Charlie, who agreed to sign the new search warrant. By 6:30 p.m. Shaw was back in Lower Oxford. The sun had long since set and the temperature was dropping. The rescue work had gone slowly during the two and a half hours she was gone. There were three buildings full of dogs to rescue, and staffers were still working in the first.

"What are we going to do with all these dogs?" Beswick asked Shaw as they headed inside Wolf's residence.

"We'll take care of it," Shaw said, but she had no idea how.

5

Filth and Fear

S HAW HAD NEVER been part of an operation this massive. From
time to time that evening, she stepped away from her other tasks
to carry out a couple of dogs herself. "Okay, punkin, we'll get you
taken care of," she said to one scared-looking Havanese as she held
the dog to her chest. "See, I told you I'd come back. I promised,
didn't I?" But the workers lacked radios to communicate back and
forth, so she had to keep making the rounds, issuing one snap decision after another and praying she was making the right calls. There
wasn't enough of her to go around.

Shortly before 7 p.m. she took a moment to phone her husband,
Bobby, to let him know she was in for a long night. He could tell she
was stressed.

Did Shaw need help? he asked.

"I'm fine," Shaw told him, but she didn't sound fine. She sounded exhausted.

He said he was on his way.

The hours ticked by. Shortly after Bobby arrived at around 9 p.m., someone delivered a pizza and left it on the top of a Jeep. "Go eat something," one of the officers said to Shaw.

For a moment, she took her colleague's advice, climbed inside the Jeep, and took a couple of bites of pizza. But this was no time to rest; there were too many dogs left to process. She stepped back out of the vehicle and returned to work.

While Shaw oversaw the rescue effort, the task of reaching inside many of the crates, pulling a dog out, and holding him or her before the camera fell to other SPCA staffers. One of them was fellow humane society police officer Beswick. A less seasoned officer might have winced at the prospect of handling unfamiliar and distressed dogs, but 53-year-old Beswick had done police work since she was 18. She'd been exposed to every horrendous situation imaginable, or so she thought. Despite her experience, she wasn't

Humane society police officer Mike Beswick. In all her years at the Chester County SPCA, she had never encountered this many neglected dogs.

prepared for the size of Wolf's kennel or the degree of misery that permeated it. As she worked to remove the dogs, mice scuttled up walls and space heaters scattered about the rooms worked overtime. She felt as if she'd stepped inside a furnace.

Cages lined the walls of every room. The rescuers started with a listless red and blue parrot, one of two found on the property. Then came a tan and white Bulldog, followed by a puppy who looked to be a Havanese-Cavalier mix. Next they brought out a female Yorkshire Terrier, a Pomeranian, two Havanese, three Bulldogs, three more Havanese, and then Cavaliers, seven of them, all but one a female. Every one of the dogs looked anxious and scared.

The animals also looked scruffy and ill. The dogs were flea-bitten, covered with lice, and suffering noticeably from scabby skin and runny eyes. Beswick struggled to remain composed as she carried out number 24, a red and white Cavalier puppy whose left eye was so cloudy and swollen it was ready to fall out of its socket. A half hour later she lifted up a tricolor Cavalier whose eye was gone entirely. Number 113, a Löwchen, had such a bad case of mange that raw, open sores covered his torso. Number 215, a Bulldog, sported an enormous hot spot—a raw, oozing open wound—on her left flank. The coats of some of the Havanese were so filthy that it was nearly impossible to distinguish their faces. One Havanese had no hair at all. The dog was covered with mange and shivering.

Beswick's heart ached for these animals. They lacked any ability to make sense of their deprived lives and had no means of escape. The mere act of extricating them from their crates required delicacy. The dogs fled to the rear of their cages and cowered. With as many as six to a crate, Beswick had to maneuver around a handful of frightened dogs to pull one out.

Green, the SPCA's office coordinator, processed the dogs while animal control officer Baxter waited at the end of the line. Once a dog was photographed, he placed it in a carrier and walked it out to a van. Baxter was new to his position—he'd been employed by the SPCA less than a year—and the suffering he saw was too painful to ignore. He stared in disbelief as the dogs, covered with fecal matter, struggled to turn around in their crates, their paws splayed and tender from standing on the thin wire bottoms. He'd never seen or smelled anything so sour, and the high thermostat setting only exacerbated the conditions. It was the dead of winter, but the heat was so intense that he quickly shed his wool jacket and turtleneck and long underwear. Before long, he was down to a T-shirt.

The first van was filled up in a matter of hours, two dogs to a crate. As soon as the vehicle was full, Baxter climbed into the driver's seat and headed for West Chester, a forty-five-minute trip. The noticeably ill dogs would bypass the SPCA shelter and go directly to an animal hospital.

Inside Wolf's house, when the noise briefly subsided, Green heard the sound of clinking glass. She searched the room and found, tucked in a corner, a laundry basket covered by a towel. Underneath,

Chester County SPCA protective services officer Craig Baxter. He was new to animal-welfare work, and struggled to cope with the squalor that stretched before him at Mike-Mar Kennel.

two English Bulldog puppies stretched in their sleep alongside a hammer, a box of nails, and two glass bowls. Had someone deliberately tried to hide the newborns? It certainly looked that way.

No one can say for certain what the tricolor Cavalier with the swoosh on her front leg saw or heard, or what she must have thought when the door swung open and light flooded the dim room. The bright light probably stung her cloudy, irritated eyes. And the voices she heard were different from the voices she was accustomed to hearing.

The people left. Then, several hours later, they returned. This time a man knelt and stuck a finger inside the Cavalier's crate. "Hang in there, little one, we'll get you out of here soon," he said. The other dogs watched with apprehension as the man picked up the laundry basket and carried it outside. When he returned, he reached up and unlatched the door to a crate on the top row. That dog, too, was carried outside.

This time the man made his way across the feces-covered floor to the Cavalier's crate. He unlatched the door, reached in, and wrapped his hands around another Cavalier, a female. "Come on, baby, come on," the man said. He disappeared with the dog. Minutes later he was back.

The tricolor Cavalier stood, frozen. Four dogs were left in her crate and the other three were huddled together, pressed as far to the rear of the cage as they could get. The little dog stared straight ahead as the man returned once more, lifted her off the urine-soaked newspapers and hugged her close. "Let's get you out of here," he said.

He carried the dog into the next room, where a woman sat at a table and a third person held a camera, waiting. The woman jotted down the barest of details about the dog. Breed: CKCS, Cavalier King Charles Spaniel. Sex: female. Color: tri.

The Cavalier was the 132nd dog to be rescued from Mike-Mar Kennel. The woman at the table wrote the number 132 on a card and handed it to the man. He held the dog on his left arm, picked up the card, and posed for a picture. The dog was still frightened, but a part of her was also curious. The instant the shutter clicked she glanced up, her melancholy eyes staring straight into the lens.

The dog had to be carried out to the van—she had no concept of a leash and refused to walk on one. An hour later, when the van left for West Chester, she hunkered down in her carrier, the same as the other dogs. For a dog who had never left her kennel, the sensations of movement must have been disorienting and scary.

Baxter had braced himself for a noisy ride, and it *was* noisy at first—the dogs yelped loudly as the journey began. Before long, though, almost all of the dogs experienced motion sickness and the smell of vomit filled the van. After that the barks subsided, and for most of the ride there was no noise at all except for the rumble of the engine. The silence, Baxter decided, was the eeriest sound of all.

A frightened Cavalier stared into the camera as Baxter helped tag her as dog number 132.

As RESCUERS WENT about the grim task of documenting his dogs, Wolf remained inside his house, sitting on his couch or at his computer and chatting with anyone who passed by. He appeared frail: Earlier, walking from his residence to the kennel, he'd grasped Green's arm as they climbed a set of steps. While other workers set up equipment, Wolf was happy to show Green decades-old photos of his prize-winning dogs and the Best in Show trophies that decorated the front room of his kennel. He claimed to have a name and a pedigree for every dog on the property.

To Green's surprise, Wolf was completely nonthreatening. He seemed calm—stunned, perhaps, by the raid, but composed. Later in the day, when Beswick slipped on a pile of feces in his living room as she was passing through, Wolf asked politely if she wanted him to clean up the mess. "Why?" Beswick responded. "There's plenty more where this came from."

Outside, Chuck McDevitt scrolled through the Rolodex he'd brought with him. Before he'd gone to work for the SPCA, McDevitt was a reporter for the *Philadelphia Inquirer*. He knew the heart-tugging rescue of dozens of frightened animals would appeal to the media. He also knew that to care for these dogs indefinitely, the SPCA would need public support—lots of it. His job was to get word out about the raid as quickly as possible. As soon as the rescue effort got under way, he began calling newspapers and TV stations.

A reporter and a photographer from the *Daily Local News* in West Chester were the first to arrive. They pulled up at about the same time as the backup troopers from the Highway Patrol. Five TV stations out of Philadelphia—6ABC, NBC10, WB17, FOX29, and CN8—showed up shortly afterward.

While McDevitt was getting word out about the raid, workers at the SPCA shelter were on the phone with neighboring shelters, asking for help. The SPCA could barely house 136 dogs, much less twice that many. The Delaware County SPCA, the Delaware State SPCA, the Pennsylvania SPCA, animal control in Coatesville, and the Applebrook Inn Pet Resort in West Chester all agreed to pitch in.

Rescuers had expected to find Wolf's kennel overrun with puppies. To their surprise, most of the dogs were adults, which was worse. These animals had languished for years with untreated afflictions, and over time minor problems had developed into major ones. Some dogs had broken legs or were visibly ill and needed immediate care. Baxter transported them to the West Chester Veterinary Medical Center. McDevitt drove to the clinic himself a Bulldog who had become violently ill after ingesting rat poison. Veterinarians at the clinic accepted thirty or so of the dogs before pleading for relief. They couldn't take any more.

In a bedroom at the rear of Wolf's house, rescuers found an English Bulldog who belonged to Wolf's son. The Bulldog was acting aggressively. She was doing her best to guard the disheveled room, where a torn-up mattress lay on the floor. "Just leave her there," Shaw told the staff. Hours later, she returned to the room, slipped a makeshift leash around the Bulldog's neck, and tugged her out. The photo taken that night of Pansy (as the SPCA later named her) showed her stretched out on her back, resisting still.

Outside, the temperature was so frosty that rescuers stamped their feet to keep them warm. Inside, Beswick was perspiring heavily. The rescue effort was exhausting work, and after ten hours on the job, Beswick was so nauseous she had to leave. But Shaw was operating on nervous energy. The rescue effort was her baby. She had to see it through to the end.

SPCA executive director Susie Spackman arrived late in the night to help, as did staffers from the Pennsylvania SPCA in Philadelphia and the Delaware County SPCA. Despite the reinforcements, Shaw was weighed down with worry; there were too many animals and not enough people to process them. Every dog taken to the SPCA would need to be examined a second time for wounds, matting, mites, and more. For legal purposes, every illness or injury, no matter how slight, had to be documented. Shaw was worn out, but her work wasn't over by a long shot.

Eyes welling with tears, Shaw turned to McMichael and said, "I don't know how we're going to do it."

Somehow, they persevered. Over the next twelve hours, Baxter alone made half a dozen trips to West Chester and back, the last of them at 3:30 a.m. Saturday. More than once he fought the urge to fall asleep on the road.

It was 4 a.m. by the time Shaw, her husband, and several workers from the Applebrook Pet Resort left Mike-Mar Kennel. Shaw drove to the SPCA and spent another hour preparing inventory lists. By the time she got home, it was 6 a.m. Too worn out even to shower, she changed her clothes, set the alarm for 8 a.m., and collapsed on the bed.

Thirty people had taken part in the rescue. Together they had removed 337 dogs, three cats, and two parrots from Wolf's premises. Added to the number of animals already housed there, the SPCA's shelter's population had tripled in size overnight, to 450 dogs. On a scale of one to ten, the Wolf case registered 100, Shaw would say later. "It was off the charts. It had all the emotions going."

6

Sorting the Dogs

B Y SATURDAY MORNING, the word was out: The Chester County
SPCA was overflowing with dogs who had been seized from
one of the largest puppy mills ever discovered in the United States.
The night before, the shelter had fielded sixty-five calls from concerned animal lovers. The new day brought hundreds more calls.
Local residents dropped off towels, blankets, cleaning supplies, and
donations. They showed up to adopt the dogs and were disappointed to learn the dogs weren't yet available. The animals were
considered legal evidence. They had to be kept in the shelter's custody until Wolf and Trottier either surrendered them or were forced
to give them up.

Shaw had slept a grand total of two hours. When the alarm
clock buzzed, she roused herself and staggered to the shower to
wash off *eau de kennel*, a potent combination of urine, feces, and fear.
It was impossible; the stench permeated her shoulder-length hair
and would linger for days, even after several shampoos. The kids

would want to hear all about the raid, but they were sleeping, so she threw on a T-shirt that said, "Happy to be Grumpy," and slipped out of the house. By 9 a.m. she was back in the office, headed for the coffeepot.

The raid was over, but the legal machinations were just beginning. The SPCA had yet to issue any charges against Wolf. If Shaw could convince him to surrender his dogs, the organization might be willing to drop the charges. That would free up the SPCA's shelter to adopt the dogs out immediately, avoiding the cost and emotional toll of housing them in a shelter for months on end.

Wolf had relinquished three dogs the night before—two Doberman Pinchers and a Mastiff. The Mastiff was old and ill. It was less clear why Wolf had given up the Dobermans; they weren't his type of breed, apparently. More important, Wolf had seemed willing to consider a wholesale surrender. "Think about it," Green had urged him. "We can probably work something out."

Without a state kennel license, Wolf could not lawfully have more than twenty-six dogs on the premises under any circumstance. But if there were three or four dogs he felt particularly close to, Green said, the SPCA might be willing to clean them up, spay or neuter them, and return them to him. Provided Wolf cooperated, that is, and gave up the rest of the animals.

Green left Wolf's property the previous night covered in grime—before entering her house, she'd stood on the porch and peeled off her clothes. But she was optimistic that the case might be wrapped up in a short time. On Saturday afternoon, she accompanied Shaw back to Lower Oxford to see whether Wolf was willing to resolve matters quickly. While they were there, Shaw also needed to go over with him the inventory of animals who had been removed the night before.

The visit went badly. Wolf pressed to keep twenty-five dogs— just enough to stay under the state-imposed limit—but Shaw had no intention of returning that many to him. She tried to reason with him, to no avail. Midway through their conversation, she and Green glanced out Wolf's window to see Trottier standing outside, behaving menacingly. Aware that he was being watched, Trottier set a bag of feces on fire on the ground next to their Jeep and began throwing leashes and gloves at the vehicle. When that failed to flush them out, he fired up a chainsaw and yelled, "They ain't getting any more." The atmosphere was so tense that Wolf eventually stepped outside to calm Trottier down. When the two women got in the Jeep to leave, Wolf got into his own car and escorted them out of the driveway to make sure Trottier didn't follow along behind.

Trottier came anyway. Minutes after Shaw and Green exited onto Highway 1, they glanced over at Baltimore Pike, which ran parallel to the highway, and saw Trottier's vehicle racing along, trying to catch up. Suddenly, their Jeep lurched to a halt. The engine was dead. "This is not happening," Shaw muttered, incredulous, from the passenger seat. She called the state police to ask for help, but a minute later, Green was able to start the Jeep up again. She mashed the accelerator and quickly managed to lose Trottier.

Wolf's unwillingness to surrender his dogs was unfortunate: It meant the animals would need to be housed indefinitely, until the case was resolved in court. That could take months. The cost of caring for them for that long a period could easily run into the tens of thousands of dollars, and all of it might be for naught; if Wolf won the case, he would get his dogs back. Absent a breeder's license, he would still need to find homes for most of the animals. But he would be free to sell them to other disreputable kennels. The dogs would probably be just as bad off as before.

BACK IN WEST CHESTER, SPCA shelter staff sorted through the dogs, determining which of them could be sent elsewhere. Each animal needed to be examined physically. The shelter put out a call for veterinarians who were willing to help.

Dogs known to be pregnant were taken to Applebrook Inn, a pet resort for dogs, cats, and other small animals. Applebrook had a fireplace where the mothers-to-be could curl up and keep warm, and it offered the added assurance that all of the animals on the premises were vaccinated. At the SPCA shelter it was anybody's guess whether Wolf's animals had all their shots.

The organization's immediate task was to parcel out a third of the dogs to other shelters. By midday Saturday, a dozen regional animal organizations responded, sending vans to pick up 135 of the dogs. The Pennsylvania SPCA in Philadelphia took 63. Others went to the Delaware Humane Association, the Delaware SPCA, the Delaware County SPCA, the Bucks County SPCA, the Humane Society of Berks County, the Animal Rescue League of Berks County, the Humane League of Lancaster County, Hickory Springs Farm Boarding Kennels, and the Montgomery County SPCA.

Twenty-five of the dogs, mostly Cavalier King Charles Spaniels, went to the Humane Society of Berks County. An officer from that organization drove to West Chester and loaded the dogs—among them the tricolor Cavalier with the swoosh on her front leg—into a van and transported them thirty-nine miles north to Reading. After six years in a cage, Dog 132 was experiencing her second road trip in twenty-four hours. Her worst days were behind her, but the little dog had no way of knowing that. She was experiencing something new, different, and scary.

Meanwhile, Wolf wasted no time launching a public relations counterassault. He told the *Philadelphia Daily News* that his dogs were living in crowded circumstances because their kennel was being renovated. He denied claims that the dogs had been living in filth and blamed the cooped-up confines of winter for the smell. "If you have a lot of dogs under one roof, you're going to have an odor," he claimed.

In an interview with the *Philadelphia Inquirer*, Wolf protested that the SPCA "took my little friends." His dogs had been well cared for, he insisted. He said he fed them strained baby food, hamburger, and cottage cheese.

"We love them. We played with them all the time," he said.

Wolf was showing no remorse. If anything, he portrayed himself as the victim. The overwhelming number of dogs on his property was evidence of his compassion, he said. If he couldn't sell a dog or find a home for it, he would simply keep it. "I kept dogs alive after I should," he told the *Inquirer*. "They wagged their tails, they ate. I'm old; are you going to put me to sleep?"

He also vowed to get his dogs back even if he had to sell his house to do it.

"All my years of devotion and love—it's horrible." Wolf told one newspaper. "It makes me sad at this point in my life I have to be in this position."

The SPCA fielded calls from several breeders who claimed to own some of the dogs taken from Mike-Mar Kennel. Wendy Trottier said she had been keeping two male dogs and a mother with four puppies at the kennel while she was out of state caring for a friend. She defended the conditions at Mike-Mar Kennel: "Any time I've been in there they were clean," she said. "I know my son cleans the cages twice a day."

Word of the raid raced through the breeder grapevine. A local terrier breeder, Ann Zevnik, told the Wilmington, Delaware, *News Journal* that she'd known Wolf a decade earlier when he bred Pekingese and Maltese. "He was a wonderful breeder, but he dropped out of showing dogs long ago," Zevnik said. The SPCA fielded several calls from people defending Wolf. "A man has a right to earn a living" was the gist of their comments. But as information sifted out about the abhorrent condition of his dogs, the criticism faded.

With the exception of Crystal Messaros, the neighbor who had complained about the foul smell emanating from Wolf's property, nearby residents professed surprise to learn that Wolf had been housing so many dogs. "In the summer, you can hear dogs barking sometimes, but you can only see a couple at a time," Harvey Stidham, who operated an auto body shop across the highway, told a reporter. Tom Rickards, who lived across the highway, told the *Daily Local News* he rarely smelled anything, "though once in a while you would get a whiff."

Green was puzzled at how Wolf could come across as intelligent and caring and yet be blind to such squalor. She marveled at his charisma. She could see he had the kind of showbiz personality that could persuade people to spend $2,500 on a puppy. And she was struck by the fact that Wolf had initially allowed Shaw and Siddons to inspect the property—something he didn't have to do.

"He had the right to say, 'No, you're not allowed to come onto my property,' but he didn't. And he allowed us to take pictures," Green said. "Why did he let them in?"

Wolf's defenders argued that he wasn't a puppy miller, he was a hoarder—a term used to describe people who collect animals, often by the hundreds, and usually keep them in deplorable conditions under the misguided belief that they are saving their lives. The SPCA's Turnbull didn't buy it. Wolf was trying to turn a profit by selling his dogs; that was the difference, in her view. By setting aside a relatively clean area in which to meet customers, he was tricking the public into believing that the rest of his kennel was in decent shape.

Shaw, too, was convinced Wolf knew what he was doing. Not only was he selling dogs, he was producing multiple breeds for profit. There was no question in her mind that he was operating a puppy mill.

Within days of the raid, Wolf erased any evidence that he and Trottier had been selling dogs on the Internet. Gone were the websites peddling the Havanese, the English Bulldogs, the Papillons, and the Cavaliers. But Shaw was one step ahead of him. She had already downloaded the ads and notified the D.A.'s office about their existence. Months later, when Wolf's attorney asked Shaw in court if she had proof that the websites existed, she was able to say that she did. "It was right there in black and white," she testified.

Wolf's refusal to relinquish the dogs left the SPCA no choice. Four days after the raid, on February 15, authorities filed a slew of charges again Wolf, Trottier, and Hills. Wolf was charged with 337 counts of animal cruelty, 200 citations for having unlicensed dogs, and 100 citations for having dogs without current rabies vaccinations.

Trottier was charged with 65 counts of animal cruelty, 50 citations for unlicensed dogs, and 50 citations for dogs without current rabies vaccinations. Hills was charged with 269 counts of animal cruelty.

The state Bureau of Dog Law Enforcement also charged Wolf and Trottier with operating an unlicensed kennel.

Turnbull had left for vacation on the actual day of the raid. When she returned a week later, she was struck by how traumatized the staff was from having worked the Mike-Mar case. Green, one of her closest friends on staff, was practically reeling from the experience.

The dogs were suffering even more. After examining them, Larry Dieter, the SPCA shelter's veterinarian, compiled a long list of their ailments. The dogs had skin problems (everything from dermatitis to mange) and eye ailments ranging from glaucoma to cataracts to severe dry eye. They had missing and rotten teeth and gingivitis, an infection of the gums. Some of their teeth were so infected that merely touching them was enough to make them fall out. The dogs' ears were inflamed and infected, and they were rife with whipworm, roundworm, and other intestinal parasites. Two of the Papillons had untreated broken bones that had healed badly, twisting their limbs. All of the dogs would need to be treated for fleas, ticks, and lice.

Among the first dogs Dieter treated was a Cavalier who had given birth to two puppies. Inside her uterus he found a third puppy, dead. The Cavalier also had a noncontagious form of mange, a cloudy eye, and a growth on her back that was either an old wound or a skin problem that had healed over and left a scaly mass. Dieter later treated a female English Bulldog suffering from pyometra, an abscess of the uterus, a potentially fatal condition. To remedy the problem he needed to spay her. When he opened her up, he found a dead puppy inside.

Aside from their physical ailments, the dogs were starved for attention. Even in horrific conditions, a little kindness would have gone a long way to make their lives tolerable, Dieter thought. It was clear to him that, despite Wolf's protests to the contrary, these dogs had been neglected not just physically but emotionally, too. Their ordeal reminded him how remarkably forgiving dogs could be. Despite their torment, these animals probably still clamored for Wolf's attention. "You can do a lot of things to the animals and they'll still come back and want to wag their tail," Dieter said.

7

A Safe Place for Dog 132

T HE FIRST THING that struck Pam Bair was the smell, an odor equal parts barnyard and sewer that assaulted her the instant she stepped into the hallway of the Berks County Animal Rescue League.

"Whoa! Is that you, Alison?" she asked with a sardonic grin.

Humane society police officer Alison Rudy acknowledged her with a rueful grimace. Rudy and fellow humane officer Katie McGlory had just arrived with a dozen puppy mill rescues from the Berks County Humane Society in Reading. The Humane Society had agreed to house twenty-five dogs from the Chester County SPCA, but quickly decided that the maximum number it could handle was thirteen. The Animal Rescue League had offered to house the rest.

All Bair knew was that the dogs had come from a high-volume breeding operation in Lower Oxford that had been busted five days earlier. The dogs had now taken their third road trip in as many days. "The journey had to be intimidating for those dogs," Bair thought as Rudy and McGlory carried in the last of the crates.

Bair ran the Rescue League's boarding kennel—the wing set aside for dogs whose owners were out of town. She also tended to pregnant dogs, orphaned puppies, and, every now and then, a group of dogs involved in a court case, which was the category Wolf's dogs fell into. The newcomers would remain at the Rescue League until the charges against Wolf were resolved, however long that took.

Inside one of the crates, a tricolor Cavalier King Charles Spaniel with enormous eyes and feathery ears trembled. A self-confident animal might have been curious about her new surroundings. She might have glanced about at the shady elms that flanked the shelter or squinted up at the winter sun. But Dog 132 wasn't noticing any of this. She cast her eyes downward as Rudy sat her crate against one wall of the wide hallway into the boarding wing, where Bair stood waiting.

Bair knelt and peered inside the crates. She counted one Havanese puppy, two English Bulldogs, and nine Cavaliers. She'd been told to expect a dozen dogs, and it looked as though all twelve were accounted for. She'd cleaned out six cinderblock kennels; the dogs were small enough to fit in them nicely, two by two. The Bulldogs could share one kennel. The Havanese could bunk with one of the Cavaliers. That left eight more Cavs, and it occurred to Bair that if she separated them by color—if she put a tricolor and a chestnut and white Blenheim in each three-by-three-foot kennel—it would be easier to tell them apart.

She had to admit, the thought of caring for a dozen new dogs at once was a little overwhelming. Bair knew something about English Bulldogs, but next to nothing about Havanese and Cavaliers. They were considered toy breeds, and when it came time for the Toy Group to trot around the ring at the Westminster Kennel Club Show, well, that's when she turned off the TV, got up off the couch, and went to do the laundry. "Toy" dogs weren't real dogs, as far as she was concerned.

Bair could see that one of the Blenheim Cavaliers was close to giving birth. Despite her distended belly, the dog looked puny and seemed overcome with fatigue. One of the mostly black and white Cavaliers, number 132, was also smaller and more sickly looking than the rest. She must have had a litter recently—her mammary glands practically swept the ground. Bair especially wanted to keep an eye on that one. She assigned the pregnant dog the kennel on the end, closest to the aisle, and the black and white dog the second kennel from the end—the dogs would be easier to see there, even from a distance.

McGlory gently lowered the crate containing Dog 132 onto the cement floor, unlatched the door, removed the foul-smelling creature, and set her down in her new home. Folded neatly and tucked into one corner of the kennel was a faded pink blanket, Bair's favorite color. In the far corner sat a bowl of clean water.

After years of living on a hard wire floor, her paws raw from being splayed out, the solid feel of the cool cement floors must have felt strange but good to the little dog. Outwardly, though, the Cavalier registered nothing; she stood motionless. Minutes later, McGlory delivered her roommate: a Blenheim Cavalier, another female. If Dog 132 recognized the other dog, she didn't show it; she ignored the Blenheim, and the Blenheim ignored her. "Oh, great," thought Bair, "now there are two dogs standing side by side like statues."

She shook her head. The Bulldogs and the Havanese would be easy enough to bond with, but the Cavaliers were going to be high maintenance. She just knew it.

EVEN THE BEST-INTENTIONED shelters can be dimly lit, smelly, and raucous—light years better than a puppy mill, certainly, but a far cry from a real home. But if most shelters could be likened to a Motel 6, the Berks County Rescue League shelter was more along the lines of a Marriott. It sat on ten acres of lush, wooded grounds crisscrossed with tree-lined walking paths. In addition to the kennels and a crematorium, the main building offered a grooming room and a surgical suite. Outside, a small barn housed a rotating parade of horses, llamas, and other large animals. On a grassy spot halfway up a bank sat a statue of St. Francis of Assisi, the patron saint of animals, and next to it was a saying of Assisi's that had been carved into stone: "If you have men who will exclude any of God's creatures from the shelter of compassion and pity, you will have men who deal likewise with their fellow men." It was a gentle reminder that any animal brought there deserved to be treated with respect.

The timing of the rescue was fortuitous. It was February, the off-season for the rescue league's boarding business. As a result, that wing of the shelter was only half full, giving Bair and her associates extra time to devote to the puppy mill survivors. It was obvious the dogs were going to need as much as attention as the staff was able to give.

The Berks County shelter usually dealt with lost or abandoned dogs, or dogs whose owners no longer wanted them. Either the dogs had grown too old and feeble, or they didn't get along with the family's new pet, or their owners had divorced and moved to apartments that didn't allow dogs. The shelter lacked the space and money to house dogs indefinitely, however. Eventually, if someone didn't adopt a dog, the animal was euthanized. For four million dogs in the United States each year, ending up at a shelter means a date with death.

The puppy mill survivors were different. They weren't going anywhere until their legal case was closed, and that could take months. Knowing the dogs were staying put for a while gave shelter techs a chance to bond with them, give them names, furnish them with toys and blankets, and even play with them from time to time.

The only disadvantage to forming such close ties was knowing that one day these dogs, too, would leave.

Fifty years old and constantly in motion, Bair had worked at the shelter for six years. Before that she'd handled claims for an insurance office, typed briefs as a legal secretary, and tended to residents of the Rainbow Home, an AIDS hospice in nearby Wernersville. She hadn't minded changing diapers for the AIDS patients—now that she was middle-aged, she actually enjoyed performing chores others couldn't or wouldn't do—but when the opportunity came to care for needy animals, she didn't hesitate to apply for it. In shelter parlance, she was a boarding kennel technician, a euphemistic title for someone who spent much of her day scouring kennels and scooping poop. The grunt work was worth doing in exchange for the chance to bestow a little kindness on a scared and lonely animal.

She'd been given little advance notice about the dogs from Mike-Mar Kennel and had no idea what kind of shape they would be in. On a hunch, she'd hauled in enormous bags of puppy food. Puppy food contained more protein than regular dog food, and protein was something these dogs were likely to need. She'd stocked up on a nutritional supplement in case the dogs were emaciated and needed to gain weight. And she had amassed a thick pile of blankets and an assortment of toys she'd picked up for pennies at a local thrift shop. The Rescue League was good about paying for things like that.

Havanese, a breed originally from Cuba, are normally happy and affectionate dogs, known for being smart, curious, and playful. Bulldogs are people lovers, too, dependable and gentle with children, while Cavaliers ordinarily are sociable, enthusiastic, and active. But while the Bulldogs and the Havanese were friendly and approachable that first day, the Cavaliers were quiet and withdrawn. The smaller dogs apparently had never interacted in any meaningful way with human beings. For all these dogs knew, they'd been moved from one puppy mill to another, and a puppy mill was a frightening place to be. At the sound of approaching footsteps, they bolted to the rearmost corner of their kennels and cringed in fear.

None of this behavior surprised Harry D. Brown III, the shelter's executive director. He'd seen enough puppy mill survivors to understand how baffling the sudden transition to life outside a cage could be. The younger dogs would adapt to their new surroundings fairly quickly, Brown suspected, but the older dogs would have a harder time adjusting. A puppy mill survivor who had spun in circles to overcome the tedium of confinement might continue to spin long after escaping a crate, for example. Brown kept a Jack Russell Terrier in his office who covered several miles during the course of a day, all of it in a three-foot radius.

Nearly every puppy mill survivor Brown encountered refused to walk on a leash; the dogs had no clue how to behave. And they were so accustomed to standing on wire that when they finally got the chance to stand on cement floors—the first solid footing many had experienced—it felt so foreign that they tiptoed. Saddest of all, these dogs had never learned to trust humans. They'd never had any reason to do so, and at the sight of strangers they practically shrank. After two or three weeks of care, some dogs began to respond, but others never came around. They remained shy and skittish for the rest of their lives.

The staff understood that Wolf's dogs needed as much TLC as they could give them. The animals were grubby and covered with infections and parasites. But it was the emotional suffering evident on the faces of Dog 132 and the others that weighed on Bair the most. The dogs were still on her mind that evening as she drove home to her century-old Victorian house in nearby Shillington, and again after dinner, when she settled onto the sofa with her own two dogs, Dudley and Odie. Basset Hounds, they were shelter rescues, adopted just in time to spare them from euthanasia. "Thank goodness neither suffered anywhere near the degree of neglect Michael Wolf's dogs experienced," Bair thought. Like most of the dogs headed for the "sleeper," the Bassets had committed the unforgivable sins of being old and inconvenient. "Now that he's five or six and housebroken and perfect, I don't have the time," is what their owners might as well have been saying when they dropped their pets off at the shelter.

There was no sense dwelling on the regrettable facts of life that came with shelter work. Bair learned early on that you just had to roll with it, because the next day would present a brand-new cat or dog who needed to be cared for. Still, it helped to be able to go home to her own fortunate dogs, whom she knew were free to lollygag away the hours until the mistress of the house arrived at the end of the day to feed them dinner. Seeing these carefree survivors always managed to bring her mood around. "You guys have no idea how good you have it, dust bunnies and all," Bair thought as she aimed a mock evil eye in Dudley's direction.

DOGS THRIVE ON routine. For Dog 132 and the other puppy mill survivors, life at the Berks County shelter would revolve around routine. The dogs were given two meals their first day at the shelter. Day two began with still more food—a small bowl of dried kibble mixed with canned food for each. Food was plentiful at the shelter. That was one of Bair's rules: As soon as a dog emptied the bowl, she told workers, fill it up again. Dog 132 picked at her portion, but she stared at her bowl as if to marvel, *Every day?*

After breakfast it was time to scrub the kennels. The dogs hadn't been at the shelter twenty-four hours and already their kennels were smeared with feces. One of the biggest perks of the boarding wing was the small guillotine doors in the kennels that, when raised, enabled the dogs to step out into a graveled run. One by one that morning, the techs opened the doors, guided the dogs outside, then lowered the doors behind them and hosed down the kennels with a disinfectant powerful enough to kill the most potent germs. They wiped the kennels down with towels and let them air dry, then raised the doors again and let the dogs back in.

The rest of the day was consumed by paperwork and physical exams, including one emergency. The tail on one of the Bulldogs had grown backward into her rectum, causing a hideous-looking abscess; the tail would have to be surgically removed.

As workers strode up and down the aisle, they ran their fingers playfully across the kennel doors and squatted down to try to connect with pair after pair of bewildered eyes. Dog 132 wasn't used to having anyone seek out her attention. Like everything else about the kennel, the friendly faces and soothing words were new and strange. They made her uncomfortable. She refused to meet anyone's gaze. Some of the other Cavaliers avoided eye contact, too, a habit that kennel tech Sandy Lambert, for one, found enormously frustrating. She was going to have trouble bonding with dogs who wouldn't even look at her.

On top of their confusion, the dogs simply didn't feel very good. That afternoon they were examined by the shelter's veterinarian, Carl Veltri. For a small dog—she weighed just sixteen pounds—Dog 132 had more than her share of ailments. A skin infection riddled her patchy coat. Her ears were infected and filled with mucus. She had a case of dry eye so advanced it had left her half blind, and her teeth were almost completely decayed. Veltri prescribed antibiotics for her skin infection and daily drops for her raw, red eyes. For now, that would have to do.

Bair fed the dogs again in the late afternoon before she left for the day. By the time she arrived for work the next morning, a fresh new odor of excrement permeated the boarding wing. The dogs' coats were filthy and full of mats, and they smelled like sewer rats. Bath time could not come soon enough. Gwen Engler, the shelter's groomer, was as eager as anyone to lather them up. Most of the dogs' physical problems could be chalked up to plain and simple dirt, Engler believed. They were covered in it. They smelled unlike anything she had ever encountered: a combination of urine and feces, certainly, and something else besides. A uniquely awful *funk*.

For months afterward, Engler savored the memories of how bedraggled the dogs looked the morning before their shampoos and how noticeably improved they looked after. She arrived early for the big job. It was doubtful any of the dogs had ever had a bath, and Engler wondered how they would respond to the billowing suds. Almost all of the dogs had skin infections. In addition, the Cavaliers all had pyoderma, tiny red bumps that covered their legs like a heat rash. Instead of a simple lather and rinse, Engler needed to treat them with medicated shampoo and let it work it into their coats for a full ten minutes to flush the hair follicles.

The groomer lined up the special shampoo on a counter next to the claw-foot tub where she had bathed hundreds of dogs over the past five years. She brought Wolf's dogs back in twos, one under each arm. Dog 132 and her kennelmate were the second pair to go. When it came her turn, Dog 132 stood quietly while Engler worked the tingling suds into her itchy skin. Ten minutes of wet lather must have seemed an eternity, but Dog 132 didn't budge. She seemed distant, detached, as if she were trying to block out the experience. As jets of warm water engulfed her, she stood immobile, frozen with apprehension the way Engler had seen other puppy mill dogs react. Some dogs would have thrashed about in the water. Not this dog. She didn't even twitch. She was resigned to letting Engler do with her whatever needed doing. The groomer was struck by how little trouble the Cavalier gave her, and also how removed she seemed. For the duration of the bath, Engler spoke tenderly to the little dog, but not once did the Cavalier gaze up at her or swish her tail in response.

Afterward, Engler toweled off Dog 132, placed her and her kennelmate in the same crate, and aimed an industrial-strength hair

Groomer Gwen Engler gives Dog 132 a soothing
bath at the Berks County Animal Rescue League.

dryer at their damp coats. Neither Cavalier reacted one way or the
other to their small confines or to the dryer's roar.

It would be months before the ammonia-laced odor would disappear from her body for good, but for Dog 132, bath day marked
a turning point. For the first time in years, the Cavalier had obtained
some relief from the eye-stinging fumes. Tears welled in Bair's eyes
when Engler brought the silky-feeling dog back to her kennel. "You
can't tell me that doesn't feel good," Bair thought as the rest of the
newly bathed dogs returned to their kennels.

Their cleanliness was short-lived. Within a couple of days of
their baths, the dogs reeked of excrement again. They thought nothing of eliminating where they lived, stepping in their own waste and,
in the process, daubing fecal matter all over the floor, the walls, and
themselves. "They don't know any better," Bair and her cohorts
told themselves each morning as they scoured the kennels yet again.
How could they? All their lives these dogs had lived five and six to
a cage, caked with feces. They'd had no choice but to tolerate the
muck.

Still, Bair couldn't bear to see any dog living in that kind of filth.
Every time she or her colleagues encountered a mess, they removed

the dogs, disinfected the kennel, and installed new bedding, even if the kennel had already been hosed down that morning. Bair vowed to do seventeen loads of laundry a day, if necessary, to keep the dogs' living quarters presentable. The lingering smell of bodily waste might stir bad memories for these vulnerable survivors, and that was something she wanted to make every effort to avoid.

A week after getting their first baths, the dogs were bathed again, and this time Engler shaved them down. It was easier to wash excrement out of a shorthaired dog, she'd decided. Dog 132 acquiesced silently as the groomer ran an electric razor carefully up and down her back and sides, across her tummy, and in and around her stubby legs, lopping off the clean but malodorous hair.

SHELTER TECHS LIVE for those milestones, those blink-and-you'll-miss-it moments when they can detect a glimmer of hope in the eyes of an abused animal. It had happened a month earlier, when a Pit Bull who'd been used as bait in a fighting ring was brought in after a raid, bloodied and scarred and lacking any reason ever to trust a human being again. In a matter of days, Prince was lavishing slurpy kisses on Lambert, grateful for the food and water she had given him, for the walks she had taken him on, and for his new and dignified name. Not all dogs rebounded that quickly, however. Some of them never turned the corner.

Kennel manager Lisa Hill struggled to come to grips with the Wolf dogs' history of abuse. It infuriated her that people could show such callous disregard for animals. Unlike Bair, Hill was fairly new to rescue work—she'd spent most of her years working in factories—and she'd never learned to move beyond the raw aftermath of cruelty that was manifested at the shelter day in and day out. She often left in tears at the end of her shift.

Bair grieved, too, for the unlucky dogs, but experience had taught her that their stories didn't always end badly. Each time a resident of the shelter found a new home, it was cause for celebration. The good news had a way of easing the sorrow of the bad.

A week passed. Thanks to Hill and Lambert, the dogs now had names. The Bulldogs were Babs and Bubbles. The Havanese was Nicolette. The Cavs were dubbed Charlotte, Thelma Lou, Betsy, Ruthie, Shirley, and Bunny. In an attempt at irony, the pregnant Cavalier was named Jolie after Angelina Jolie, who was as gorgeous as this Jolie was homely. For the next four and a half months, Dog 132 would be called Wilma. Her kennelmate was Patty.

From the start, the two puppies in the group, Babs and Nicolette, were energetic and cheerful. They hadn't endured the misery of puppy mill life long enough to be traumatized. Betsy, the smallest of the Cavaliers, had a ravenous appetite for some reason; the techs needed to watch to make sure she didn't steal her kennelmate's food. The nine remaining dogs had been penned up for so long that they needed to test their new world cautiously, at their own pace. It was possible to win over a dog who'd been neglected and abused as long as Wolf's animals had, but it wasn't going to happen right away. These dogs were as emotionally damaged as any Bair had seen.

Two weeks after the dogs' arrival, Jolie gave birth to a litter of puppies and refused to have anything to do with the squirming newborns. Bair found them lying cold on the cement floor of the kennel the next morning. She tried everything she knew to keep them warm, but within a week all six of the puppies were dead. She couldn't blame Jolie for rejecting her babies. The poor dog had borne litters all her life. She was worn out.

Still, the death of the puppies inspired Bair anew to demonstrate, over and over, that she was *there* for these dogs. Whenever she had a few minutes to spare, she stepped inside a kennel, lay down next to its inhabitants, stroked their coats, and cooed to them non-stop. The shower of attention conveyed a powerful message: *You're a good dog. You're special. Somebody loves you.* The payoff would come, she knew.

Change did come, gradually. By early March, the dogs looked healthier. Their coats were growing back in, albeit slowly. Their bodies had begun to fill out. Their eyes were starting to lose that awful dullness and take on a little shine.

The dogs also appeared to appreciate their clean kennels, even if they kept soiling them. Once nighttime temperatures crept above fifty-five degrees, workers left the guillotine doors open day and night, and a couple of the dogs took advantage of the arrangement to go potty outside. They seemed to like having clean kennels. They were housetraining themselves.

Over time, the puppy mill survivors lost their fear of water. For the first weeks at the shelter the dogs were shampooed weekly, then monthly after that. They loosened up in the tub and learned to turn around for Engler with just a little prodding. Back in their kennels, they cuddled up with their blankets. Toys, stuffed or squeaky, were less of a hit. The puppies adored them, but the older dogs couldn't grasp the purpose of lavishing attention on an inanimate object. The blankets, though, were something else entirely. After years of living on wire mesh, the dogs grew to cherish the soft layers of warmth. They had no idea Bair was color-coordinating the blankets with the color of the dogs' coats, but the tenderness she brought to the task was evident.

The dogs needed as much socializing as they could get. Bair and her co-workers made it a practice to greet their wards as they passed back and forth during the course of a day. Frequently a tech would kneel down, reach some fingers through a chain-link door and stroke a face or squeeze a paw. The staff addressed the dogs by their newly given names, and in a matter of weeks some of the dogs began to answer back. Instead of retreating to the rear of their kennels, they trotted forward at the sound of someone's approach, stood up on their hind legs and wagged their tails. To Lambert, watching their personalities emerge was like watching a flower bloom—something you would expect to see in a puppy, but rarely an adult dog.

Dog 132 hung back. She still soiled her kennel and still stepped in her own feces. Emotionally, she remained maddeningly out of reach. She paced back and forth, seldom responding when staffers greeted her by name. The techs knew from experience that dogs were capable of a wide range of emotion: anticipation, gratitude, anger, fear, jealousy, exuberance, love. But Dog 132 seemed too closed off to feel anything but numb. She was so tiny, so devoid of personality. Some of the dogs came around nicely, Hill noticed. Some didn't. Number 132 didn't.

Veltri later estimated Dog 132 to be 6 years old. She'd been born in a crate, reared in a crate, and forever after confined to one. At last she'd been liberated. Finally she was in a safe place, a place where she was getting plenty of food and, even more special, human compassion. Yet she seemed incapable of deriving pleasure from any of it.

For centuries, scientists and philosophers debated the capacity of animals to suffer fear and pain. The staff at the Rescue League didn't need to be told what modern-day studies have concluded: that neglected and mistreated animals do feel pain, and not just physical pain but emotional deprivation, too. The techs saw the effects of abuse firsthand. And they knew that while many dogs were able to get over the past, some never would recover. Which camp would Dog 132, Wilma, fall into? They were starting to wonder.

8

The Case Goes to Court

A SSISTANT DISTRICT attorney Finnegan stood aside as Shaw rolled open the wooden doors that led into the Chester County SPCA shelter. The women threaded their way past the wing full of adoptable dogs—the part of the shelter the public got to see—and stepped through another doorway, into the building's back half. The noise was deafening. Before them stretched a succession of runs, a seemingly endless row of cinderblock and chain-link cells. Inside each kennel were nine or ten Havanese, Cavaliers, English Bulldogs, and Papillons, 200 dogs in all. And those were just two-thirds of the dogs taken from Mike-Mar Kennel. Another 130 or so had been parceled out to other facilities.

Finnegan had braced herself to see a roomful of animals, but the reality was startling. "Holy s——t, Cheryl, that's a lot of dogs," she said.

Lorraine Marie Belfiglio Finnegan, 47, was a senior lawyer with the D.A.'s office, a mother of four and a dog person. No one needed to explain to her what was wrong with this picture. Her indignation already ran high.

She'd taken a circuitous career route. After graduating from Southwestern University law school in 1983, she worked for the D.A. for six years before leaving to try her hand at insurance-defense law. She'd returned briefly to the D.A.'s office before the Mommy Track beckoned and she dropped out of the workplace to start a family. For eleven years, between breast-feedings, she practiced law at her kitchen table: family wills, estate matters, that sort of thing. In 2001, she returned to Chester County as an assistant D.A., one of thirty who worked out of the courthouse downtown. Her reintroduction to the courtroom was trial by fire—her first case involved some skinheads who had robbed and stabbed a bar patron to death—and she'd been inundated with assignments ever since. She commuted an hour each way from the suburb of Drexel Hill, and in spite of all the ball-juggling she made it work, somehow, by focusing on her job when she was on the job and on her family the instant she left the courthouse at the end of the day.

Her husband, Ed, was a public defender in nearby Delaware County and understood the pressures that came with her job. The kids—Danny, 15; Catherine, 14; Emily, 12; and Jacqueline, 8—realized, too, that if Mom could make it to their special events, she would, but those occasions would be rare.

The first few days after the raid, the atmosphere at the SPCA shelter was chaotic as staffers and volunteers processed dogs, shipped some out to other shelters, and organized provisions for the dogs who remained. Finnegan deliberately waited until things settled down before driving out to meet with shelter officials about the case.

Six days after the raid, on the morning of February 16, 2006, Finnegan left the Chester County Courthouse, climbed into her Honda Civic, and headed east of town. Ten minutes later she turned left onto Phoenixville Pike. The SPCA was a third of a mile down the road. Before visiting the dogs, she met with SPCA executive director Spackman, operations manager McMichael, animal protective services coordinator Turnbull, and Shaw. They walked

Chester County assistant district attorney Lori Finnegan was assigned to prosecute Wolf and his partners, to win justice on behalf of the dogs.

her through the details of the raid. Then it was their turn to listen as Finnegan described the options that existed for going after Wolf.

The bad news was that the animal cruelty charges filed against Wolf, Trottier, and Hills were classified as summary offenses. In Pennsylvania, a summary offense was considered less serious than a misdemeanor—more along the lines of a traffic violation—and did not warrant a jury trial. The case would be decided by a district judge instead. Still, the animal cruelty charges were numerous, and they could add up. Each charge carried a fine of anywhere from $50 to $750, imprisonment for up to ninety days, or both.

The SPCA officials were adamant that Wolf be prosecuted fully and that none of his animals be returned to him. Not one.

Ideally, Finnegan told them, the rescuers would have confiscated some of the key evidence the night of the raid. The garbage cans full of soiled newspaper, for instance, would have made for a memorable exhibit in court. Wolf's computer likely contained a treasure trove of information that could have been used against him. Instead, rescuers were focused so intently on removing the dogs that they had overlooked the significance of Wolf sitting at his computer the night of the raid. There was no telling how much evidence he'd destroyed right under their noses.

At least Shaw had the presence of mind to videotape Wolf's compound before the raid got under way. The grainy footage appeared dark on the small screen; when Shaw played it for Finnegan, the prosecutor had to lean forward to make out any details. She asked if she could take the tape with her. Absolutely, Shaw said. For the next couple of months the prosecutor would view the tape over and over, determined to document every remnant of filth and rubbish in every room.

The evidence against Wolf, Trottier, and Hills seemed abundant, yet Finnegan hadn't lost sight of Wolf's once-formidable reputation in dog-show circles. Until she was assigned to the case, she'd never even heard of Wolf. She'd never been to a dog show, and she knew nothing about puppy mills. Her family's Pomeranian and Sheltie were beloved pets, not trophy winners or birthing machines. But people who knew of Wolf spoke of him with near reverence. To win the case, Finnegan needed to peel back his glamorous veneer to reveal the miserable conditions inside his kennel, conditions dog show judges never got to see. She needed to emphasize the lice, mange, and other afflictions suffered by Wolf's dogs; the untreated broken legs found on several of the animals; and the urine-slick floors that the dogs who were allowed to run loose slid about on.

The Wolf case had one thing in common with murders and child abuse investigations: The victims were mute, incapable of describing the crimes against them. To compensate, the evidence presented in court needed to be clear, persuasive, and overwhelming. She needed to nail the coffin shut.

Because of the enormity of the case, district attorney Joe Carroll assigned Finnegan an assistant, her officemate, Kate Wright. Wright's family had owned a Husky while she was growing up. She doted on her brother's Toy Fox Terrier–Jack Russell mix and her grandmother's Cocker Spaniel, and she still mourned the recent death of her sister's Husky to Coonhound syndrome, a disease that attacks the nerves near the base of the spinal cord, causing a fast-moving paralysis. For now, anyway, the 28-year-old prosecutor's life was too hectic to accommodate a dog of her own.

Finnegan compiled a long list of potential witnesses she planned to call to the stand. She interviewed Shaw, Beswick, Green, and others who had taken part in the raid. She met twice with Siddons, the dog warden who accompanied Shaw on the initial visit to Wolf's home. Finnegan also wanted to question the veterinarians who'd treated the dogs in the days afterward. She asked Wright to interview the vets by phone and determine which two or three could best articulate their findings on the witness stand.

Among the vets Wright selected was Ravinda Murarka, a veterinarian with the Pennsylvania SPCA in Philadelphia. Murarka, who was of eastern Indian background, spoke with a deep accent—the judge would need to pay close attention to understand him—but his knowledge of dogs was exhaustive. His job gave Murarka a chance to witness the most egregious forms of animal abuse, and yet even he had been struck by the neglect suffered by Wolf's dogs. He would make an excellent witness, Wright believed.

Wright also chose Bryan Langlois, a veterinarian at the Humane League of Lancaster County, which had taken in several of Wolf's dogs, and Larry Dieter, the veterinarian for the Chester County SPCA. A fourth vet, Amy Parkman of West Chester Veterinary Medical Center, had cared for some of Wolf's sickest animals following the raid and was able to provide valuable background about the skin infections, the ear and eye infections, and the other diseases and parasites she found in some the dogs.

STORIES ABOUT MIKE-MAR KENNEL continued to trickle in after the raid. Customers reported purchasing puppies only to discover later that the dogs were sick. In some cases buyers spent thousands of dollars trying to heal their new pets. The calls were interesting, but they didn't yield anything that could be used in the Wolf case.

Information gathered during the raid provided ample enough evidence. As they built their case, Finnegan and Wright covered their office walls with charts and photos of Wolf's compound and piled related documents in stacks around Finnegan's desk. The fate of the neglected dogs began to consume them in a way run-of-the-mill cases seldom did. Finnegan had handled animal cruelty cases before, but she'd never seen dogs shake with fear the way Wolf's dogs had. How could a man who'd spent decades lavishing attention on show dogs demonstrate such blatant disregard for his "babies"—hundreds of them left at home in reeking filth?

Once a week, usually at the beginning of her day, Finnegan drove out to the SPCA shelter to visit Wolf's dogs. Some days she was content to kneel outside a single run and observe the dogs inside. Other days she walked up and down the aisles, checking on as many of the dogs as she could. When she had the time, she would open up a kennel door, sit on the cement floor, and let the wary but curious inhabitants wander over to her. The visits stirred in her a jumble of anger, sadness, and pity. "If we fail to convict this man of animal cruelty, the lives of his dogs won't ever change," she thought to herself. "They'll live out their days in cages smaller than the ones they're in now."

She tried in some small way to let the dogs know someone cared, and each time she visited she went out of her way to thank the SPCA staff and volunteers for their hard work. One person she almost always encountered was her boss's daughter, Jennifer Carroll, a college student who was considering veterinary school. Carroll showed up to perform whatever chore needed doing, including scrubbing floors. On the drive to work afterward, Finnegan asked herself if there was something she could be doing to move the case along a little faster.

Nearly everyone at the shelter had shifted their duties to help care for Wolf's dogs. Officer Beswick had offered to handle most of the new investigations so that Shaw could prepare for the trial and handle any issue that arose with Wolf's dogs. Managing the fallout from the case had become a full-time job in itself. Throughout the day, Shaw fielded phone calls from veterinarians and others involved with the dogs' care. She worked closely to substantiate the evidence Finnegan planned to present in court. If she couldn't nail the evidence, Shaw worried, the dogs could wind up back at Wolf's. "No holes," she kept telling herself. "If I lose, all those animals lose, too."

WOLF WAS BUSY planning his own strategy. He'd hired a team of lawyers led by Eric Coates of Oxford. Coates had a rapport with the judge and would act as the spokesman for the group. The other attorneys—John Alice of Philadelphia and Charles Iannuzzi of nearby Woodbury, New Jersey—had litigation experience. Iannuzzi had a track record of representing alleged animal abusers.

Publicly, Coates pooh-poohed the allegations against his client. "Michael loves his dogs," he told one newspaper. "He'd go overboard to treat them as pets. The ones that needed vet treatment, he was tending to. It was not out of control."

Behind the scenes, the lawyers asked for repeated delays in the trial. Each time a specific court date was suggested, one or another defense attorney claimed to have a conflict in his schedule. The earliest date the two sides could agree to was April 11.

Once the date was set, the defense attorneys pressed for a deal that would allow Wolf to keep as many as sixty of the dogs. Finnegan and Wright refused to entertain the possibility. The idea of sending any of the dogs back to Mike-Mar Kennel struck the prosecutors as unconscionable. The dogs had lived in squalor long enough.

Publicity about the Wolf case continued to spread. In the first couple of weeks after the dogs' rescue, newspapers and television stations filed dozens of stories about the plight of the dogs. The SPCA fielded 3,000 calls from animal lovers offering to donate money, purchase dog food, drop off supplies, or give the dogs new homes. Animal lovers from across the country wrote to Finnegan and Wright urging them to win justice on behalf of the victimized dogs. The prosecutors taped the letters to the walls of their office; they were a daily reminder that the outcome of the case would have ripple effects not just in Chester County, but nationwide.

The American Kennel Club also weighed in. AKC board chairman Ron Menaker cited the raid on Wolf's kennel as an example of the need for stronger federal oversight. Despite disciplinary action by the AKC, Menaker said, Wolf had continued to operate a large-volume kennel "under the radar."

"This is a pattern we see all too often," Menaker added in a statement. "Breeders stop registering with us in order to avoid inspection after we take disciplinary action against them. Unfortunately, however, many of these people continue breeding and sell dogs, and register them with a for-profit registry that has no inspection requirements to monitor care and conditions standards."

His comments drew a stinging rebuke from Margaret "Peggy" Mickelson, a breeder and veteran AKC judge. In a lengthy e-mail she sent to an Internet chat site about Cavaliers—which was swiftly forwarded to other sites—she accused the AKC of willfully ignoring the problems at Mike-Mar Kennel while continuing to accept registration fees paid by Wolf.

"[Wolf's] facility has been notorious in the dog world for many, many years, AKC inspection or not," Mickelson wrote. "The only reason AKC is doing anything publicly now is because the world is aware of the conditions. . . ."

For years, Mickelson added, "it was known that [Wolf] kept Pekingese in rows of wire crates stacked one on top of the other so that the rows were five wide and four high, with no flooring to prevent feces and other excrement from falling from top to bottom. The Pekes were never out of the crates except to be bred and to whelp . . . and when there got to be too many, he simply put them down [himself], in terrific numbers, and started keeping the younger ones in the same fashion."

She ended her e-mail with a flourish. "This whole matter disgusts me from *any* view, and everyone connected with this fiasco should be hung up by their genitals, if they all have them. And that includes the AKC and Mr. Menaker."

AT 9 A.M. ON Tuesday, April 11, the case against Wolf, Trottier, and Hills got under way in the town of Oxford. Presiding was judge Harry Farmer Jr., the same judge who had signed the search warrant authorizing the raid.

The courtroom was so tiny that the defendants had to sit behind their attorneys, in the front row of the spectators' gallery. Behind them was Trottier's mother, Wendy. Ten SPCA staffers, representatives of other animal welfare organizations, and a camera operator for a television station filled the rest of the seats. Onlookers unable to find a seat were told to leave. The judge refused to allow spectators to stand in the rear.

Anyone who came expecting instant fireworks was disappointed. At the outset, Farmer questioned the need to have a separate attorney for each defendant. "You got two counsel. Why do you need him here?" he asked, referring to Iannuzzi. After the judge finally acquiesced, the defense then moved to suppress the search warrant the SPCA had used to enter Wolf's property. The breeders' attorneys also asked Farmer to recuse himself from hearing the motion on the grounds that he'd signed the search warrant authorizing the raid and might need to be called as a witness. This was news to Farmer. Nobody had told him they intended to call him to the stand. "Now, all of a sudden, you are alleging I have a conflict and, you know, I'm a potential witness. Am I or am I not?" the judge said.

Farmer refused to recuse himself, but the rest of the morning was consumed by the motion to suppress the search warrant. Two days before the raid, Coates argued, Shaw and Siddons had reached an agreement with Wolf whereby he would have a veterinarian examine and vaccinate his dogs, an understanding Coates said Shaw neglected to disclose to the judge when she requested the search warrant. Coates also argued that Shaw took more animals from Mike-Mar Kennel than she had identified in the warrant.

That point was true, but it didn't constitute grounds for dismissing the case. Finnegan called Siddons to the stand. She asked her to describe the powerful odor of ammonia that struck her when she'd first stepped into Wolf's home two months earlier.

"The smell was overwhelming," Siddons testified. Throughout the visit, she said, her eyes watered, she had problems breathing, and she had to retreat three times to compose herself enough to continue.

Inside and outside of Mike-Mar Kennel, Siddons said, she saw heavily matted dogs and feces. Excrement littered the deck outside and overflowed from the dogs' pens inside. In one of the rooms, soiled newspaper spilled out of a fifty-five-gallon trash can.

When she first glimpsed Trottier and Hills, Siddons said, they were "furiously trying to clean." Asked what she meant by that, she said, "trying to clean before somebody else gets in there. In other words, being very quick about it, because they knew it needed to be cleaned."

Coates saw an opening.

"If you have to clean for 137 dogs . . . if you want to do it twice a day, you have to move pretty quickly, right?" he said. "You don't clean a pen and the dog waits twenty-four hours or forty-eight hours to urinate or poop. It happens all day long, is that right?"

"Yes," Siddons responded.

"But [the defendants] are not expected to stand there and clean up after every waste, are they?" Coates said.

He interrupted again after Siddons described seeing four dogs each in pens approximately two and a half feet by three and a half feet in size.

"So it wasn't a crowding situation?" Coates asked.

"No, not as far as size of the dogs was concerned," the dog warden replied.

Coates asked if Siddons was present when Shaw contacted the veterinarian, Tom Stevenson, to verify that he'd had an appointment with Wolf the day of the inspection, but hadn't made it for some reason or another. Siddons said she was aware that Stevenson showed up the next day.

Later, Coates asked, "Have you ever cleaned pens before?" Finnegan objected, so Coates rephrased the question. "Can you tell me which of these dogs appears to be the object of cruelty?" Under questioning by Iannuzzi, Siddons conceded that at the time she and Shaw left Wolf's property that afternoon, she had no plans to remove the dogs.

Siddons stepped down from the witness stand. Other than describing the acrid air inside Wolf's kennel, she hadn't done the prosecution any favors.

Finnegan next called Shaw to the stand. The prosecutor walked the officer through the events of February 8—how, upon exiting the van, she'd seen approximately ten dogs in the front yard of the kennel, a handful of dogs in the gated area of the rear residence, several Cavaliers sitting on the couch inside Wolf's home, and back rooms filled with cages full of dogs. At the rear of Wolf's house was a deck covered in feces. It, too, was overrun by Bulldogs and Cavaliers.

"Describe what you noticed about the dogs," Finnegan said to her.

"There were several that were heavily matted," Shaw replied. "There appeared to be feces, dirt imbedded into the mats. A lot of the dogs had clouded-over eyes. There were a lot of dogs that had a green mucusy-type substance coming from their eye area."

Some of the crates lacked water. In crates that had water, the insides of the bowl were ringed with slime. The cages were soiled by waste. The smell was overwhelming, Shaw reiterated.

After touring the house and the kennel, Shaw issued Wolf a notice of mandatory corrections, she testified. He needed to provide all animals with clean drinking water, a clean and sanitary environment, and veterinary care for their skin and eye infections. He needed to remove the matting and the dirt from all of the dogs, and he needed to reduce the number of dogs on the premises, possibly by surrendering some of them each week to the SPCA. In any case, Wolf needed to provide documentation for the animals' whereabouts.

Coates cross-examined her. "Do you know what happens to water containers when there is a lot of iron in the water?" he asked.

"No, sir," Shaw replied.

"If I told you that there was high iron content in the water, that it would make containers turn brown—"

"Objection," Finnegan said.

"—It gets brown," Coates finished.

The defense attorney noted that in the report Shaw filed the day of the inspection, she described the matting and mud on the dogs, but failed to mention the presence of any feces. Coates accused her of ignoring her agreement with Wolf and instead seizing the animals and filing charges against him.

Coates also faulted Shaw for failing to obtain search warrants for two separate properties from the outset. "All they had to do was do it right, but they didn't," Coates told the judge. "There's enough taint there to say that everything has to go—all the pictures, all the photographs, all the dogs, everything . . . because they didn't give you all the facts."

The judge didn't buy it. The inspectors may have had an understanding with Wolf, but that didn't preclude them from returning to remove the dogs, Farmer said. He denied the motion to end the trial and recessed court until 1:30 p.m.

9

Proving Cruelty

MICHAEL WOLF'S ATTORNEYS had failed to stop the trial. Now, finally, prosecutors could get to the heart of the cruelty charges. Assistant D.A.s Finnegan and Wright felt good about their prospects of winning. They were confident Judge Farmer would find Michael Wolf, Gordon Trottier, and Margaret Hills guilty as charged. The lives of 333 dogs, 2 cats, and 2 macaw parrots rested on the outcome.

Spectators filed in after lunch, and Judge Farmer reconvened court. Finnegan recalled Siddons to the stand. She testified that she had been a dog warden for the state of Pennsylvania for ten years and during that time had inspected 160 or so licensed kennels twice a year. That amounted to roughly 3,200 inspections, if anyone bothered to do the math.

Finnegan needed to undo the damage Siddons had inflicted that morning when, under questioning, she said she hadn't initially planned to remove any dogs after leaving Mike-Mar Kennel the day she and Shaw paid their unannounced visit.

"Have you ever observed the conditions that you saw on February 8 that these dogs were living in?" Finnegan asked.

Just once before, Siddons said, in a case involving fewer dogs.

Think back to the afternoon in question, Finnegan said to her, "What is your opinion as to the conditions that you observed?"

"Overwhelming, unacceptable," Siddons responded. "Certainly, by the department's regulations, it would not be tolerated."

"And in leaving the premises on February 8, were you concerned for those dogs?" Finnegan asked.

"Yes."

Mission accomplished. Siddons stepped down.

Finnegan next called Shaw, her star witness. The prosecutor dimmed the lights of the courtroom and turned on Shaw's videotape of the kennel. She left the volume on at first. As the camera panned room after room stacked with dogs inside Wolf's residence and kennel, frenzied yelps blared from the speaker. Finnegan waited a minute or so and then switched off the sound. She wanted the judge to concentrate not on the noise but on the squalor: dogs scrabbling for attention in crates draped in dried feces. She wanted him to focus on the overcrowded rooms and the rusty water bowls sitting in the crates. Even without any sound, the footage was powerful.

As the tape continued to roll, Finnegan turned back to Shaw.

"How would you describe that cage there?" she asked as the camera closed in on a small plastic crate.

"It's a carrier."

"How many dogs are living in that carrier?"

Wolf's lawyers objected. No one had said the dogs were living in the crates.

Finnegan asked Shaw again to describe the cages. She said they were filthy and appeared to be coated with dried feces. A number of the crates lacked any sort of water container, and the water buck-ets that were present were covered with slime.

The videotape kept rolling. Minutes later, the camera panned the interior of a different building. "Officer, can you recall what you're trying to show us in those photos?" Finnegan said.

"The filth of the cages," Shaw repeated.

"What was the condition of the cages that you're photographing?"

"Filthy, soiled newspaper. The animals' waste. The feces that was on the wires and the grates."

Outwardly, Shaw managed to look composed. Inwardly, she was wracked with anxiety, certain she would stumble, say the wrong thing, and cost the prosecution the case. "Who knows what might come out of your mouth?" she silently chided herself. "The way you remember things might be different from the way someone else remembers them."

Finnegan next called Ravinda Murarka, the veterinarian with the Pennsylvania Society for the Prevention of Cruelty to Animals, which had taken in sixty-three of Wolf's dogs. The organization had spent nearly $8,000 treating the medical problems of the animals over the last two and a half months, not counting room and board, Murarka said.

"Almost every dog was emaciated . . . the majority were infested with the fleas," he testified. "Ten of them . . . they have a very seri-ous skin problem . . . allergic dermatitis. And we had to treat for at least two to three weeks."

Was there a causal relationship between the conditions observed on the videotape and the health conditions of the dogs? Finnegan asked.

"Yes . . . they are kept in highly unhygienic conditions," Murarka said. "And what I observed is that that could perpetuate to the skin problem when the dogs were stained with the feces and urine." The conditions might also cause worms and pneumonia, he added.

The mood in the courtroom was tense. Under cross-examination, Coates asked the veterinarian how long it would take for a dog to contract fleas. In high temperatures, they could hatch quickly, Murarka said—in as little as four to five days.

Coates asked Murarka what evidence he had that the dogs he examined weren't already being treated. They could have been treated for fleas on February 9 and still had fleas on the eleventh, the day they arrived at the Pennsylvania SPCA, the attorney said.

No, that wasn't possible, Murarka said. If the dogs had been treated, he would have noticed dead fleas in their coats. "The way the dogs were infested with the fleas, they were crawling all over the place," the veterinarian said. "If they are treated, the condition of the dog would not have been like that."

Coates surmised that perhaps the dogs had acquired fleas on February 10, the same day they were removed. Murarka dismissed that theory, too. "I don't know how somebody can pour that much quantity of the fleas on the dog," he said. He added that dogs develop allergic reactions to the fleas' saliva only after a long infestation.

The defense was trying to muddy Murarka's testimony, but the judge was not confused. "It takes the fleas to bite the heck out of the dog until he gets it," Farmer interjected from the bench.

Coates moved on. He questioned the cause of a congenital hernia found in one dog. He commented that congenital hernias can develop regardless of how a dog is treated. Murarka agreed, but said that hernias left untreated can cause problems later.

Coates then asked about a 3-year-old Papillon of Trottier's who had been taken in by the Pennsylvania SPCA and was described as being dirty and missing hair. "What caused the hair loss?" he asked.

Murarka responded that a skin infection and allergies to fleas could cause a loss of hair.

Coates asked about a dog of Wolf's who died on February 15, four days after the Pennsylvania SPCA took her in. An autopsy showed the dog died of pneumonia, Murarka said. Coates asked if that was an common occurrence when a dog is 10 to 12 years old. "Normally not," the veterinarian replied. He said the ill dog must have contracted some kind of upper respiratory infection.

Coates noted that several of Wolf's dogs were missing teeth. He suggested that older dogs often lose teeth, and this time the vet agreed.

Seizing an opening, Coates asked, "It is fair to say that with regard to all these dogs in here that went to Philadelphia, there are some of them that were dirty and they needed grooming. Some of them had tartar on their teeth. Some of the older dogs were suffering from congenital whatever or losing their teeth, like we do when we get old. Some of them may have had mange. But mange is a treatable condition, is that right?"

"Yes, sir," Murarka responded. "But there are ten dogs that have the skin problem."

"When you have that many dogs, is that unusual for skin problems and mange to develop?" Coates asked.

"Yes."

Coates was finished. Prosecutor Wright had just one final question. "How do dogs react to having fleas?" she asked.

"They scratch. They feel discomfort," Murarka replied.

The next witness was Bryan Langlois, the veterinarian at the Humane League of Lancaster County. He described the dry eye condition found in a number of Wolf's dogs who had been sent to his facility. All but four of the animals had chronic skin conditions that were most likely caused by fleas. A number of the dogs were diagnosed with intestinal parasites, several had diarrhea, and some of the dogs were a little underweight; he would not call them emaciated, Langlois said. Finally, a number of the dogs had very serious and chronic ear infections.

Asked if he saw anything unusual about the environment the animals had come from, Langlois said, "The feces that is caked on the cage doors is not something that would be cleaned twice a day. Feces do not dry that quickly."

Coates pressed him on that point. The discoloration on the cages looked like rust to him, he said.

"It can appear as rust," Langlois responded, "but to me, it looked like caked-on feces."

The problems he found were all treatable, Coates countered. The dogs were responding to treatment. They were going to get better. "They are not going to die from these things," he said.

"There was nothing at the time that I saw them that indicated that they were in imminent risk of death, no," Langlois agreed.

Finnegan rose to redirect. She asked Langlois to enumerate the many steps taken to treat the dogs. All of the dogs with lice were shaved down, the vet said. Those infested heavily with mites were dipped with lime sulfur, an insecticide. Their ears were flushed out, they all received dewormers, and they were started on medication.

One puppy had to be euthanized. "It came in bad shape," Langlois said. "Cold, hypothermic, in a little bit of shock." He said the medical issues he diagnosed were directly caused by the unhealthy sanitary conditions found at Mike-Mar Kennel.

Larry Dieter, the veterinarian for the Chester County SPCA, was the next witness. Dieter had been out of town when the dogs were brought in and didn't see them until six days after the raid. He found them suffering from a long list of maladies, he said. In his opinion, the dogs had "definitely not" received adequate veterinary care at Wolf's kennel.

The veterinarians' testimony had set exactly the tone Finnegan hoped for. She recalled Shaw to the stand. The prosecutor asked her to describe the conditions Wolf was instructed to remedy by February 10. Shaw ticked off three steps: Wolf was supposed to provide veterinary care for the dogs, clean their kennels, and provide them adequate water.

"Had that been complied with on February tenth when you reexamined this home?" Finnegan asked.

"No," Shaw said.

Earlier she'd testified that during the initial visit to Mike-Mar Kennel, she phoned Wolf's veterinarian, Tom Stevenson, and told him he needed to come to the kennel prepared to inoculate 100 dogs. Under cross-examination, Shaw said she had asked Stevenson to vaccinate the dogs because Wolf was unable to produce paperwork showing that any of the animals had been vaccinated. She said she requested documentation from Stevenson but never received it. The veterinarian did not return her phone call until after the raid. When he finally did so, Shaw wasn't in, so he left a message. She never actually spoke with him, Shaw said, so Stevenson couldn't confirm how many dogs he saw. Shaw added that she informed Wolf during the initial visit to his kennel that she planned to cite him for having unvaccinated dogs.

She stepped down, and Finnegan stopped there. It was late afternoon, a good breaking point. The hearing had lasted much longer than anyone anticipated; Shaw alone spent three hours on the stand. The judge adjourned matters for a week, until the following Friday.

Outside the courthouse, Coates told reporters the case was going about as he expected. "I feel good for Gordon and Michael, but I feel real good for Margaret. I don't think they have a good case for Margaret," he said. He reiterated that Wolf loved his dogs and simply had too many of them. The breeder had considered turning the dogs over to rescue leagues, Coates said, but not to the Chester County SPCA.

"I hope the people at home will wait till all the evidence comes in before they make a decision, which is what the court will do," the lawyer added.

• • •

A WEEK PASSED. On April 18, court reconvened in Oxford. Once again, the courtroom was standing room only. The prosecution had four more witnesses to call. The first day of the hearing had given Finnegan and Wright a better sense of how aggressively the defense team would try to downplay the poor health of Wolf's dogs. His attorneys would try to make the state prove that every single dog taken from Wolf's property had been neglected or abused.

But Wright convinced Finnegan that it wasn't necessary to parade every dog into the courtroom to prove the prosecution's case. They could easily show that the environment at Mike-Mar Kennel was so filthy that every dog was at risk. Every single cage was encrusted with feces, the ammonia fumes were pervasive, all the bowls were filthy, and there wasn't a single dog who didn't suffer from fleas, dermatitis, and matting. A number of the animals were worse off than that.

Finnegan called forward SPCA humane society police officer Beswick, who described walking into Wolf's home the day of the raid. The judge had heard similar testimony, but Beswick was able to paint a fresh image of the misery.

Opening the door, she said, she was greeted by an odor so pungent, "I felt like a brick had hit my face. . . . It burned my eyes and throat . . . the stench was overwhelming." The temperatures were so hot she had to escape the building every fifteen minutes in search of fresh air, she added.

The condition of the cages "was horrendous," Beswick went on to say. "There were feces, there was dirt, there was vermin in these cages. Dogs were filthy."

She told of slipping twice on excrement and how Wolf, witnessing her fall, apologized. She described seeing one Bulldog whose hind legs were splayed on the floor, unable to stand. Later she carried out a Cavalier King Charles Spaniel whose eyes were so infected they appeared ready to rupture. She said Wolf asked her, "Is that dog dead?"

Many more dogs had paws caked with feces, Beswick testified. The dogs seemed wary and unsocialized. Some were visibly sick. She described seeing mice scurry across the floor, up the door, and down the hallway. By the time she left the site, she felt physically ill. The conditions "broke my heart."

At one point during her testimony, Beswick paused, glanced up, and for a split second made eye contact with Wolf. He was seated across the courtroom, behind his attorneys, wearing a black suit, red shirt, and red and white tie. The eyes that stared back at her were vacant. She saw no remorse in them, no concern.

Beswick turned back to the judge. "All my time I was a law enforcement officer, I have never seen conditions so deplorable, so atrocious," she said.

SPCA office coordinator Green followed her on the stand. She, too, described encountering a stench in Wolf's residence—an ammonia smell "that triggered a gag reflex . . . you could actually feel it burning your lungs. It was very overwhelming."

Green conversed with Wolf at length while the rescue effort was under way, she said. She said Wolf tried to impress upon her his concern for the dogs. Hoping to elicit more information from him, she responded sympathetically; anyone in his situation would have trouble keeping up with that many animals, Green told Wolf. Clearly, he had gotten in over his head. She said Wolf described to her his plan to fix up his house and sell the property. She suggested he might be better off bulldozing the house instead.

"Why was that?" Finnegan asked.

"Because of the condition of the house being covered in feces," Green said. "Just filth everywhere . . . a combination of dirt and feces everywhere you looked. . . . I couldn't possibly fathom how you could get the stench from his residence out."

Green had helped process more than 200 of the dogs. Finnegan asked her to step down from the witness stand, walk over to the diagram of Wolf's property, and mark with an X the two spots where she'd found baskets of puppies. It had occurred to Finnegan that a visual diary, compiled through photos and testimony, might best capture the chronology of the raid. Green pointed out the room in Wolf's residence where she found half a dozen Cavalier puppies slumbering inside a closed plastic basket, on top of which someone had placed a half-empty bag of dog food. She identified the adjacent room where she found two English Bulldog puppies in another wicker basket covered with linens.

Under cross-examination, Wolf's defense attorneys questioned the fact that, although she had no training or expertise, Green had been given the responsibility of deciding the condition of each animal. She only noted obvious problems, she said, and she had assistance with that task. It didn't take a veterinary license to see pus seeping out of a dog's eye or that an animal had a bleeding lip, Green said. The defense also noted that she never described any dog as emaciated.

Suzette Nicolini, a volunteer with the Chester County SPCA, was next on the stand. She testified about seeing a white board in Trottier's room that said, "Lightening's Papillons." Written on the board was an indecipherable list of names and dates—Trottier's attempt, apparently, at keeping track of which dogs had been bred to which.

Jennifer Danby, kennel manager at the Applebrook Inn pet resorts and a former SPCA employee, also testified briefly about her role in the rescue. Finnegan saved for last Kimberly Williams, an animal control officer for the Delaware SPCA, who arrived late the night of the rescue to help process the remaining dogs. She dealt mostly with the Papillons—sixty to seventy of them chockablock in an unventilated basement room measuring roughly twelve by fifteen feet.

"A lot of them had missing fur, skin conditions of some kind, gooky eyes, runny noses, I'll say birth defects: malformations of how their feet should be and things like that," Williams testified. She said she saw dogs running loose and stepping in fresh feces, mashing it on top of old, matted excrement. The temperature in Trottier's basement was "hot and sticky and humid and nasty."

Finnegan was elated with Williams's performance on the stand. Her vivid descriptions left no doubt that Wolf was abusing his animals. She was the perfect witness to wrap up the prosecution's case.

Now it was the defense attorneys' turn. But Coates, Alice, and Iannuzzi called no witnesses. Not Wolf, Trottier, or Hills. Not even Stevenson, the veterinarian.

In her closing arguments, Finnegan emphasized the neglect that had been the hallmark of Wolf's operation. By law, she said, Wolf, Trottier, and Hills were required to maintain the health and well-being of their dogs. Clearly, they had not done so. Unable to speak for themselves, the dogs had been forced into confinement, "and not only imprisonment but imprisonment in filth," at considerable risk to their health.

She asked that Wolf, Trottier, and Hills be sentenced to a day in jail apiece for each of the 337 animals in their care. She asked the judge to fine the defendants, order them to pay restitution of $256,000, and require them to forfeit the animals to the SPCA so that they could be adopted out to new homes.

"We need to send a message of incarceration, even if only one day for one dog, or even one ninety-day sentence," Finnegan said.

The defense argued that the Commonwealth of Pennsylvania had failed to identify which dogs were unlicensed or unvaccinated and therefore were unable to prove every element of every charge. The allegations of poor hygiene weren't shown to be intentional, Wolf's attorneys said. They said the animals' ill health could be attributed to old age or other reasons.

"They cleaned the pens every day, at least once a day," Coates said of his clients. "When you have that many dogs running around there's going to be a mess, and you can't clean it twenty-four hours a day."

Attorney Alice described Wolf as "a knowledgeable individual about dogs. It was not his desire to be neglectful or to cause harm." Wolf had so many dogs because he couldn't bear to part with them, his attorneys said. He doted on them so much that he fed them hamburger and cottage cheese.

The attorney for Hills said that none of the dogs belonged to her and asked that charges against her be dropped entirely.

Wright listened to the defense team's rationale with a rising sense of incredulity. These dogs had subsisted in filth. They had been mangy and sick. Did that not constitute cruelty and neglect in the eyes of the defense? She found it astonishing that anyone would try to argue it did not.

The hearing was over. Farmer announced that he would issue his ruling the following Friday, April, 28, and adjourned the court.

Earlier, during a break, Wolf had commented to a reporter that it was natural for his buildings to smell bad. He blamed the SPCA officers for some of the disarray. "They trashed my kennel," he said. But as he exited the courthouse this time, Wolf avoided reporters, said nothing, and left.

10

The Breeder Appeals

T HE NEXT WEEK crawled by. Finnegan and Wright still felt posi-
tive they had mounted a persuasive case and would carry the
day in court. The question in their minds was whether Wolf and his
cohorts would drag matters out by filing an appeal. Finnegan was
all but certain they would.

The morning of April 28, Farmer wasted no time delivering his
verdict. He found Wolf, Trottier, and Hills guilty on all counts of
animal cruelty against 333 dogs, 2 birds, and 2 cats. He ordered Wolf
to forfeit the animals to the Chester County SPCA. And he held Wolf
liable for restitution and court costs—the sum of which now totaled
$358,357. Trottier was ordered to pay fines and restitution to the
SPCA of $85,438. Hills was found liable for $83,499 in fines and
ordered to help Wolf pay $240,000 in restitution to the shelter.

Farmer forbade Trottier from owning animals for sixteen years.
Hills was barred for sixty-six years, and Wolf was banned for life
from owning animals, the judge said.

Farmer stopped short of putting the defendants behind bars; that would have been unrealistic, he said later. Even so, he had handed down the toughest sentence in the history of puppy mills, and SPCA officials were ready to celebrate. "We would have liked to see jail time, but we're very happy with what the judge has decided," McDevitt said afterward.

The victory was short-lived. The defendants had thirty days to appeal the ruling, and Coates announced immediately that Trottier planned to do just that. Asked what he thought would happen to the dogs until then, the attorney shrugged, "I guess they'll just sit there until the appeal's heard."

Twelve days passed. On May 11, Wolf's lawyers appealed the case to the Chester County Court of Common Pleas.

"We think the judge made mistakes," was Coates's explanation.

Finnegan groaned inwardly at the news. She knew all too well how easily summary appeals could get tangled up in the system. It might take anywhere from two to six months for a new trial to get under way. Even then, the decision wasn't necessarily final. Wolf's attorneys could appeal that finding to State Superior Court and to the State Supreme Court after that. The case could take years to resolve.

Almost three months had elapsed since the dogs were rescued. Tens of thousands of dollars had gone into housing them, treating their illnesses and injuries, and helping prepare them for new lives. The dogs were beginning to recover emotionally from their ordeal, but there was a limit to the amount of attention harried shelter workers could give them. For everyone's sake, the dogs needed to move on to permanent homes, and soon.

The shelters were braced for summer, the season when their populations tended to swell. Asked by one newspaper if the SPCA's resources were so depleted the organization might consider reaching a deal with Wolf, McDevitt didn't rule it out. "I guess that could be a possibility," he said.

Unbeknownst to the prosecutors, they had an advocate in Edward Griffith, the common pleas judge who was now in charge of the case. Griffith could have let matters languish. But he was acutely aware of the sprawling support system that had been erected to safeguard Wolf's dogs. He made it clear he had no intention of letting the case get dragged down any further by delays.

Griffith got Finnegan, Wright, and Wolf's attorneys on a conference call. He was clearing his calendar, the judge informed them. They'd better do the same. He'd already picked a date for the trial, June 19, and he insisted the lawyers commit to it. There would be no delays like the kind that had stalled the first trial.

Wolf's lawyers appeared chastened. It was obvious the judge wasn't going to tolerate any tomfoolery. His insistence on moving forward quickly did not bode well for them.

Five weeks passed. On the day the new trial was scheduled to get under way, the defense team suddenly informed the prosecutors that they were willing to work out a deal. The announcement caught Finnegan and Wright off guard, but they grabbed at the chance to resolve matters once and for all. Now all that was left was to hammer out a settlement.

The hearing had been moved to the main Chester County courthouse in West Chester, to courtroom number 1, the largest venue available. It had double the seating of any other courtroom, and on this day it was brimming with reporters and spectators.

Finnegan notified Griffith that a settlement looked possible. Then she and Wright met with the defense team in a nearby conference room to hash out details. They needed to decide the terms of Wolf's, Trottier's, and Hills' convictions, the fate of the dogs, and the conditions by which future inspections of Wolf's property could take place. The parties also needed to determine the level of fines and the amount of restitution the defendants would pay. Nearly every animal welfare organization that had taken in some of Wolf's dogs had produced a different tally of room-and-board costs and medical expenses they had incurred; arriving at the total was going to be a task in itself.

The defense attorneys kept insisting that one of Wolf's sons be permitted to keep a dog, despite the fact that the breeder himself would be banned from having any. Finnegan and Wright were equally adamant that no dog could be kept in Wolf's home, period.

Before signing off on any agreement, Finnegan needed to run it by SPCA executive director Spackman. Spackman was amenable to a settlement of some sort. Her desire to see Wolf punished was tempered by the realization that the sooner the case was resolved, the faster the animals could be adopted out to real homes.

Finnegan also needed to make certain the terms of the agreement were satisfactory to Joe Carroll, the district attorney. The back-and-forth dragged on for hours. Griffith grew tired of waiting. At one point he called the case to the courtroom. Give us just a little more time, Finnegan asked.

Around 2 p.m., following a late lunch, the judge invited all of the attorneys into his conference room. He wanted to know the status of the case—whether talk of a settlement was genuine or the defense attorneys were merely pulling his leg. Gamesmanship of that sort had been known to happen.

The settlement was very real, the parties assured him. If that were the case, Griffith laid down a stipulation of his own: There would be no dogs in Wolf's house, he said. Period. End of story. If any animals did, in fact, turn up, Wolf would be charged with violating parole.

The afternoon wore on. Wolf's attorneys continued to propose changes to the terms. Wright was new to this kind of behind-the-scenes dealing and frustrated by the delays. The prosecution's case was solid—they had no need to negotiate—and yet Wolf's attorneys kept trying to call the shots. Late in the day, when the defense team tried to insist on yet another new provision, Wright ripped up a draft agreement in front of them, ready to call it quits. Finnegan stared at her in disbelief. "You can print that again, right?" she asked. If the agreement fell apart, the case would go to trial a second time, something Finnegan wasn't about to let happen. Wright regained her composure and left to reprint the document.

In another conference room, managers of the various shelters that were housing Wolf's dogs were gathered, ready to list by number the dogs who needed to be adopted. Veterinarians waited, having taken off the day in anticipation of being called to testify. The prosecution had arranged for as many as ten of Wolf's dogs to be brought into the courtroom, if necessary, to help make their case. Shaw waited in the corridor outside, anxious for updates.

Finally, the prosecutors emerged. A deal had been reached.

The defendants never showed even the slightest remorse. They acted as if the filth and squalor of Wolf's kennel represented the typical conditions at large-volume breeders. But Spackman got the sense that Wolf was frightened at the possibility of going to prison and that his trepidation gave prosecutors some negotiating power they might otherwise have lacked.

Despite the agreement, Finnegan didn't feel nearly as confident this time around. It was one thing for the attorneys in a case to agree to a settlement. Having the defendants themselves sign off on the terms was another thing entirely.

She notified Griffith that the two sides had come to terms, and court was reconvened. The courtroom fell silent as the prosecutors strode in, followed by the defense attorneys and Wolf, Trottier, and Hills. Representatives of the SPCA and the other animal welfare groups filed in as well. Finnegan stood before the judge and outlined the terms of the agreement. It was a watered-down version of the sentence Farmer had imposed two months earlier.

Farmer had held Wolf liable for nearly $360,000 in restitution and court costs, and forbidden him from owning animals ever again. Under the new agreement, Wolf would plead guilty to sixty counts of animal cruelty. He would be fined $6,300 and, within a year's time, pay $122,157 in restitution to the Chester County SPCA. Wolf would be banned from having contact with animals for fifteen years, during which time he would be subject to investigations by the Pennsylvania dog warden and the Chester County SPCA. His property would be inspected regularly to make certain he had no animals.

Wolf stood as the judge addressed him. "Mr. Wolf, you've heard Ms. Finnegan outline the terms of a plea," Griffith said. "Do you accept those terms?"

Finnegan held her breath. Wolf could decide right that minute to back out of the deal. She closed her eyes with relief when he answered, simply, "Yes."

Trottier and Hills also pleaded guilty to sixty counts each of animal cruelty. Trottier agreed to pay a fine of $3,000 and restitution of $31,304.50 to the SPCA. Hills agreed to pay a fine of $3,000 plus court costs. Each would serve fifteen years of nonreporting probation, during which time they would be banned from having contact with animals.

Griffith ratified the agreement reluctantly. As diluted as the deal was, it contained two key components: first, that the Chester County SPCA would be reimbursed; and second (and more important) that the dogs were free to be adopted out.

It was the end of the road for the case. There would be no more appeals.

Shaw was thrilled by the outcome. Minutes before the hearing, when she learned that Wolf planned to plead guilty, she'd thought, "No, he's not going to do it." When she watched him stand before the judge and admit his guilt, she let out a silent, triumphant cheer. Finnegan had done it—she'd gone after Wolf with a passion, and as a result, the dogs were saved. "She was the bright light in this whole thing," Shaw said later.

Afterward, Wolf stood on the steps outside the courthouse, unwilling still to take responsibility for his misdeeds. "It's sad that it

Some of the dozens of cards and letters prosecutors Lori Finnegan and Kate Wright received from across the country thanking them for helping convict puppy mill breeder Michael Wolf.

has to end this way," he told reporters. In court, attorney Alice had said Wolf expected to sell his property and would pay the restitution and fines from the proceeds. Outside the courtroom, Wolf said he had no idea how he would come up with the payments.

Finnegan kept her comments brief. She'd never stopped thinking about Wolf's dogs, she told reporters. Their fate was what mattered most. "I'm happy the animals are going to go home"—to real, permanent homes, she said. "I'm hoping that every one of these puppies can now be treated royally compared to where they've been. They're all really beautiful animals, and they're going to require a lot of spoiling."

11

The Soft, Cool Feel
of Grass

FOR FOUR MONTHS, Shaw had watched over nearly 200 of the dogs from Mike-Mar Kennel. She checked on them each morning when she arrived at the Chester County SPCA and again each evening before she left for the day. She sat on the floor with the dogs, petted them, and reassured them, "Everything's gonna be okay."

Bearing that responsibility had proved to be more stressful than any assignment she'd ever taken on before. But watching the animals blossom emotionally more than made up for it. She would never forget the day a few weeks earlier when she tossed a couple of tennis balls to the Bulldogs. She did it on a whim, not expecting much of a reaction. To her surprise, the dogs went wild for their brightly colored new toys. They nosed them, tossed them around, and chased after them madly. Watching them, Shaw smiled so much her cheeks hurt.

That evening, after she told her husband, Bobby, about the dogs' antics, he got on eBay and ordered a thousand tennis balls, enough to shower the dogs with them. Then Shaw went to Kmart and bought a cartful of Christmas toys that had been marked down to twenty-five cents apiece.

If the Bulldogs preferred the tennis balls, the Cavaliers and the Papillons favored the squeaky Christmas toys. The toys helped bring them around. Now, when Shaw climbed into a kennel to sit, the dogs cuddled in her lap. Their coats still reeked of urine, but the odor didn't bother her. "Just for them to come out of their shells like that, it was great. It was so great," she said.

And now that Wolf and his partners had pleaded guilty, the case was over. Done. Soon the dogs would be leaving the SPCA and all the other shelters they were scattered in, destined for permanent homes at last.

Animal lovers across southeastern Pennsylvania and Delaware who had followed the case were just waiting for the go-ahead. The dogs had been in custody for 138 days. They deserved good homes, and local residents were more than ready to provide them. It didn't hurt that instead of going for upward of $2,000, these dogs would be available for just an adoption fee.

A few issues remained, however. Several breeders had stepped forward to claim some of the Bulldogs and the Havanese. SPCA staff needed to resolve who owned which dogs. They also wanted to screen would-be adopters before sending them home with any of the puppy mill dogs. These animals were going to require patience and work; people looking to adopt them needed to know that. SPCA spokesman McDevitt reminded the public that none of the dogs was housetrained or accustomed to walking on a leash.

"We've had these animals for five months and we want to make sure they go to loving, permanent homes and people are willing to make a lifelong commitment," he said.

Finally, the shelters needed to microchip the animals, examine them medically again, and give them each a bon-voyage bath.

The case had cost the Chester County SPCA $256,000, much of which it managed to recoup through donations. Other shelters asked to be reimbursed for the costs they'd incurred caring for Wolf's dogs, but the Berks County Animal Rescue League, the shelter that took in Dog 132, refrained from doing so. The Rescue League didn't even ask to be reimbursed the $1,600 it spent on surgery to repair Babs the Bulldog's ingrown corkscrew tail. Executive director Harry D. Brown III knew what it was like to have to ask other shelters to house rescued dogs until a case was resolved. A couple of years earlier, his organization had removed fifty-two Pit Bulls from a bad breeder and had to parcel thirty-two of them out to other shelters. He wouldn't have wanted those shelters calling him up and saying, "You know how much it costs me to keep your dogs?" and he vowed not to do that to the Chester County SPCA.

Brown had given the SPCA his word that his shelter would help out as long as needed. "Financially sometimes it gets rough," he acknowledged. "I always look at it this way: As long as we have enough to survive, we're happy. We're not looking to have a three-million-dollar bank account. If, by the end of the week, my bills are paid and my employees are paid, even if there's nothing left, we're okay."

His lone request to Chester County was that, when the time came, the Animal Rescue League be allowed to find homes for the twelve dogs it had taken in. The dogs had been through hell already. He wanted to make certain they had the best chance possible to enjoy what remained of their lives.

The following week, the *West Chester Daily Local* announced that on Thursday, June 29, the Chester County SPCA would begin adopting out sixty of Wolf's Cavalier King Charles Spaniels and twenty-five Papillons. The adoption fee of $100 included an examination by one of more than seventy-five local veterinarians who had stepped up to care for the dogs, and would also pay for vaccinations, deworming, and spaying or neutering. In fact, instead of going home directly with their adopters, the dogs would be taken to a veterinary office, spayed or neutered, and then released.

On Monday, June 26, the *Reading Eagle* ran a similar article about the puppy mill dogs being kept at the Animal Rescue League. The newspaper recounted the story of Wolf's dogs for readers who weren't familiar with the case. Accompanying the article were three photos of Cavaliers. Two of them showed the dogs getting shampooed. The third showed Pam Bair sitting outside a run, hugging three of the Cavaliers. One of the dogs was in her lap and two more were standing on their hind legs, gazing up at her with soulful eyes. Interested parties were asked to fill out an application, including information about their income, housing, and pet history.

SIX WEEKS EARLIER, the veterinarian for the Berks County Animal Rescue League, Carl Veltri, had treated the dogs again. At 2:34 p.m. that day, a vet tech carried Dog 132 into the examining room. The paperwork filed that day listed her as Invoice Number 166008. It noted that she was a Spaniel, Cavalier King Charles. Color: Unknown. Female. Weight: 16.8 lbs.

The Cavalier's teeth were in sorry shape, rotted down to quarter-moon-shaped stumps. Veltri pulled all but five of them. The cost of the dental work came to $198.20, but the veterinarian discounted his fee by $99.10. The Cavalier was better off with no teeth than with bad ones. Shelter techs had realized belatedly that she and several of the other dogs were having difficulty chewing their food because of their worn-down teeth. Besides that, all the built-up bacteria on their teeth threatened to work its way into their systems, causing heart and kidney disease.

After her teeth were pulled, Dog 132 was able to chew her food more easily. The medication and baths eased her itching skin, and the eyedrops curtailed the stinging in her eyes. Physically, she was starting to come around. But Bair was looking for something more intangible in this little dog. A flicker of trust in her new caregivers, perhaps. A recognition, however subtle, that life might, in fact, offer a bit of promise.

The dogs had their kennelmates, but they needed to socialize with other dogs, too. A few weeks into their stay, the shelter staff decided to spring them from their kennels, two dogs at a time, to explore the rest of the boarding wing. Dog 132 avoided human contact on the days she was let out, but she sniffed noses tentatively with the other dogs as they peered out of their kennels, and after a time she trotted down the aisle in the direction of the kitchen and the laundry room. "Finally," Bair thought, "she's acknowledging there's life beyond her cinderblock cell. We're making progress."

One afternoon Bair placed four of the Cavaliers, Dog 132 included, in one of the larger kennels at the far end of the boarding wing. In no time the dogs seemed delighted to be in one another's company.

No one knew what made the difference. They only knew that after two and a half months in their care, Dog 132's personality finally began to emerge. The efforts of the kennel techs were starting to pay off. Sandy Lambert, one of the techs assigned to the boarding wing, was struck by the difference just five minutes of attention could make in the life of a rescued dog. Once they got over their fear, Wolf's dogs seemed grateful for everything they'd been given.

One sunny afternoon in April, the techs escorted six of the dogs to a grassy area at one end of the Rescue League building and—for the first time since their arrival—turned them loose. The dogs sniffed one another. They'd been in close proximity to their former kennelmates, but were seldom able to actually see one another. The dogs began checking out the soft, cushiony grass. Their paws were no longer tender; it had been weeks since they had been forced to stand on wire. Still, the spongy ground must have felt miraculous.

And the smells! Dogs' noses are up to 100,000 more sensitive than humans', and the grass offered a cornucopia of aromas to investigate.

Minutes passed. The dogs seemed baffled. They watched and waited, perplexed. The grass felt wonderful, but now what? If this were a Disney movie, Dog 132 would have picked up her paws and begun to frolic in the warm spring sun. She would have rolled on her back and mouth-wrestled a playmate as her dangly ears lay stretched on the ground.

But in truth, no one remembers the tricolor Cavalier doing anything dramatic that day. Only that she mingled. She sniffed her surroundings. In her own quiet way, she seemed to enjoy the chance to explore a tiny patch of the outdoors.

"Who knows?" Bair thought to herself when her colleagues herded the dogs back inside. "Maybe she'll come around someday."

12

Deciding on a Dog

LINDA JACKSON HAD never been crazy about dogs. She'd tried to overcome this; four years earlier, she'd given in to her kids and purchased a celebutante–style Yorkshire Terrier puppy. It hadn't worked out. At two and a half pounds, Spike had an ego the size of a Bull Mastiff. He soiled the carpet, chewed holes in Linda's sixty-dollar leather sandals, and bolted out of the house every chance he got. And he yapped incessantly. One night, when a friend called, the kids were hollering and Spike was barking so loudly that Linda could barely hear herself. "What is *going on?*" her friend asked.

Finally, Linda had had enough. She returned the Yorkie to the neighbor she'd bought him from, and Spike ended up with a new owner who was much more forgiving of the little dog's high-maintenance personality. But 15-year-old Ryan, 12-year-old Erika, and 9-year-old Julia were furious that Mom had given Spike away. Linda felt horrible.

When Julia announced that the family was going to get another dog to replace Spike, Linda refused to consider it. "No, we're not going to get another dog," she corrected her daughter. "We failed this one." Besides, the family still had a cat, an affectionate gray shorthair with green eyes. Kitty would have to do.

But Julia was relentless. She constantly played Nintendogs, a video game in which players feed and walk virtual dogs, even guiding them through obedience training. And night after night, Linda watched her youngest sprawl on the couch with a children's book about dogs, researching the perfect breed for their family. "How about this one?" Julia would ask, showing her a picture of a Corgi. "How about this?" pointing to a demure-looking Dachshund. All three kids lobbied for an English Bulldog.

"I'll know the right dog when I see it," Linda told them.

By the time Julia showed her a picture of a Cavalier King Charles Spaniel, Linda's resolve had begun to soften. She had to admit, the little dogs with the large, expressive eyes and dangling ears were appealing. They were the size she preferred—twelve to eighteen pounds—and their personality seemed ideal. Cavaliers were considered intelligent, loyal, cheerful, and even-tempered. They were renowned lapdogs, said to have so captivated Britain's King Charles II in the mid-1600s that he'd issued a decree allowing the diminutive spaniels to enter any public building in England. Cavaliers' charm was indisputable.

"Breed buzzwords: Gentle. Affectionate. Sporty," the chapter of the book on Cavaliers said. Accompanying the description was an illustration of a Cavalier and a bubble of words above it that had the dog saying, "I get my best exercise getting on and off laps."

All right, Linda told the kids, she would check into a Cavalier. But ten minutes of research on the Internet and she wished she'd never opened her mouth. Cavaliers were a flavor of the month, it turned out. A registered puppy from a reputable breeder could easily run $1,500 or more. There was no way Linda could afford to spend that kind of money.

Scrolling online one evening, she stumbled across what sounded like a good deal: Cavalier puppies for sale for $700, plus $200 for shipping. But the breeder in Texas acted evasive when Linda contacted her to ask about her kennel. And the idea of shipping a dog sight unseen made Linda uneasy; friends warned her against transporting a puppy hundreds of miles. If something went wrong with the puppy, what recourse would she have? Suddenly, what had sounded like a bargain now seemed too good to be true. "Face it," she told herself, "a Cavalier just isn't in the cards."

She was debating how to break the bad news when, on her way to work the next morning, she stopped, as she usually did, at a local coffee shop in her hometown of Lebanon, Pennsylvania, and reached for the *Harrisburg Patriot-News*. The rack was empty; the paper hadn't arrived. She picked up the *Reading Eagle* instead—the local paper for a bigger metropolis thirty-seven miles east of Lebanon. Linda rarely went to Reading and had no interest in news from that area. But as she flipped through the paper, a large photo on the cover of the Lifestyle section caught her attention. It showed a woman surrounded by Cavalier King Charles Spaniels, all of them standing on their hind legs and clamoring for her attention.

The Cavaliers were among 337 purebred dogs and other animals who had been rescued from a puppy mill—a shoddily run commercial kennel forty miles away. Some of the dogs were being housed at the Animal Rescue League of Berks County shelter, south of Reading. The breeder had pleaded guilty to animal cruelty and agreed to give up his dogs. In a matter of days, once the legal hurdles were cleared, the dogs would be available for adoption.

Linda thought quickly. Her job as development director at the local YMCA didn't pay a fortune; she was always trying to figure out how to pay the bills. Getting a dog would be another expense. But she wanted to make her kids happy. A puppy mill rescue might just be the way to go. She couldn't afford a purebred dog any other way.

This *Reading Eagle* photo of shelter employee
Pam Bair surrounded by Cavalier King Charles
Spaniels caught Linda Jackson's eye.

She jotted down the number for the shelter and dialed it as soon
as she got to work. The woman who answered confirmed that the
dogs would be available in a matter of days for a small fee. She
directed Linda to the shelter's website, where she could download
an adoption application form. Linda should submit the form and
keep calling back to see when the dogs were available, the woman
told her.

Linda filled out the application, sent it in, and was notified a
couple of days later that she qualified to take one of the dogs home.
The shelter had one Havanese, two English Bulldogs, and nine
Cavaliers from the puppy mill. If she got in line soon enough, she
could choose one of the Cavaliers. For several days she phoned the

shelter every morning to see if Adoption Day had arrived. Not yet, she was told. Try again tomorrow.

On Thursday, June 29, she phoned again, expecting to hear the usual "Sorry, keep calling." To her surprise, the woman told her that the dogs were ready to go. "First come, first served," the woman said, "so get here as quickly as you can."

Linda glanced at her watch. Fund-raising season was in full swing at the YMCA; this was hardly a convenient time to disappear on personal business. But the chance to adopt a Cavalier took precedence. She ducked out of the office, backed her sedan out of the parking lot, and threaded her way east through town and out onto Highway 422.

The shelter was only forty miles away, but the highway was narrow, just two lanes, and traffic was stop-and-go the entire way. Two-story brick houses lined the road. Along certain stretches, turn-of-the-century row houses sat only a few feet from the pavement, so close you could practically reach out and shake hands with people relaxing on the front porch. The drive would take an hour or more.

When she reached the town of Sinking Springs, ten miles out, Linda called the shelter to make certain some Cavaliers were left. The voice on the other end sounded apologetic. "I'm so sorry," the woman told her, "we just adopted out the last one."

There has to be a mistake, Linda thought. She hadn't driven all this way for nothing. She stepped on the accelerator. She had to see for herself that all the Cavaliers were gone. If they were, she'd think about getting another breed of dog. Any dog; by now it didn't matter what kind. She was on a mission that day to bring home a pet.

As she got closer to the shelter, she asked herself again if she really wanted to bring home a new pet. Dogs were work. You had to walk them. You had to board them when you went away. "The kids want a dog, sure, but I'll be the one who winds up taking care of it," she thought. "There's no getting around that."

It was noon when she turned off the bypass, followed a curving road for a few hundred yards, and drove up the driveway to the Animal Rescue League facility. She parked her car and entered the main door. She'd never been inside an animal shelter before, and the pungent aroma of the place—a combination of disinfectant and smelly dogs—filled her with second thoughts. Linda was buoyed by the sight of a shelter tech holding a red and white Cavalier. "Is that one of the dogs you're adopting out today?" she asked.

The woman nodded.

The receptionist had been mistaken after all! The Cavalier looked healthy for a puppy mill survivor, and she was beautiful— just like the dogs Linda had seen in the Reading paper.

Immediately, though, another tech who overheard the exchange called out that that dog had been spoken for. But they did have one left.

Pam Bair had left to run some errands, so Linda missed the chance to talk with the staffer who knew these dogs best. The tech came around from behind the counter and invited Linda outside, where the last remaining dog was waiting in a fenced-in, graveled run. Linda knelt down and peered through the chain-link fence. Looking back at her was a black and white lump with coffee brown eyes. She wasn't anything like the striking animal Linda thought she would find. Her coat might have been pretty once—her back and sides jet black, her chest and front legs the color of snow—but her hair had been clipped short and was bone dry. One of her eyes bulged out slightly and looked cloudy, as if she had cataracts. And her nipples were so distended they nearly touched the ground. Linda had never seen anything like them.

The shelter tech opened the door, reached in, picked up the dog, and set her down in the aisle next to Linda. "Ugh," Linda groaned to herself, "this dog stinks." She smelled like a combination of fear, confusion, and despair.

Wilma, as the staff called her, was believed to be 6 years old. Part of the puppy mill's breeding stock, she'd had one litter of puppies after another, and an absence of veterinary care had caught up with her. She had a recurring skin infection. Her ears were clogged with mucus. She suffered from dry eye and needed eyedrops every day. The cloudiness in her right eye had permanently damaged her eyesight. And her teeth were so rotten that the shelter's veterinarian had pulled most of them. She had only five teeth left.

Those were the problems the shelter had been able to diagnose. The Cavalier could always develop more. "Be aware you may have to spend thousands of dollars on this dog," the shelter tech warned.

Linda said nothing. She had just gotten rid of one problem dog. Now she was contemplating another dog who sounded like a medical train wreck. One more thing to complicate her life.

The Cavalier turned slowly and approached Linda. Fleetingly, the white tip of her black tail swung to one side and then the other. "At least she's friendly," thought Linda. "She's not cowering." She petted the little dog gingerly. In a gentle voice, the tech reached out to caress the Cavalier, too. "That a girl." A moment passed and Linda, hesitating, picked up the dog and sat her on her lap. Almost by instinct, the dog leaned against her. Linda was struck by the endearing way her feathery ears framed her face.

Linda thought about her promise to the kids. She had assured them that if and when the rescued Cavaliers were available, she would get in line to adopt one. Now, here she was, cradling the last dog left. How could she think of leaving the shelter without her?

She looked down at the dog. The Cavalier's cloudy brown eyes gazed back. Something about her petite little face was pathetic but also endearing. Linda couldn't resist it.

"You know what?" she heard herself say. "I'll take her."

The tech nodded, pleased. "You hear that, Wilma?" she said. "You've just found a new home." She lifted Dog 132 out of Linda's arms and clutched her to her chest.

Linda had already completed the paperwork. She'd stated in writing that she owned her home, that the dog would live inside, and that she agreed to have her spayed. She listed the name of her veterinarian and a reference. The information filed that day noted the vaccinations Wilma had been given, but left some questions unanswered.

Housetrained? Unknown.

Good with children? Unknown.

Good with other animals? Unknown.

This was no time for second-guessing. Linda excused herself, walked to her car, and retrieved the small plastic cat crate she had brought from home. The shelter tech carried the Cavalier to the lobby to wait for her return. As soon as Linda stepped back inside, the employee handed her Dog 132. She watched as Linda first tried to coax the dog into the crate and, when that didn't work, gently push her inside. The latch on the crate was broken, but the little dog made no attempt to step back out. She'd spent most of her life in confinement. She knew the drill. She crouched for several seconds and then laid down obediently and stared out.

"If you decide you don't want her, you can always bring her back," the tech said.

Linda thanked her and said goodbye. She crossed the parking lot, placed the crate in the rear seat of her car, got in behind the wheel, and started the engine. Almost instantly the dog's putrid odor filled the car. The shelter's groomer had bathed all the dogs in preparation for Adoption Day, but this one was going to need another bath, maybe two or three, before she smelled good enough to hug close.

Linda drove out of the parking lot and retraced her route down the winding road. She had just pulled onto the fast-paced bypass when she felt the Cavalier's presence next to her. Silently the dog had scrambled out of her crate, climbed down off the backseat, and scampered on top of the leather console between the front seats. She was standing at Linda's elbow, wobbling. Before Linda could stop her, the dog half-jumped, half-fell into her lap.

Linda grimaced. The papaya-colored sundress she was wearing—the all-cotton sheath that was such a chore to iron—would have to be washed now. She thought about setting Dog 132 down in the passenger seat, but the little dog dug in her nails. She wasn't going anywhere. Linda, touched by her tenacity, let her stay.

Halfway home, she decided to drop by and show her new find to her friend Cathy, a former colleague of hers at the Y who lived just off the highway. Linda had kept Cathy up to date on her search for a dog, and Cathy, an ardent dog lover, was eager to meet her friend's new pet.

On the outskirts of town, Linda phoned Cathy and moments later pulled alongside her house. Cathy was waiting. She had read about King Charles Spaniels on the Internet. The long-eared, multicolor dogs were adorable. Cathy loved the history of the breed, too. Linda was incredibly lucky to have found this dog at no cost, Cathy told her.

Then Linda stepped out of the car holding her new dog, and Cathy winced at the sight of the dull-coated creature with the distended belly. Linda knew what she was thinking: She looks like a cow. "She's going to need a breast lift," she said aloud, and the two women laughed.

Months later, Cathy confessed that the Cavalier had looked so sickly that she wasn't certain the dog would survive. But outwardly she forced a smile. "Maybe she'll come around," she said finally, and Linda smiled back. Leave it to Cathy to put a sunny spin on something she clearly thought was a mistake.

The two friends chatted briefly before Linda got back on the road. This time she didn't bother putting the Cavalier in the crate. She had to admit that, despite the smell, the warmth of the dog's scrubby little body on her lap felt good.

Linda had never thought of herself as a dog person. Growing up in Cumbola, a village in the thick of Pennsylvania's coal country, she, her sister, and their mother had owned a couple of Toy Poodles, first Gigi and then Tina. But while the dogs were allowed inside the family's modest row house during the day, they were forbidden from jumping onto the furniture, so the girls never cuddled with them much. At night, or any time the family left the house, the dogs were locked in the basement, often for long stretches. They were paper-trained and didn't have to go outside. In hindsight, Linda was struck by how much of the dogs' lives were spent in the dark.

For reasons she couldn't explain, Linda had always preferred cats. She'd doted on Puddy, a striped tabby she and her ex-husband had adopted from the pound when they were still dating. Before her own children came along, Puddy was her baby. Uncharacteristically for a cat, he loved to go on car rides, and consequently he went everywhere with Linda. When, years later, he was struck by a car and crawled under a neighbor's porch to die, Linda was overcome with grief.

Still, something felt right about taking this needy little dog. Linda thought back over the events that had led to this moment. The fact that the Harrisburg paper hadn't been delivered to the coffeehouse that morning, for one; if it had, she never would have learned about the rescued Cavaliers. Then, when she'd called the shelter that morning, she had been told it was too late. Yet she'd driven there anyway to discover Dog 132—the puppy mill survivor no one else wanted—waiting.

Maybe in some odd, serendipitous way this was destined to be. She was meant to have not just any Cavalier, but this particular dog, problems and all. "And here she is sitting in my lap," Linda thought. "She likes me, too."

13

Overwhelmed

It was after two by the time Linda arrived home. She'd been missing in action for three hours now. If she dropped the Cavalier off at her house, she could slink back into the office and spend a couple of hours calling prospective donors. Not exactly a memorable welcome for a new pet, but it was the best Linda could do.

She pulled into her driveway, got out of the car, set the dog down in the grass, and quickly went up the two stairs to the back door. "Come on, let's go inside," she called out. The Cavalier toddled along behind her, stopped at the steps, and stared up at her, confused. "My gosh, she has no idea how to climb stairs," Linda thought. She was about to reach down and scoop the dog up when the Cavalier solved the problem on her own by clambering up a small bank by the side of the steps. It struck Linda that the dog wanted to follow her badly enough to find a way.

Inside, Linda set a bowl of water on the floor. The Cavalier stood motionless. Linda knelt beside her and offered her a couple of treats. "Good girl," she said, stroking her. "You're in your new home now." The dog accepted the treats but stood stiffly, too confused to explore.

Linda spent several more minutes talking to the dog before she placed the crate on the floor beside the dining room table, helped the Cavalier inside, and braced the broken door. The crate was too small, but she didn't want to give the dog the run of the place just yet. She wasn't housetrained. "You take a nap now, sweetheart," she told the little dog. "I'll be back soon."

A little after five, she left work and swung by a friend's house to pick up the kids. Ryan, Erika, and Julia were spending the week at golf camp at a public course. Linda had told them a Cavalier might be available, and they were waiting with a flurry of questions.

"Did you get the dog?" Erika wanted to know as soon as she climbed into the back seat.

"What dog?" Linda teased.

Erika raised her voice in exasperation. "You know. The dog you said you were going to get!"

"I don't know," Linda replied. "We'll have to see."

She'd never been terribly good at keeping secrets. Grinning, she glanced in the rearview mirror and confessed that yes, she'd adopted a dog. And yes, it was a Cavalier. But she has a couple of problems, Linda warned.

She explained that the dog had come from a puppy mill and had led a difficult life. Okay, the kids nodded. She has some skin problems, Linda said. She's going to need to take medicine to clear them up. The kids shrugged. No big deal. And she has an ear infection. *And* some eye issues. Okay, okay, the kids said.

Also, Linda told them, she has almost no teeth. The kids stared back at her incredulously. "No teeth?"

"If you don't like her, I can take her back," Linda said matter-of-factly. She wanted the kids to feel as if they had some say in the matter. They seemed mollified.

Even before they laid eyes on the new dog, the kids bandied about possible names. Wilma, everyone agreed, sounded like somebody's fusty great-aunt. Julia suggested naming her Princess or Precious. "Keep going," Linda said. They considered Checkers or Oreo, but neither sounded right.

"How about Gracie?" Erika said, finally. *Gracie.* Linda liked it. It sounded right for the little dog. Gracie it would be.

When they arrived home and saw their new pet, the kids were ambivalent. Gracie was clearly anxious to be sprung from the carrier. Julia opened the latch and reached inside to pull the dog out. Inadvertently, she felt the dog's protruding nipples. "That's disgusting!" she said, drawing her hands back.

The kids stood back to watch Gracie explore her new surroundings. But the wide open space of the living room was too much for the little dog. She stood still, petrified.

Linda needed to throw together something for dinner. She left Gracie in the care of the girls. Julia, determined to connect with the Cavalier, attached Spike's old leash to her and tugged her out the

Gracie had a new home that offered plenty of space to explore. For a dog accustomed to constant confinement, the freedom was overwhelming.

back door to go for a walk. Julia walked slowly, but Gracie resisted every step of the way. She did everything she could to turn her sixteen-pound body into a dead weight.

From the kitchen window, Linda watched as her daughter inched down the sidewalk with their new pet. Erika and Ryan stayed behind. They were unimpressed. To Ryan, the Cavalier looked like a frightened stuffed toy—not at all the kind of dog you could toss balls to or wrestle with. To Erika, Gracie was too scared to be much fun.

After supper the girls helped Linda bathe Gracie, and that night, when Linda went out on a date with her boyfriend, Eric, they took turns holding and dressing Gracie in doll gowns. The little dog remained apprehensive. She wasn't used to this much attention.

Erika and Julia weren't sure they wanted anything to do with her, either. The Cavalier still stank, not of feces, as she once did, but of some sort of medicine, like she'd been dipped in flea powder. They sat on the floor with her because they didn't want her anywhere near the furniture.

"Well, should I take her back?" Linda asked late that evening as she leaned against the doorjamb of the girls' second-floor bedroom. Erika and Julia agreed that no, they guessed she should stay. Despite Gracie's smell, the girls had sandwiched her between them on Erika's bed, and that's where she stayed until the alarm clock buzzed the next morning.

At school that day, Erika complained to her friends that the family's new pet was boring. Later she told Linda, "I was expecting a normal dog. Why can't you get a normal dog?"

The family vet, Robert Kezell, wondered the same thing. Two days after Linda brought Gracie home, she took Gracie in for a checkup. The Cavalier cowered on the cold metal counter as the veterinarian looked her over carefully. The clinic's medicinal smell seemed to exacerbate her fear. Kezell picked up on her anxiety, looked at Linda, and shook his head.

"This poor dog," he said.

It turned out Gracie had a staph infection on her chest. Kezell prescribed antibiotics to treat it. Her left ear canal was partially closed, thanks to chronic infections. The vet showed Linda how to massage the sides of the dog's ears to work out the mucus. The dog suffered from anemia, and her eyes were in bad shape. Scar tissue clouded her right eye, and Kezell diagnosed both eyes as being severely dry; Linda would need to put drops in them daily to ease the pain.

Kezell's good news was that Gracie's heartbeat sounded strong. Cavaliers as a breed were notorious for dying from mitral valve disease, a heart condition that causes blood to flow backward into the atrium. The prevalence of mitral valve disease in Cavaliers is about twenty times that of other breeds. By the time they are 5 years old, more than half of all Cavaliers have developed mitral valve disease, and nearly all develop it by the time they are 10—if they live that long. The average Cavalier only lives to be 7 or 8. As far as Gracie was concerned, though, so far, so good, Kezell said.

Still, he wanted to make it clear Gracie did not get a clean bill of health. "I want to run some blood work," the vet told Linda. He also asked, "How far do you want to go with this? She could be really sick and you could wind up spending a lot."

For a moment Linda said nothing. "Let's clear up the obvious things and then we'll reevaluate her," she said finally.

How naive she'd been to think a dog from the pound might truly come problem free. Despite that, Linda already felt attached to her vulnerable new pet. For now, anyway, she had no desire to learn whether Gracie's health was more fragile than she already knew. What mattered, right this instant, was that, for once, this deserving little dog felt safe and comfortable—and that she be given every chance possible to enjoy a better life.

14

Too Scared to Play

N o question about it: Gracie was a cutie. Her coat of jet-black-against-snow-white hair (with just a pinch of the red that made her a tricolor) was striking; her feathery paws were adorable; and those long, curly ears made complete strangers want to reach out and take her in their arms.

But if the newest member of the Jackson family possessed anything approximating a personality, Ryan, Erika, and Julia couldn't detect it. The kids had expected the Cavalier to frolic about the house, chase after toys, and bond with them instantly, the way a pet dog was supposed to do. They figured she'd connect with them in that special, primal way dogs have, that together they'd be a *pack*.

In nearly every instance, Gracie came up short. She was unsure of her surroundings and too bewildered to enjoy herself. She didn't seem to comprehend what it meant to have fun. She just sat there, day after day, like a furry blob, camped out in an out-of-the-way corner of the kitchen.

The kitchen was the nerve center of the household. It's where Linda and the kids exited out the back door and reappeared through it several times a day. It was the gathering place for the family, where conversations took place and—most important—where meals were consumed, including Gracie's. Mealtime was the highlight of the day for the little dog, the one time she showed any spark. If Gracie had had to fight for her food in the puppy mill, it was no wonder the sound of kibble hitting plastic brought her running. Linda had never seen a dog inhale nourishment so quickly.

The first couple of days after adopting Gracie, Linda kept her in the cat carrier when no one was home. Gracie wasn't housetrained, and Linda wasn't about to let an untrained dog wander loose through the house. But after a couple of days, the sight of the Cavalier practically stuffed inside the carrier wore thin. Linda brought up from the basement a plump, fleecy bed, the kind with a puffy border designed to make a pet feel protected and safe. She'd bought the bed for Kitty, the family's elegant gray cat, but in typical feline fashion, Kitty had never once deigned to use it. Affectionate and friendly, Kitty much preferred the intimacy of someone's lap.

Gracie took to the bed right away. It was her very first possession, something she didn't have to share. No one had to coax her to curl up in it and claim it as her own.

The solution, unfortunately, was short-lived. As soon as Kitty observed Gracie in her bed, she decided to reclaim it for herself. The bed was just big enough for one animal, so when Kitty took over, Gracie found herself displaced. Linda remedied the situation by buying Gracie another bed, just like the first one. Now Kitty's bed remained in the kitchen, and Gracie's bed was positioned a few feet away. After all that accommodating, Kitty lost interest in the bed all over again. She went back to her perch on the windowsill. From there she could gaze out at the birds and squirrels that fluttered and scampered about the patio, and also keep an eye on the bashful Cavalier below.

As far as anyone knew, Kitty was the first cat Gracie had ever been exposed to. The two animals mostly sidestepped each other, but occasionally Gracie would get too close, the cat would swat her, and the little dog would skitter away.

It wasn't just Kitty. Gracie seemed uncomfortable around other animals, period. She was especially afraid of Baxter, a Golden Retriever who lived a few doors down. At a neighborhood picnic one afternoon, Baxter discovered Gracie sitting on Linda's lap and came galloping over to say hello. He was a gentle dog who wouldn't have dreamed of hurting her, but Gracie had no way of knowing that. She panicked, and from then on she bared what few teeth she had left at Baxter whenever he came around.

If doggy playmates weren't an option, surely the Cavalier would enjoy having a toy or two. Linda's boyfriend, Eric Walter, picked up at the grocery store a plush leopard-print bone that looked irresistible. A few days later the family presented Gracie with a second toy, one that squeaked. Gracie had no idea what to do with either. She left them alone.

Erika was right: Gracie wasn't a normal dog. Even so, the family kept trying to treat her like one. For help, they turned to Eric, who was a dog lover from way back. Just recently he'd had to put down his 17-year-old dog, Barley, a large and lovable mutt. Helping acclimatize Gracie to her new home eased the grief of losing Barley. Eric helped Linda understand that, first and foremost, dogs liked routine. In fact, they thrived on it. Gracie would adapt more quickly to her new life if she could count on being fed at the same time every day and taken outside to go to the bathroom on a regular schedule, Eric said. So far, that wasn't happening.

The family drew up a loose schedule. In a matter of days, Gracie learned that each morning, shortly after she awoke, Linda would take her outside to go potty. After that, Gracie traipsed after Linda while she made coffee, showered, and dressed. Gracie stayed by her side until she walked out the door. While Linda was gone for the day, the kids, home for the summer, were available to take Gracie on walks, feed her, and let her out. Linda had decided to give Gracie one meal a day, around 2 p.m., in hopes of reducing the number of times she needed to go outside.

In time, the Cavalier learned that she could count on Linda to return home at the end of the day. Linda would change out of her work clothes and begin preparing dinner, often by grilling something outside. It didn't matter what she did; Gracie never left her side.

The best time of the day came at the very end, when Linda finally sat down to unwind. If she was especially tired, she would stretch out on the sofa. Gracie would look up at her, Linda would reach down to pick her up, and together they would snuggle. Gracie wanted to burrow in as close as she could to the woman who had given her a home.

The Jacksons worked at encouraging Gracie to explore her new world. At first, she didn't seem terribly interested in leaving the comfort and safety of her bed. Maybe she was too timid to check out her surroundings. Or maybe she was apprehensive at the thought of feeling her way around in rooms she had trouble seeing. Inside the house, she kept bumping into furniture. Outside, on walks, she tended to stumble when she encountered a curb.

A couple of weeks passed before she finally began to venture around the house, taking first a few steps into the living room, then around the corner to the front hallway, down the hall past Ryan's room, a bathroom, and back to the kitchen. The full circle might take a human five seconds to navigate. To a small dog unaccustomed to freedom, it could easily take five minutes.

There was plenty to sniff along the way. The living room was carpeted and full of smells. Scents undetectable to humans were all over the floral couch and the pair of side chairs. From the far end of the living room, Gracie could veer right into the front hall, which was tiled—a different type of floor to master. A flight of stairs led from the entryway to the second floor, but Gracie didn't begin to know how to negotiate them, so she passed them by. She sniffed her way past Ryan's room, which was filled with the athletic-sock aromas typical of a teenage boy. Next, she passed the bathroom, where the fragrance of scented soap wafted out. Finally, at the end of the hallway was the kitchen, a buffet of aromas, the most tantalizing room of all. After years of inhaling the lung-piercing fumes of urine and feces, these ordinary, run-of-the-mill scents must have been a pleasant surprise.

Learning to climb the stairs was a major challenge. Gracie wasn't used to them: a seven-inch step was a significant obstacle to the Cavalier. The family approached the problem methodically. Linda would climb the stairs and then call to Gracie from the top. From down below, Julia and Erika would hold the dog and show her, step by step, how to climb up. Gracie finally learned to get to the top, but going back down again was another story. She would stand at the head of the stairs and whimper for help. Several weeks passed before she overcame her fear and learned to climb up and down without help.

Walks were equally challenging. Some dogs who had spent years in a crate might relish the chance to walk on grass. But to Gracie, after a lifetime of stepping on hard wire, grass was disconcertingly soft. It wasn't long before she overcame her misgivings and began to enjoy sniffing all things outdoors: the grass, the bushes, the calling cards left behind by dogs who had strolled by before her. Most days, the promise of enticing smells combined with some pulling, tugging, and cajoling was enough to entice her to circle the block. But she followed on a leash reluctantly, her paws pressed into the sidewalk to discourage anyone from pulling her too far. The entire excursion might take ten minutes, and when she arrived back at home, she was exhausted. Linda had to remind herself that Gracie's muscles were weak; she was unaccustomed to exercise. For her, a walk around the block was the equivalent of a three-day trek.

The walks were one tool the family used to instill in Gracie the fundamentals of housetraining. While Linda was at work during the day, the kids took turns taking the Cavalier outside to do her business. Over and over they tried to enforce the message. "Go potty, Gracie. Go potty," they said, hoping she would associate the words with going outside. When she did as told, they praised her effusively—"Good Gracie. Good girl!" and Gracie wagged her tail enthusiastically. She devoured applause in any form.

Despite that, a lifetime of going wherever and whenever she needed would take months to undo. Gracie had never had a chance to develop the instinct most dogs have to eliminate somewhere other than where they live. She'd been stuck in a crate; she'd had no choice. Linda knew this when she adopted Gracie. But now that the dog was living in her house day and night, her inability to distinguish outside from inside was distressingly apparent. Time and again she would squat on the champagne-colored carpet in the living room, near tables or chairs, and within seconds she'd had another accident. She didn't recognize this as a misdeed and therefore didn't try to hide it. Linda lost count of the number of times she had to have the carpet shampooed.

Beneath all that timidity and fear was a dog full of whimsy and charm—Linda was sure of it. She'd glimpsed it the day she'd picked Gracie up from the Berks County shelter and the little dog had crawled into Linda's lap in the car. But friends of the family weren't convinced. Instead, everyone wanted to focus on Gracie's "weird" right eye.

Erika's friends winced at the sight of it. The neighbors pointed it out, too. Even Linda's financial adviser zeroed in on the imperfection when Linda dropped by his office to show Gracie off to him and his wife. What was she doing with this crazy-eyed dog? He asked jokingly.

Gracie's right eye *was* abnormal. It was cloudy, as if someone had colored the inside with a silver crayon. And it protruded slightly, a side effect of her keratitis, or dry eye.

Linda wasn't bothered by Gracie's milky, scratched eye. To her, it was a permanent reminder of the suffering the Cavalier had borne. Harder to overlook was the peculiarly pungent smell that suddenly flared up six weeks after Linda brought Gracie home. She'd never smelled truly clean, despite weekly baths, but this new odor went above and beyond. Now she reeked like a sack of rotten potatoes. An experienced dog owner would have known immediately what to suspect, but Linda was mystified. The smell wafted from Gracie's hind end, where she had a callous—the result, Linda assumed, of having sat for so many years on wire. Maybe the callous had gotten infected, she thought, so she repeatedly shampooed Gracie's rear. The odor remained.

Finally, Linda gave up. She took her to Dr. Kezell, who within minutes was able to diagnose and solve the problem. Gracie's anal sacs, the glands that lined the inside of her rear end, were infected and full—as full as any the vet had ever seen. In a matter of minutes he was able to express the foul-smelling substance. Problem solved.

It wasn't Gracie's fault she had stunk up the room, but her malodorous condition didn't exactly endear her to the kids. They flatout didn't like Gracie, they informed their mother a month or so after Linda brought her home. The Cavalier wasn't any *fun*. Early on, when Ryan had tried kneeling on the floor to play with Gracie, it scared her silly. Even the sound of his voice seemed to make her tremble. "What is up with that dog?" he said, frustrated.

The girls made no attempt to hide their disappointment. Over and over Julia tried to get Gracie to sleep with her, but each time the little dog jumped off the bed and went in search of Linda. Both Julia and Erika missed Spike, the Yorkie Linda had given away a year earlier. "Spike was my favorite dog," Erika said. "He liked me and only me."

The girls evidently had banished from memory Spike's less appealing traits, Linda thought to herself. Spike was tiny but loud, and even a little bad-tempered. He had a bad habit of biting ankles, and he wasn't housetrained either, even after *five* years, no matter how diligently Linda had worked with him. Spike never stopped hiking his leg against the furniture; it didn't matter which room.

But Linda was frustrated, too. She'd jumped through hoops to get the kids this new dog—and not just any dog, but the breed they'd clamored for. What she'd ended up with was a dog who had next to no teeth, had trouble seeing, and smelled. Who, worst of all, wanted nothing to do with the children she was supposed to adore. "What is up with this?" Linda wondered to herself.

One morning, lulled into confidence, she left Gracie in her bed, went downstairs to make coffee, and came back upstairs to find a wet circle on the bedspread. Another accident from this accidental dog. But that's when it dawned on Linda that despite all of Gracie's problems, Linda hadn't for a second regretted adopting her. She wasn't put out with her the way she'd been with Spike. She felt sorry for Gracie, but at the same time she also admired her. Some dogs who have been mistreated become angry or mean-spirited. Gracie

Linda and Gracie take a moment to share each other's company. They bonded quickly.

was just the opposite. She was loving and appreciative. Cheerful, even.

Watching Gracie emerge from her trauma gave Linda a feeling of contentment, too. There was a lot about this little dog she didn't know, but she could see that Gracie approached each new day with a sense of optimism and hope. Gracie's tail said it all. It swished back and forth, back and forth, as if she were thinking, "You know what? Life's not so bad after all." And the more the family praised her, the harder it wagged. Before long, the Cavalier had earned herself a new nickname: Miss Happy Tail.

15

Learning to Trust

Linda wasn't the only person to experience difficulty rehabilitating a survivor from Mike-Mar Kennel. Many other adopters struggled with their new pets, as well. Pam Bair adopted Jolie from the Berks County Animal Rescue League, and the dog seemed distant and dazed. Alycia Meldon's dog, Abby, was so petrified of people that she hid beneath chairs. Mike and Laura Hewitt ran up thousands of dollars in veterinary bills treating their dogs, Baxter and Duffy. And Susan Krewatch battled a series of illnesses with her two Cavaliers, Lily and Bella.

Pam had kept her eye on Jolie, the most pitiful of the twelve Wolf dogs she'd taken care of at the Animal Rescue League. If Gracie was puny, Jolie, believed to be 7 years old, was worse. Months after her rescue she was still underweight, her skin scabby and itchy, her coat patchy and dull. She had a heart murmur. She suffered from dry eye. She was deaf, the result of too many untreated ear infections. She'd been debarked, a procedure in which the

vocal cords are severed or removed. Puppy mill dogs were sometimes debarked by shoving a plastic or steel tube down the dog's
throat. And Jolie had so many of her teeth pulled that her tongue
hung like a limp lollipop from one side of her mouth.

On top of all that, Jolie was an emotional wreck. Like Gracie, years
of bearing litter after litter had rendered her withdrawn and shell-
shocked. Pam wondered if dogs could suffer from post-traumatic
stress disorder. If so, Jolie was a textbook example. During the dog's
entire stay at the Animal Rescue League, Pam worried that when the
time came to adopt her out, Jolie's new owner might find her too much
of a challenge, give up on her, and turn her back in. The only way
to prevent that from happening was for Pam to take Jolie herself.

Divorced for a couple of years, Pam already had a houseful of
pets: two rescued cats, Rudy and Boomie, and two Basset Hound
rescues. The Bassets, Dudley and Odie, were appealing in a laid-
back sort of way. They radiated that air of gratitude all rescue dogs
seem to exude. Now, to Pam's surprise, she had overcome her bias
against toy breeds and fallen headlong for the Cavaliers. She
couldn't help it. They were such cheerful, optimistic little creatures.
They loved everything and everybody. An unfamiliar dog could be
growling and barking two feet away, and a Cavalier would waltz
right up and say hello.

"You can't pick who you fall in love with," Pam reminded herself.

She liked the fact that Cavaliers seemed thoroughly attached to
the people in their lives. The healthy ones acted that way, at least.
She had to admit, she hadn't detected that quality in Jolie. But she
suspected that if she worked hard enough, she could crack the shell
that encompassed this disturbed little dog. She was prepared to give
Jolie all the affection in the world to bring her around.

To Pam's relief, the Bassets welcomed the Cavalier, and the cats
were indifferent. From day one, everyone seemed to understand
that the newcomer in their midst was a little needy and more apt to
take up Pam's time. Dogs and cats alike were willing to give Jolie as
wide a berth as she needed to adjust to her new home.

Pam dived into her new project. Priority number one was to make the Cavalier as comfortable as possible. Pam put drops in her eyes daily, as she'd done for the last several months. She soaked Jolie's dry food to make it easier to chew; she'd started that practice in the shelter and it had made a difference. She began mixing ground flaxseed into her food to relieve her itchy skin. In a matter of weeks, Jolie stopped scratching and her coat began to thicken and shine.

The tougher challenge was to rehabilitate the Cavalier emotionally. Pam was determined to make up for lost time, to give Jolie the kind of attention she'd gone without those first seven years. That meant hugs and kisses—lots of them—copious amounts of lap time, and plenty of sweet-talking of the sort that had pulled some of Wolf's other dogs out of their shells.

In the morning when Pam left for work, Jolie would curl up on the couch and fall asleep. When Pam came home at the end of the day, Jolie was often in the exact same spot, still nestled and still napping, as if for the first time in her life she felt safe enough to really relax. Sometimes Pam left her undisturbed for an hour or so while she started supper and tended to her other pets. Once Jolie was awake, Pam dropped everything to spend time with her. She could see the little dog starting to respond and didn't want to ease off now.

Pam's devotion to rescue dogs—this need to try to compensate for their dismal past—was draining at times. But she derived every bit as much meaning from the relationships as she put into them. More, really. Dogs saw people at their very worst. They didn't mind how bad you looked when you got up in the morning or were sick. They loved you anyway.

For the first six months, Jolie remained distant. For better or worse, she seemed to have no expectations whatsoever. She was no trouble at all—so well-behaved that a month after Pam adopted Jolie, she began accompanying Pam to work three or four days a week. The Cavalier would while away the day in the kitchen of the Rescue League's boarding wing, dozing contentedly in Pam's chair. The only thing that roused her was the scent of a treat—a pig's ear, a rawhide chew, or a marrow bone filled with meat and fat. The treats felt good to her gums; she gnawed on them for hours. Pam delighted in seeing Jolie enjoy something so intently. "If this dog wants ten pig's ears a day, by God, she's going to get them," she decided. At this stage of Jolie's life, Pam wasn't about to deny her anything.

The treats helped draw out Jolie's personality. She was unaccustomed to such culinary luxury and willing to do whatever it took to keep it coming. At home, all three dogs got bones, but Jolie was obsessive about them. If Dudley happened to leave his bone on his bed for even a minute, Jolie would jump off the couch, race into the dining room, steal the bone, and hop back on her perch, purloined treasure clamped firmly between her jaws. If Dudley came looking for his bone, Jolie would growl and Dudley—easily three times her size—would give up the fight.

Jolie wasn't housetrained, but she learned the rules by watching Dudley and Odie go outside. If Pam was going to be gone all day, she put down a potty pad for Jolie and the little dog quickly adapted to it. After years of being mired in her own excrement, she seemed eager to have a separate place to do her business. It wasn't necessary to put her in a crate to prevent her from soiling the house.

The outpouring of affection and a safe, loving environment made all the difference. Six months after she came home with Pam, Jolie seemed liberated emotionally. She carried herself with a newfound sense of pride and confidence. Overnight, it seemed, Jolie wasn't frightened of anyone or anything, including Sullivan, the Husky next door. Despite their difference in size, the two dogs hit it off. Jolie would walk right up to Sullivan and sniff his snout, and he would let her. For the first time, Jolie began to wag her tail and approach life with a Cavalier's trademark blend of curiosity and cheerfulness.

TWENTY-THREE MILES away, in Wilmington, Delaware, 56-year-old Alycia Meldon had a more difficult experience.

Alycia was looking for a Pekingese to rescue. She'd taken in two before and fostered others, one of them a stray who'd been struck by an Amish buggy in Lancaster, Pennsylvania, and tossed into a ditch. Alycia was drawn to the glorious autumn-colored coat and gentle nature of the Pekingese breed, and the needier the dog, the better. Alycia lived alone and liked working with animals who'd been abused or thrown away. She'd choose a mistreated animal over a healthy, well-adjusted puppy any day.

A friend of Alycia's who'd been following the raid on Mike-Mar Kennel urged her to check out the dogs who were seized. Wolf was known for raising Pekingese, and who knew? Any number of his Pekingese might be in need of new homes.

When Alycia found out there were no Pekingese among the Wolf rescues, she began looking elsewhere. But none of the Pekingese rescue groups within an hour's drive of her had any dogs available, and the groups that were farther away had a standing rule against adopting out dogs to anyone living more than fifty miles away.

After several months of searching, Alycia was ready to give up. "Maybe I'm not supposed to have a Pekingese this time around," she thought. She read more about the Wolf case. Wolf no longer had Pekingese, but he did have several dozen Cavalier King Charles Spaniels. Cavaliers were known for being sensitive and caring—the perfect lap dog. And in a matter of days, some of them would be in need of a home. Alycia's interest was piqued.

The morning of July 6, she arrived at the Chester County SPCA at 7:30 a.m. for round two of the adoptions, hoping to get a Cavalier. Twenty-five people were ahead of her. She waited seven hours, but when she finally reached the front of the line the Chester County SPCA staff announced that the last available Cavalier had been taken. Feeling like a bride abandoned at the altar, Alycia left.

Despite her disappointment, she was impressed by the compassion the SPCA had shown in caring for Wolf's dogs. Two days later she drove back to the shelter with a bouquet of sunflowers to give to the staff. When she explained her situation—how the Cavaliers had all been taken by the time her number was called—the woman behind the desk looked up at her and smiled. "We've got one," she said. An adoption had fallen through the day before. A Cavalier was available after all.

The staffer ushered Alycia into a private room and went to get the dog. She was a Blenheim, but her chestnut and white coat was cut short and stained yellow, and she was thin. The little dog crouched beneath the chair the staffer was sitting in, a look of utter terror on her face. She refused all entreaties to come out. Unaccustomed to attention, she urinated on the tile floor.

Alycia was undeterred. She got down on the floor, too, talking to the employee and the dog in the gentlest possible tones. Finally, the Cavalier inched out from under the chair, but only to try to crawl up the legs of the kennel worker. Tenderly, Alycia reached out and lifted her up. The dog stiffened her legs and drew her head as far away from Alycia as she could. Alycia continued to speak to her softly. It seemed only natural that a dog in this circumstance would be fearful and shy. She'd take her, Alycia told the staffer. The woman carried the dog back to her pen so that she and Alycia could finish the paperwork.

On the ride home, the Cavalier cried the entire way. Alycia carried her crate into the kitchen of her Cape Cod house, unlatched the door, let the dog out and informed her that she had a new name: Abigail. For the first time, the little dog glanced up at her. A few minutes later, Alycia took her to the backyard and set her down. Suddenly, Abigail was curious. She began sniffing the air, the ground—the dozens of scents humans can't begin to distinguish. The smells were new to her, and she was entranced. Within minutes she dropped on her back and rolled around on the fresh, cool lawn. "This is the first time she's ever been on grass," Alycia thought. She watched her explore with a combination of pity and wonder, tears rolling down her face.

There were the usual physical ailments. Abby's teeth were so rotten they hung loose. Alycia's veterinarian initially thought Abby's jaw was broken; he wound up pulling all but seven of her teeth. And housetraining her was an ordeal. Abby eventually learned to go outside, but teaching the 4-year-old dog the fundamentals of cleanliness took every ounce of patience Alycia possessed.

Abby's emotional issues, though, were more serious. All of Alycia's previous rescues had struggled to overcome various problems, but it soon became apparent that Abby was way more disturbed. She frantically fought any attempt by Alycia to clean her ears—as if, in a previous life, she'd been handled roughly around her head. If Alycia reached toward her hind end, Abby curled up into a tight ball, terrified. And she was extremely protective of her space. She would consent to lie on the sofa next to Alycia as long as Alycia heeded an ironclad rule: no eye contact. If Alycia sat perfectly still and fixed her gaze elsewhere, Abby might edge close or crawl up Alycia's shoulders, but only under those conditions. Yet Abby suffered separation anxiety, too. If she sensed that Alycia was getting ready to leave the house, she would retreat to the farthest corner and shut down.

Her aversion to being touched from behind, her refusal to make eye contact, and her desire to hide out in a corner from time to time are typical behaviors of puppy mill dogs, Michelle Bender and Kim Townsend wrote in "Rehabilitation of a Puppy Mill Dog," a paper that has been widely published on the Internet. Rescue veterans with years of experience, they wrote that dogs living in puppy mills are seldom handled, and when they are, the experience is unpleasant—they're being vaccinated, dewormed, or carried to a new cage to breed or whelp puppies.

"Many mill dogs will try to always face you, not trusting you enough to give you easy access," Bender and Townsend wrote. "The most common posture we see in mill dogs is the 'freeze'; the dog will initially try to escape you, but when they realize there is no escape, they simply freeze up—rigid like a statue—and accept their 'fate.'"

Alycia understood all that. But Abby wrestled with deeper emotions her owner couldn't begin to fathom. She would sometimes whimper all night long, inconsolably. Alycia wondered if her distress had anything to do with the fact that the gestation period for a dog is sixty-three days. Was Abby conjuring up memories of being bred or of giving birth? There was no way to tell. Dogs live in the present as best they can, Alycia knew. But she also believed that bad experiences could become ingrained in an animal's psyche and never completely fade away.

Over time, Abby came around. In spite of her problems, she and Alycia bonded quickly. The sofa was Abby's favorite spot, but she would jump off of it and go in search of Alycia if Alycia disappeared anywhere else in the house. Abby didn't mind spending time in her crate. Being enclosed on all four sides gave her a feeling of security, and if Alycia needed to confine her for a few hours, Abby would step inside her crate willingly. She was so quiet and well behaved that Alycia soon began taking Abby to work with her in the afternoons, the way she'd done with her previous dogs. Alycia worked as an executive administrative assistant for a business consultant. Abby's crate sat ten feet from Alycia's desk; the dog spent most of her time there napping or chewing on a bone. The door to the crate stayed open.

At obedience class, Abby hid behind Alycia's legs but somehow managed to learn to sit, stay, and come. At home she figured out how to stand at the back door and bark, spinning in a circle, when she wanted Alycia to let her out. She loved the outdoors. The backyard was the place she was most apt to let down her guard and act the way a dog ought to, with no worries or cares. As soon as Alycia opened the door, Abby would race toward the edge of the low-lying deck, soar through the air, and hit the ground running, her shoulder-length Cavalier ears flying out behind her.

In time she seemed almost normal, with one exception: Abby never overcame her fear of other people. She felt comfortable around Sandy Wood, the woman who ran the boarding wing at the veterinary clinic where Abby sometimes stayed, but that was it—no

Abby, a Cavalier rescued from Michael Wolf's puppy mill, with her new owner, Alycia Meldon. With the help of Alycia, Abby overcame some but not all of her issues.

one else got close. She remained skittish and fearful. Years after her rescue, she jumped at the slightest noise—a door opening or an object hitting the floor. She learned to reach her front legs out for Alycia, but every now and again she cringed when Alycia came close. Her years in the puppy mill would haunt her forever.

Which, of course, made Alycia love her all the more. Her life was much fuller with Abby in it, she said. "I'm so thankful for this little miracle."

UNLIKE PAM AND ALYCIA, Laura and Mike Hewitt dealt one-on-one with Wolf. They met him just days before the raid on Mike-Mar Kennel. Laura, a retired speech-language pathologist, and Mike, a vice president for Dupont Safety Resources, had recently lost their two rescued dogs: Mattie, a Keeshond, and Lucie, a Sheltie-Corgi mix. This time around, they wanted a Cavalier. Two of them, as a matter of fact. Laura had researched the breed and was convinced the friendly, diminutive dogs would make ideal pets.

The Hewitts' veterinarian referred them to Susan Krewatch, another client who had Cavaliers. She passed along contact information for Wolf. Laura checked out Mike-Mar Cavaliers on four different websites. One of them, breeders.net, featured four photos of Cavalier puppies and the assurance that the kennel was home to "over 200 champions in several breeds."

"My goal is to own the very best quality dogs that are healthy and happy," Wolf wrote. "I have decided to sell my puppies as pets only not to breeders or exhibitors. The dogs are the happiest being a beloved pet."

Laura contacted Wolf, and over the next two weeks they e-mailed back and forth several times. He could tell she was a dog person, Wolf wrote. But when Laura asked to visit his kennel in person, Wolf kept putting her off, saying that he needed to undergo dialysis or that it simply wasn't a good day to visit.

Finally, he relented. On February 7, 2006, the Hewitts drove the fourteen miles from their home outside Newark, Delaware, to Lower Oxford. They arrived the day before Cheryl Shaw and Maureen Siddons made their unannounced inspection of Mike-Mar Kennel and three days before the dogs were seized.

It was close to 4 p.m. when the couple turned in to Wolf's driveway. The landscaping was overgrown, and it seemed peculiar to Laura that there were no signs advertising the kennel. But any doubts she had were erased the minute Wolf opened the door to the kennel building and half a dozen Cavaliers scampered out. The dogs surrounded the couple, begging for attention. Their friendly nature seemed like a good sign, although oddly, the dogs emitted no sound when they barked. Wolf brushed it off when Laura asked him about it. He simply said the dogs were well-behaved.

The breeder ushered the couple into the viewing room, a living room-like area decorated with threadbare furniture. He spoke at length about his show days at Westminster and pointed out photos of his champion dogs. Talk turned to breeding, and Wolf lamented the proliferation of Pennsylvania's Amish-run puppy mills. "He deplored the Amish because of how they deceived the public," Laura recalled. "He went into a whole dissertation" about their irresponsible practices.

The Hewitts were more interested in the two litters of puppies that were piled together on a velveteen bed inside an open-topped wire pen. Laura leaned over to play with the wide-eyed dogs. It was good to see her interacting with the puppies, Wolf said. He said a couple had dropped by in a limo earlier that week to check out his dogs, but after neither the husband nor his wife bothered to actually handle the puppies, Wolf said, he refused to sell them a dog. The Hewitts later met other customers of Wolf who said he had told them the same story.

Laura asked the breeder how old the puppies were; he said he couldn't remember. She cuddled two puppies—a Blenheim with sleepy eyes and a tricolor dog. She was smitten, just as she'd suspected she would be. The Cavaliers were every bit as adorable as she had hoped. What's more, they were available immediately. It had taken the couple weeks to get their last rescue dog.

Laura asked if the Cavaliers were AKC-registered. Wolf no longer did business with the AKC, he told her. He said he raised his dogs not for breeding, but to be pets.

That didn't matter. Laura was definitely interested in the two pups she'd picked out. They'd call the chestnut and white Cavalier Winston, she decided, and the tricolor dog Wallace. Wallace came from another litter and was about two weeks older than Winston.

Winston seemed to be congested; mucus spilled from one of his eyes. Laura borrowed a towel from Wolf to wipe the mucus away. The dogs' hearts and eyes had been checked, Wolf assured them. They were healthy and good to go.

He had a deal for the Hewitts, he said. Normally he charged $1,500 each for the puppies, but he would sell them the pair for $2,000. That sounded reasonable—the price was considerably less than the $3,000 a breeder in Baltimore was asking for a single Cavalier. The Hewitts' only problem was that they planned to leave town in a few days. If they paid him a deposit, would Wolf be willing to hold the puppies until they returned? He agreed to do so, provided the couple paid extra for food. Mike wrote Wolf a check for $500, Laura snapped several photos of the dogs, and the couple left.

On the way home, the Hewitts stopped off for dinner and Laura excused herself to go wash her hands. In the bathroom she glanced down at the black wool coat she was wearing. She'd deliberately worn black to see whether the puppies shed. There wasn't much hair, but the coat smelled nasty—almost as bad as the mushroom barns in nearby Avondale when the farmers flung open the doors.

"I can't get this smell off me," Laura commented to her husband. She had to have the coat dry-cleaned the next day.

Laura wished Mike-Mar Kennel had been cleaner. But despite the odor, she and Mike were sold on the Cavalier puppies. Two days later, excited about her new pets, Laura e-mailed Wolf to let him know she had already sent some of the pictures of the puppies to family and friends. Now their friends were asking questions, like what were the puppies' birthdates? Where did their parents and grandparents come from, and what information could Wolf share about them?

The puppies "were all so loving and cuddly that I got overwhelmed being in puppydom and doggy kisses that I didn't even use the list of ?s that I had prepared!" Laura wrote. She closed by saying, "Thanks so much for your help and in the breeding and raising of such loving and precious dogs!"

Thirty-four hours later, Laura turned on the eleven o'clock news and watched, astonished, the coverage of the raid on Mike-Mar Kennel. The station showed footage of rescuers carrying hundreds of dogs out and loading them into vans. Where in all that chaos were Wallace and Winston? she wondered. Laura felt as though she'd been kicked in the chest.

She phoned the station, NBC10 in Philadelphia, and tracked down the reporter who was working the story. The Chester County SPCA was handling the raid, he told her. That night Laura wrote the SPCA a lengthy e-mail explaining that she and Mike had put down a deposit for two of the puppies taken from Wolf's kennel. The following morning the couple drove to the SPCA shelter, ready to claim Winston and Wallace. The staff had bad news: The puppies were considered evidence in the case against Wolf. They would need to be kept in custody until the matter was resolved.

As far as Laura was concerned, the puppies were already part of her family—and now she and Mike might not see them for months. The predicament brought back painful memories. Seventeen years earlier, Laura and her first husband had one child and had arranged to adopt a second. Laura spent five months bonding with the biological mother; she even attended Lamaze classes with her. But four days after the woman gave birth to a little girl, she decided to reclaim her baby, and the couple were forced to give up the child.

In an e-mail dated February 13, Mike informed Wolf that he had stopped payment on the deposit he'd left with him four days earlier. "We feel dismay, disappointment, anger, and shock in what the media has reported, and our decision was extremely difficult to make," Mike wrote. A few days later, Wolf's attorney, Eric Coates, returned the Hewitts's check with a brief note saying the puppies weren't available for now but that he hoped they would be in the near future.

The Hewitts remained concerned about the puppies' welfare. Laura stayed in touch with Chester County SPCA staff, and four and a half months later, when the dogs were ready to be adopted out, Laura arrived at the shelter early to claim the Cavaliers. Becky Turnbull pulled her out of the line to tell her there was more bad news. The puppies had been ill the night they'd been taken from the kennel, and neither had survived.

To try to make up for the couple's loss, Turnbull gave Laura first pick of some other Cavaliers, puppies who had been newborns when the raid occurred and were now barely 5 months old. Laura again chose two males, this time a Blenheim she named Baxter and a black and tan dog she named Duffy. She knew she'd made the right choice when the moment they were released the puppies scampered to her, jumped into her arms, and covered her with kisses.

The Hewitts mourned the loss of Winston and Wallace, but Baxter and Duffy quickly stole their hearts. They had been rescued early enough to escape the trauma of puppy mill life. They were spared the fear and lack of socialization that plagued the rest of Wolf's dogs.

Physically, though, the dogs were a nightmare. Both had ear mites and bad teeth, even though they were still puppies. Baxter had a hernia that required surgery. Two weeks after the Hewitts brought the puppies home, the hair on Baxter's face began to fall out. He was diagnosed with demodectic mange, a condition that can be hereditary but frequently is caused by a dog's weak immune system. He suffered hair loss across his entire face. In a matter of weeks, he developed a worse form of the disease, sarcoptic mange—mites tunneling into the outer layers of his skin, causing it to become crusty

It was love at first sight for Laura Hewitt and her two new Cavaliers, Duffy and Baxter.

and scaly and itch constantly. For weeks, Baxter buried his inflamed head in Laura's chest, whimpering. And because the dogs slept with Laura and Mike, Laura herself contracted sarcoptic mange.

Eventually the Hewitts got the mange under control, but their dogs went on to experience a succession of other ailments. Duffy's biggest problem was worms. He had every kind imaginable. His immune system was so fragile that two days after he went home with the Hewitts, he collapsed. That's what happens with puppy mill survivors, the couple's veterinarian told them. In crowded and stressful circumstances, their adrenaline races at such a high pitch that when the dogs finally start to settle down, they fall apart.

Both Cavaliers suffered from gastrointestinal problems. In a matter of months, constant eruptions of blood, vomit, and diarrhea ruined the white carpet in the couple's spacious home. It wasn't uncommon for Laura to take one or both dogs to the vet three times a day. In the first year alone, the Hewitts spent nearly $10,000 fighting an array of health problems in their dogs.

HAD SHE FORESEEN the ordeal she would undergo—not to mention the troubles the Hewitts would experience with their dogs—Susan Krewatch never would have recommended Wolf.

She first visited him in 2004. She'd located him online and liked the fact that Wolf lived only about twenty minutes from her house in Hockessin, Delaware. His place was a little dirty and smelly, but not enough to sound any alarms. That first visit, Susan purchased a tricolor female she named Lily. Lily seemed healthy, so six months later Susan returned to buy a second Cavalier, another tricolor she named Bella.

Bella had problems immediately. Susan's vet found a corneal abrasion on one of Bella's eyes, dead ear mites in her ears, and patches of missing hair. A few days later the puppy developed bronchitis. Her body wouldn't tolerate antibiotics, so Susan had to hold an inhaler over the dog's nose to clear out her lungs. She confronted

Wolf about the problems over the phone. He agreed not to cash the $200 deposit check Susan had left him, and she was satisfied. Two hundred dollars covered the vet bill.

Bella eventually regained her health. But three years later, Lily developed a heart murmur and painful urinary tract infections that wouldn't go away. The infections made her so sick that her eyes glazed over and she could hardly walk or lift her head. She turned out to also have *E.coli* and *Pseudomonas*, serious bacterial infections. Exploratory surgery revealed worse problems. Lily had just one kidney and, on top of that, a recessed vulva, a condition that could enable urine to pool in the folds of her skin, triggering bacterial growth. A surgeon operated on her vulva, but problems continued. Then Lily's vet determined that she had subluxation, a partial dislocation of the bones in her hind legs. "But don't worry about that now. That's the least of your worries," the vet told Susan.

Too late she realized she'd been dealing with a puppy mill. The signs were all there: Wolf's house was filthier and smelled worse every time she visited. He kept trying to sell her male puppies—presumably so he could keep the females for breeding purposes. The last time Susan visited him, she brought along Lily and Bella, and Wolf proudly showed her his kennel: a building filled with dogs in stacked crates. He seemed not to notice that the floors of the building were awash with urine. Susan's own dogs were skating about on the slippery floors, and Lily began drooling uncontrollably, a sign of acute stress.

Susan was horrified by the rank conditions, and told Wolf so. "I said, 'Michael, this is terrible. There are too many dogs to a cage. They aren't even able to walk around and turn around.' He said 'Oh, no no. We're cleaning. They're not usually like this.'" Susan bathed her dogs when she got home that day and vowed never to go back. A year later, though, despite what she'd seen, she recommended Wolf to the Hewitts.

"He just kind of sucked me in," Susan recalled years later. "He said, 'You know I love dogs more than people'—that kind of stuff. And he made a big fuss over the dogs—the ones I saw."

16

Tackling the Puppy Mills

R OBERT O. BAKER understood better than anyone how widespread the hidden world of puppy mills had become.

A former stockbroker from St. Louis, Baker, 59, began chronicling abuses in horse and dog racing and dog theft rings in the late 1970s. He wrote the book *The Misuse of Drugs in Horse Racing.* In 1980, after *60 Minutes* featured his work, the Humane Society of the United States (HSUS) hired him to look into puppy mills.

His assignment was straightforward: Find out whether the federal Animal Welfare Act was making any headway in improving conditions at commercial kennels. The U.S. Congress had passed the law in 1966 and expanded it four years later to establish minimal standards for the care, housing, sale, and transport of dogs, cats, and other animals held by dealers or laboratories. Large-scale breeding kennels were now required to be licensed, and federal inspectors were supposed to inspect the kennels once a year. But the HSUS kept hearing anecdotal evidence that, ten years after taking effect, the law wasn't making much of a difference. Dogs were still being inadequately housed, poorly bred dogs were still winding up in pet stores, and customers were still being victimized.

Baker got a job selling kennel supplies and equipment to brokers and breeders, which provided a crash course in the how-to's of large-scale dog breeding. From time to time he also approached kennel operators on the pretext of buying a dog. Breeders weren't always fooled; in Missouri, he was shot at by a kennel owner who discovered him on her property with a television camera crew. But most breeders had no problem letting him view their operations up close.

He quickly discovered that far from being hampered by the Animal Welfare Act, puppy mills were flourishing. Breeders routinely flouted the law's minimum standards. In kennel after kennel— sometimes old chicken coops—he saw dogs confined to cages so small they could barely turn around, visibly hungry, and diseased. Pennsylvania's farmers didn't have chicken coops, so they housed their dogs in old washing machines and refrigerators or tied them to oil drums or abandoned cars, unprotected from the elements.

The lengths to which breeders were allowed to skirt already lenient regulations astounded Baker. For example, even though excrement was supposed to be removed regularly from a dog's cage, federal inspectors were told not to issue a citation unless the fecal buildup was more than two weeks old. Inspectors typically let matters go three to four weeks before they cited a breeder. And left on their own, breeders tended to let the excrement build up even longer. Not until piles of fecal matter rose so high off the ground that they brushed the wire bottoms of the rabbit hutch-style cages was anything done, and then breeders remedied the problem by simply moving the hutches. It wasn't unusual to see heaps of excrement dotting area farms; the heaps were never removed.

Worn-out dogs were killed and thrown away like garbage. In Missouri, Baker stumbled onto a kennel owner in a back field who was shooting to death about thirty American Eskimo Dogs and

Samoyeds. The breeds weren't as popular as they'd once been, and they'd stopped selling. Baker identified himself as a supplier, so the breeder didn't think to cover up his actions. He assumed Baker would regard the killings the same way he did—business as usual.

Gradually, Baker pieced together the rise of puppy mills: how large-volume commercial dog breeding surfaced in the Midwest after World War II as mom-and-pop pet stores began to give way to corporate franchises; how marketing experts hired by the corporations had concocted an easy way to lure customers by putting adorable puppies in shop windows.

Americans' rising prosperity escalated demand for purebred dogs, and the advent of shopping malls multiplied foot traffic past pet stores. Having a pet shop in a town meant families no longer had to search the want ads or drive out to a farm to examine a litter. At a pet store, they could choose from a variety of breeds, and once they picked out a dog, the supplies they needed—collar and leash, food, toys—were right there, too. Moreover, buyers could charge their purchases on a credit card, something amateur breeders weren't set up to handle. Pet stores made it so easy to acquire a dog that many families found themselves buying one on impulse. Roughly half of the consumers who later complained to the HSUS about buying a sick dog admitted that they had left home that day with no intention of getting a pet.

The AKC registered these pet shop dogs by the tens of thousands. Between the mid-1940s and 1970, the number of registrations jumped from 77,000 a year to 1 million.

To meet the demand, brokers who supplied puppies to the stores needed a steady supply of dogs. They zeroed in on Missouri and Kansas, centrally located states that were home to hundreds of small, isolated farms. Breeding puppies was a boon to Midwestern egg farmers who'd been edged out by large corporations. Farmers could put their empty chicken coops to use by housing dogs in them instead. The U.S. Department of Agriculture encouraged raising puppies as a way for farmers to supplement their income.

In the 1950s, department store chains such as Sears Roebuck and Co. and Montgomery Ward were selling Poodles and Dalmatians alongside tool chests and bicycles, and puppy mills spread into Arkansas, Iowa, and Oklahoma. By the late 1970s, they were migrating east into Pennsylvania, putting them hundreds of miles closer to pet stores along the eastern seaboard. In 1981, a puppy broker from the Midwest held a demonstration in Lancaster County to show Amish and Mennonite farmers how, with little experience or investment, they could raise puppies for profit; several hundred farmers attended the workshop.

In the 1970s and early 1980s, dog brokers and pet stores dealt only with puppies that were registered with the AKC. Amish and Mennonite farmers didn't understand how to fill out the AKC's paperwork, however; their registration applications were filled with errors and, as a result, were frequently denied. To remedy the problem, the AKC sent field agents to Lancaster County to teach these breeders the proper way to register their dogs.

"Without the active assistance of the AKC, Pennsylvania puppy mills would have never been established," Baker maintains. In fact, the Pennsylvania Federation of Dog Clubs, composed of member clubs of the AKC, was so livid over the AKC's involvement that its president, Dotsie Keith, met with Baker and the Federation of Humane Societies to help draft the state's original Dog Law. The legislature passed it in 1982.

By now, though, the industry was mushrooming. Across the country, breeders used the cachet of AKC registration papers to sell purebred puppies, and the AKC collected hundreds of thousands of dollars in registration fees. While nobody was looking, dog breeding exploded into a multibillion-dollar industry, profitable for operators but at the expense of millions of mistreated dogs.

Throughout the 1980s, the HSUS worked to rein in reckless breeders. With a camera in his pocket, Baker trespassed onto many properties to document abuse. By calling ahead and asking when a breeder was going to be home, he was also able to find out when they were going to be away. He steeled himself to avoid eye contact with the animals and focus instead on recording as many grim details as he could. "You're just there to obtain evidence and get out," he recalled. In a matter of several grueling months, he visited 284 kennels.

Armed with Baker's research, the HSUS was able to push through some improvements. Pennsylvania and a few other states passed laws of their own to monitor large-volume dog breeding. Local humane societies frequently followed up on Baker's investigations by filing animal cruelty charges against breeders.

In Kansas in the late 1980s, Baker led state attorney general Robert Stephan on a tour of licensed kennels. Stephan was so sickened by them that he prosecuted some of the breeders himself. He called the worst offenders the Dirty Thirty. Breeders across the state shut down their operations rather than risk finding themselves in Stephan's crosshairs. The number of puppy mills in Kansas plummeted from nearly 1,200 to fewer than 300.

Meanwhile, the HSUS launched a campaign against Docktors Pet Center, the largest pet store chain in the United States, after discovering the stores were routinely selling sick dogs to customers. All 300 Docktors stores wound up closing as a result.

In 1993, Baker left his position as chief investigator for the HSUS to become a field investigator first for the Companion Animal Protection Society, and then for the Humane Farming Association. By 2005, he had visited more than 800 puppy mills and helped bring charges against dozens of breeders. He had done all he thought he could do and was ready to turn his attention elsewhere. He shipped a quarter-century's worth of archives, including some 800 photos, to fellow advocate Libby Williams, the cofounder of New Jersey Consumers Against Pet Shop Abuse, or NJCAPSA for short.

A year later, though, Baker was pulled back into the fray. Pennsylvania governor Ed Rendell was getting ready to crack down on puppy mills, and the American Society for the Prevention of Cruelty to Animals (ASPCA) asked Baker to step in and help.

Elected to office in 2002, Rendell had spent his first term trying to reverse the state's high unemployment rate and jump-start its stagnant economy. He injected money into tourism and agriculture and launched a series of green initiatives to clean up rivers and streams and reclaim polluted industrial sites. The rumpled, self-confident officeholder had an ambitious agenda and was running for reelection in the fall. His schedule was on overload.

But Rendell was also a dog lover. He and his wife, Marjorie, a federal judge for the U.S. Court of Appeals' Third Circuit, had two Golden Retrievers adopted from rescue groups. No one needed to remind the governor that Pennsylvania was one of the top puppy-producing states in the country—infamous for the nickname Baker had bestowed upon it as the Puppy Mill Capital of the East. Roughly 2,500 kennels were licensed by the state to house anywhere from 26 to 500 dogs apiece, and hundreds more unlicensed kennels festered under the radar. In Lancaster County alone, Amish and Mennonite families operated 300 kennels, the largest concentration of puppy mills in the United States.

The proliferation of large-volume dog breeding was already a prickly subject with the governor. When a certain billboard surfaced along the Pennsylvania Turnpike one morning in February 2005, Rendell was downright mortified. The billboard showed a family of tourists decked out in Hawaiian shirts, riding gaily in a convertible, and in nostalgic, 1950s-era typography, the words, "Welcome to Scenic Lancaster County." Below that it said, "Home to hundreds of puppy mills. Learn more about Pennsylvania's notorious puppy mills. Visit these websites: mainlinerescue.com; stoppuppymills. org."

Rendell decided to form an ad hoc committee to study the success of the state's dog law. In January 2006, Baker met with the governor and agreed to serve on the panel. He was intimately familiar with Pennsylvania's statutes; four years after helping push through passage of the Dog Law, he'd promoted a state puppy

lemon law designed to compensate buyers who unwittingly purchased sick puppies.

The ad hoc committee consisted of representatives from the
attorney general's office, the ASPCA, a veterinarian, and several
ordinary citizens. To Baker's surprise, not everyone on the committee favored revamping the dog law. Several members blamed the
problem on a few bad apples and overblown media coverage. "Even
the person representing the governor's office was terrible," Baker
said. "She made the comment that as long as there were poor people without health insurance, why were we worrying about dogs."

To convince them otherwise, fellow committee member Marsha
Perelman, a businesswoman from Philadelphia's affluent Main Line
and an ardent animal lover, hired an undercover investigator to document conditions at puppy mills. Baker followed up with more detective
work of his own. He also turned to his friend Williams of NJCAPSA.

Williams, 55, had plenty of evidence to share. A passionate dog
lover, she'd spent the last half-dozen years collecting and dissemi-
nating every iota of information she could find about Pennsylvania's
puppy mills. She attended conventions for breeders, stayed abreast
of Dog Law Advisory Board doings, and kept track of problem
breeders who ran afoul of the state Dog Law Bureau. She focused
on Pennsylvania because, of the seventy-plus pet stores in New
Jersey that sold puppies, as many as half sold dogs brought in from
the Keystone State. The rest were trucked in by brokers from the
Midwest.

From her ground-floor office in her home in southwestern New
Jersey, operating mostly on her own dime, Williams helped seek
recourse for consumers who'd purchased ill or dying puppies from
breeders or pet stores. She dug up kennel inspection records and
passed along to consumers the information necessary to file a complaint. Every once in a while she wrote the complaint herself.

Posing as an uninformed buyer, Williams wangled her way into
more than a dozen Pennsylvania puppy mills. She wanted to see for

Animal welfare advocate Marsha Perelman and veteran puppy mill investigator Bob Baker reach out to pet a puppy mill survivor. By 2006, Baker had visited more than 800 substandard kennels across the country. He knew better than anyone how weak and ineffective the laws governing kennel operators were.

herself if the appalling rumors she'd heard about these outfits were true. Not one of the dogs she saw in intensive confinement behaved normally; the animals either barked furiously or crouched in their cages, shell-shocked.

In 2005, Williams helped rescue eighty mixed-breed dogs when the broker died and his widow contacted her organization. The dogs were several months old and looked happy and socialized in their pens, but as soon as anyone reached in to pick them up, they were terrified—frozen, she recalled. At another puppy mill, a friend accompanying Williams furtively called her attention to a mother dog pacing about in a cage, a dead puppy hanging from her mouth. Elsewhere in the barn, breeding dog after breeding dog lay on wire floors, nursing puppies. Years later, Williams was still haunted by the memory of the mother dogs refusing to make eye contact. "They looked down as if they were ashamed—as if to say, 'I'm not even worthy of having you look at me,'" she said. "They just looked so spent." She shook her head at the thought that, weeks later, unsuspecting buyers would spend up to $1,500 apiece for the puppies produced by these overbred dogs.

Pennsylvania's kennels were nothing short of scandalous. Newspapers had repeatedly exposed the conditions. Between 1991 and 1996, the *Pittsburgh Press*, *New York Times*, *Philadelphia Inquirer*, and *New York Post* detailed the fetid environment, particularly in kennels operated by the Amish. To the surprise of many, Amish farmers admitted openly to raising dogs as livestock—they confined them to tiny cages and destroyed the breeding animals as soon as they

Libby Williams and Sweetie, a Gordon Setter who found a new life with her after ten years in a dilapidated kennel.

stopped producing. The *Post* described dogs caged in dimly lit barns—filthy, covered in feces and so broken in spirit they were "unresponsive to a visitor's presence and voice." The stories prompted the passage of the puppy lemon law, but did nothing to curtail the poor breeding practices.

Pennsylvania's 1982 law wasn't working, in large part because it wasn't being enforced. Breeders were ignoring space requirements and, worse, denying veterinary care to their dogs. When a dog became sick or injured, it simply languished; it cost the breeder too much to take the dog to the vet. A breeding dog's reward for producing litter after litter was to be shot dead around the age of 5 or 6.

The state laws created a situation that made it difficult, if not impossible, to nail unscrupulous breeders. Pennsylvania's dog wardens had the authority to inspect licensed breeders. But it was police officers employed by nonprofit humane societies who actually enforced the state's animal cruelty law. Unless they had a warrant, however, humane officers weren't allowed to enter private property to determine whether any cruelty had taken place. It was a classic Catch-22: The people who were permitted to see the problems were not allowed to do anything about them. In theory, dog wardens could inform humane officers of a problem, but few did.

The relationship between dog law officials and the breeders had grown far too cozy, as far as Williams was concerned. A bureau official later conceded that instead of reprimanding breeders for committing violations, wardens were more inclined to help them comply with the rules.

Pennsylvania had fifty-three dog wardens, and needed more. Money wasn't an issue. The state earmarked revenue from dog license sales to pay for enforcement, something most states didn't do. But Pennsylvania wasn't spending the money: Its Dog Law Bureau was sitting on a $14 million surplus.

The state's puppy lemon law needed tightening, too. Buyers who unknowingly purchased a sick or diseased dog had the right to return the puppy for a refund, exchange it for another dog, or seek reimbursement for veterinary bills up to or equal to the purchase price of the dog. But the law didn't go far enough for families whose new pet turned out to have a life-threatening illness such as parvovirus or pneumonia; dog owners quickly racked up hundreds, if not thousands of dollars more in vet bills than they could ever hope to get back in the form of a refund.

The governor's ad hoc committee said breeders should be required to pay all of the veterinary bills associated with a sick puppy. The committee also said the attorney general's office should survey veterinarians to determine which kennels ill puppies were coming from, and publicize the puppy lemon law more aggressively to make sure buyers understood their rights. The absence of veterinary care provided to dogs in commercial kennels was the system's single biggest failure, Baker believed.

Aware that animal welfare advocates took a dim view of their practices, commercial breeders had become more careful to conceal their operations. Where once hutches full of dogs could be seen from the highway, the cash crops were now hidden inside low-slung metal barns. Some commercial breeders refused to deal with the public at all—they sold their dogs to brokers instead. A few breeders admitted to Baker that they knew people would be horrified if they saw their facilities up close.

THE RAID ON WOLF'S kennel occurred a month after Rendell formed his ad hoc committee. The nasty details of Mike-Mar Kennel filled newspaper columns and the airwaves. This time the governor decided to go public with his discontent. In March 2006, a month after the raid, Rendell told the *Philadelphia Inquirer* he was considering a shake-up in the Bureau of Dog Law Enforcement. While he was at it, he announced another bold move: he planned to fire all fourteen members of the state Dog Law Advisory Board. The board was made up of dog breeders, veterinarians, representatives from animal welfare groups, animal research entities, sportsmen, and pet shop owners, and had no real enforcement authority. The group had convened just three times since Rendell took office. Rendell said the board had not been active enough, and the ASPCA chimed in, faulting the bureau for hiring too few dog wardens, failing to train them properly, and failing to report cruelty violations to humane society police officers.

Behind the scenes, the ad hoc committee offered another recommendation: that Rendell should empower the state's dog wardens to continue monitoring breeders whose licenses had been revoked. The governor agreed. If the wardens had possessed that authority earlier, they could have stopped Wolf long before the Chester County SPCA was forced to step in, the governor said. "People say we lie down on kennels, but here they did the right thing [revoking Wolf's license], and the guy goes back in business and we never know about it," Rendell said. "Once we close a kennel, we should go back and do spot checks."

The message to breeders was unmistakable. Moreover, Rendell was just gearing up. On October 17, 2006, seven months after the raid on Mike-Mar Kennel, the governor held a press conference on the steps of the Chester County Courthouse to propose a sweeping overhaul of the state dog law. Flanking him were Chester County SPCA board president Sandra Thielz and humane society police officers Cheryl Shaw, Michele Beswick, and Rebecca Robers. Also on hand was one of the dogs rescued from Michael Wolf's kennel— a colorfully bedecked Cavalier King Charles Spaniel named Cricket—embraced by her new owner, Amy Dluhy of Chester Springs.

"We are taking strong steps to protect consumers, reputable breeders and kennels, and the defenseless animals whose health and welfare is at the heart of this important issue," the governor said.

He announced that Jessie Smith, a twenty-year veteran of the attorney general's office and former president of the Harrisburg Area Humane Society, would fill the newly created position of

Pennsylvania Governor Ed Rendell greets Amy
Dluhy and her Cavalier, Cricket, after announcing
a sweeping plan to overhaul the state's puppy mills.

special deputy secretary for dog law enforcement in the Department
of Agriculture. Rendell named Jeffrey Paladina as special prosecutor for dog law enforcement. And he appointed a team of four kennel compliance specialists to make sure the kennel provisions of the
dog law were carried out.

Among other things, the governor wanted the state legislature to
give dog wardens the authority to seize dogs in distress. While cruelty charges were pending, the breeder in question would either
have to pay for the care of the dogs or forfeit ownership. That would
help head off the kind of stalemate the Mike-Mar Kennel raid had
created. And the secretary of agriculture would be required to
revoke the license of any kennel owner convicted of cruelty. Not
only that, but the license would be withheld for ten years.

The legislative proposals were one thing, but it was Rendell's
regulatory wish list that incited breeders most. The governor wanted to double the size of cages in all kennels, require that all dogs be
exercised for at least twenty minutes a day, and establish minimum
standards for lighting, temperature control, ventilation, air movement, bedding, sanitation, slope of ground, and flooring materials.
Breeders would be required to keep more detailed records.

Finally, Rendell announced a special team to improve state dog law enforcement, and he named sixteen people to the Dog Law Advisory Board. The new members included representatives from agriculture, breeders, dog club officials, veterinarians, and others. Their first assignment was to review changes to the state dog law. The board planned to meet before the proposed regulations were published so that all concerned could review them before a sixty-day comment period got under way.

"This is just the beginning of our efforts to strengthen the dog law," the governor said. "I encourage the public to play an active role in this important and ongoing process."

Three weeks later, Pennsylvania voters reelected Rendell, a Democrat, to a second term with 60.4 percent of the vote over former Pittsburgh Steelers star Lynn Swann. Anyone who thought the puppy mill issue was nothing more than campaign rhetoric, to be shelved once the election was history, was in for a surprise. The following month, the governor was on hand when nearly 300 people crowded into the Farm Show meeting hall in Harrisburg for the first gathering of the new Dog Law Advisory Board. The board members faced a gauntlet of anger from small-scale and large-volume breeders alike over the proposed regulations, which they said were cumbersome, expensive, and unenforceable.

A decade earlier, the Pennsylvania Federation of Dog Clubs had urged passage of the puppy lemon law, but now it opposed cracking down on puppy mills. "This document would not allow me to keep a litter of puppies next to my bed because it is not a washable room," the federation's Nina Schaefer said.

Ken Brandt, a former state representative who now headed the Pennsylvania Professional Dog Breeders Association, argued that dog breeding had helped keep Amish and Mennonite families on the farm. Many of them would be forced out of the dog business and unable to pay their mortgages, he said. He also warned that tougher regulations might encourage breeders to operate without a license as a way of avoiding laws they couldn't afford to obey. "There's a demand out there for dogs," Brandt said, "and that demand will stay."

The chorus of opponents included Cynthia Miller, a delegate to the AKC. She said inadequate enforcement of the existing law appeared to be the problem, and she cautioned that tougher regulations could prove more burdensome and could "make things worse." Shelters and rescue groups weren't happy, either. They said the paperwork required by the new rules would engulf them, and the move to bigger cages would limit the number of dogs they could rescue.

Rendell responded that shelters and small breeders would be exempt from some of the rules, but he acknowledged that some of the largest kennels in the state might feel the hit. He said his goal was not to get rid of Pennsylvania's kennels, however.

Meanwhile, the ad hoc committee came back with two more key recommendations. The first was that the state hire a special prosecutor to handle egregious cases of animal abuse and neglect. The second was that the inspector general's office investigate the worst violations of the dog law. Rendell agreed. He said Pennsylvania's current law had left dog wardens "undermanned and outgunned." The wardens weren't equipped with law degrees and couldn't begin to compete against private attorneys hired to defend kennel owners charged with violating the dog law.

In January 2007, the governor's office began circulating sixty-seven pages of proposed new dog regulations. Breeders launched a new outcry. Twelve thousand people sent in comments.

The legislature would have to approve the changes, and opposition was swelling. But support was building, too. Baker joined one hundred animal welfare advocates on the steps of the state capitol building to urge a tougher dog law. They produced as Exhibit A a three-legged West Highland Terrier named Aidan. A former breeding dog, his leg was sliced off by his owner when it got caught in a wire fence.

For months, the *Philadelphia Inquirer's* capitol reporter, Amy Worden, had exposed the loopholes bedeviling the state dog law. Now the *Allentown Morning Call* weighed in with an exhaustive series that demonstrated just how loosely the dog law was enforced. The newspaper analyzed 20,000 inspection records compiled over a three-year period and concluded that state dog wardens were often a kennel owner's best friend. Even when dogs were confined to cramped cages filled with dirty water bowls and feces, and even when diseased or dead dogs lay about, breeding and boarding kennels were virtually assured of a passing grade. Despite rampant problems, more than 90 percent of Pennsylvania kennels got perfect ratings in all twenty-six categories. Because it had no idea how to analyze its own data, however, the Bureau of Dog Law Enforcement itself hadn't fully realized the extent of its dismal track record.

As an example, the *Morning Call* cited the case of Long Lane Kennel in Lancaster County. The dog warden assigned to the kennel had cited it twice in March 2006, but nevertheless had rated it as satisfactory. Later that year, other inspectors and a cruelty investigator with the Humane League of Lancaster County found conditions so terrible at Long Lane that they confiscated twenty-three dogs, one of whom had to be euthanized. Among other things, the kennel was strewn with feces and had a broken heater and exposed wires.

Then there was breeder Aaron Burkholder of Kutztown, who had been cited for thirty-one violations over the previous three years. Even when the dog warden filed five criminal citations against Burkholder, he continued to sell nearly 200 dogs a year. "If you have a good product, you'll have sales," Burkholder said.

At Bear Track Acres in Bucks County, dog warden Verna North noted dismal conditions. Water in the dog bowls was frozen. Some of the more than two dozen dogs lacked food. There was no bedding, the temperature fell below regulations, and North found fecal matter in every one of the runs. She gave owner David

Greenlaw a week to correct the problems. A week later the kennel had been cleaned, but the dogs still had no bedding or heat; the temperature had now plunged to a bone-chilling eighteen degrees. Yet despite those deficiencies, the dog warden gave Greenlaw satisfactory ratings in both her reports.

The most shocking finding of all was the sheer size of the state's breeding industry. In Pennsylvania alone, nearly a million dogs had been sold in 2006. The *Morning Call's* website offered a link to state inspection records, so in a matter of clicks, readers could troll the records for themselves. Soon afterward, Rendell announced the creation of a similar new online database that would enable consumers to access inspection records for every dog kennel licensed by the state.

Cori Menkin, senior director of legislative initiatives for the ASPCA, scoured the databases and discovered that rescue shelters were being inspected nearly twice as often as large commercial kennels. Shelters that received state money for rescuing stray dogs were required to be audited quarterly. Even so, the bureau's priorities made no sense, Menkin said. Large-volume breeders were the problem, and in all practicality the large-volume breeders were being ignored.

17

A Bond Develops

THE SUMMER OF 2006 was winding down fast. In a matter of weeks, Linda Jackson's kids would be back in class at Lebanon Catholic School. (Ryan was a high school sophomore, Erika an eighth-grader, and Julia was in fourth grade.) The timing of Gracie's adoption had worked out nicely; for those first few weeks in her new home, she was able to enjoy the kids' company. The Cavalier insisted on Velcroing herself to Linda the first hour of the day, waiting patiently outside the shower and pacing back and forth between the makeup table and the closet while Linda got ready for work. But by 7:45 a.m. Linda was out the door, and for the next eight hours it was up to the kids to look after their new pet.

Gracie wasn't exactly high-maintenance. Ordinarily, a new dog might attempt a little mischief—chew a stray sock, steal a sandwich off the kitchen counter, sneak out an open door. But Gracie was accustomed to the most draconian of rules: no trouble-making, no calling attention to herself. Two months after her arrival, she still behaved as if the old rules applied. The family's previous dog, Spike, would not have thought twice about bolting out the front door or rifling through a closet for a forbidden item. Gracie was too timid to even consider it.

Her faulty eyesight was partly to blame. Those dry, scratched eyes seriously hindered her vision. Even after she felt comfortable exploring, she was mostly content to stretch out and wait for the end of the day, when Linda walked through the door.

Yet even a bashful dog needs basic care—someone to let her out on potty breaks, feed her an afternoon meal, and maybe take her on a short walk. Ryan made an effort to help out, but Gracie was terrified of him. When he tried to hold her, she writhed to be put down. Instead, Erika and Julia handled most of the chores. Feeding Gracie was no problem. As she circled in anticipation, the girls would fill her bowl full of dry food and set it on the floor. The same dog who had picked at her kibble at the shelter now inhaled it, even though no other dogs were around to steal her meal.

Letting her out for a bathroom break was a fairly straightforward task, too, although Erika occasionally had to remind herself that Gracie was outside. The backyard wasn't fenced, and there was nothing to stop the Cavalier from meandering. Erika discovered that the hard way one afternoon when she let Gracie out, went back inside to pour herself some juice, and then answered the phone. A girlfriend was calling to chat. The two girls talked for some time, and after they hung up, Erika decided to call another friend. By the time she remembered to check on Gracie, the dog had disappeared from the backyard.

Overcome with guilt, Erika called Linda at work to tell her the bad news. Linda panicked. She was just about to rush home to scour the neighborhood when a neighbor three doors down phoned to ask, "Did you just lose your puppy?" Crisis averted. But it was now apparent that Gracie was capable of roaming after all. She did so several times before she finally settled in.

Walking her was a challenge all its own. Gracie liked the *idea* of going on a walk. She lit up at the words "bye bye," the phrase that signaled a walk was imminent, and she learned that if she went over and stood by her leash, which hung on a hook inside the back door, she might hasten matters along. Once outside, though, her resolve melted. She strained against her leash to return to the house, to that safe space where life's hurdles were surmountable. The Jacksons had to remind themselves that for years, all Gracie had known was a two-by-four-foot cage. The four rooms that comprised the first floor of their brick house were enough of a brave new world to last her a lifetime. To Gracie, those rooms offered an endless supply of alluring corners and hallways. There was even the occasional surprise, like the insouciant smack of Kitty's paw. In contrast, the kingdom that lay beyond the back door was so vast that it was intimidating.

Erika persevered with the afternoon strolls. Having to tug Gracie along was more than a little annoying. It wasn't as if there wasn't anything *better* Erika could be doing. She took singing lessons and loved nothing more than to practice her music. Or she could be hanging out with friends. Nevertheless, most days she managed to coax the Cavalier up the hill on South Thirteenth Street, right on Elm Street, right again on Twelfth, and back around by way of Poplar. Like clockwork, Gracie still bumped into almost every curbside they encountered, and if they happened to meet another dog on the sidewalk, her tail instantly disappeared between her legs. Still, she derived some enjoyment from the outings. Her flattened nose went into overdrive—she sniffed every bush, tree, and light pole they passed. And just to make certain the other dogs in the neighborhood knew she'd made the rounds, she left her calling card early and often.

SIX MONTHS FLEW by. By Christmas, Gracie was behaving differently, in a good way. Maybe it was the hot pink collar that showed off her striking coat. Maybe it was the play-sleep-eat schedule she had learned to rely on day in and day out. Maybe it was the deluge of kisses she received first thing each morning and last thing each night, just before she lay her head on Linda's pillow and fell asleep.

Whatever the reason, Gracie was morphing into a more confident dog than the pitiful creature Linda had brought home the summer before. The same sweet innocence was still there, but overnight, it seemed, she'd begun to assert herself. If she liked something, she let her family know about it. If she didn't like something, she was pretty good at letting them know that, too.

The first time she let out a bark, it startled Linda. It wasn't like Gracie to pipe up. The family had grown accustomed to having a silent dog—as if by keeping quiet, Gracie could deflect attention and not be forced to leave. Faced with anything new or unfamiliar, she retreated quietly. The day she finally opened her mouth and made noise, it occurred to Linda that her raspy-sounding *woof* didn't sound like a bark at all. It sounded more like a scratchy piece of sandpaper. "Oh my goodness," Linda thought, "she must have been debarked." Whatever she'd experienced, Gracie had responded by shutting down altogether.

Now, years later, she felt self-assured enough to bark again. She began to yelp at any sound that struck her as frightening or unusual. She barked at Ryan and also at the hum of the microwave oven. Her vision may have been damaged, but her sense of hearing was tightly tuned.

Despite her protectiveness, she was starting to open up to outsiders. She befriended the Jacksons' cleaning lady, Kim Kessler. Kim came every other Friday to scrub, dust, and vacuum, and she made a point of doting on the shy little Cavalier, giving her treats and even taking her for short walks. In no time, Gracie stood on her hind legs and fluttered her paws with excitement at the sight of Kim coming through the door.

After several months, Gracie also warmed up to Linda's boyfriend, Eric, a printer with the Hershey Company. He spent most weekends with the family. His easygoing manner was a soothing antidote to Gracie's anxiety. She wasn't nervous about going on outings with Eric; he'd walk her a mile at a stretch and let her take her time to explore anything of interest she came across. Gracie normally slept with Linda, but when Eric was around, she knew better than to try to wedge between them. Gracie just went to sleep in her own bed.

Her days of bearing litters were over. As part of her agreement with the Berks County Animal Rescue League, Linda had Gracie spayed. After that, her appearance improved greatly. Her scarred right eye still bulged—Linda continued to put drops in both eyes every morning. But the postpartum belly-drag disappeared. The patches of baldness grew in, as well. Her coat, shaved at the shelter to minimize dirt, grew back with a thick, wavy sheen.

After six months, Gracie finally got the hang of doing her business outside, not in. And once she learned the do's and don'ts of housetraining, she never again had another accident. She also learned a couple of tricks. Erika taught Gracie to sit, and together, Linda and the girls instructed her on the fine art of bestowing kisses. "Gracie, gimme kiss," they'd say to her, over and over. The first time she licked Linda's face obligingly, they were so full of praise— "Yay, yay, Gracie!"—that before long she was dispensing kisses nonstop. When Linda dropped Erika off at camp the following summer, the nurse fussed over the Cavalier in Linda's arms, but wanted to know, "She's not a licker, is she?" He wasn't terribly interested in having a rough tongue lap his shins. Linda was about to warn him that, as a matter of fact, Gracie did indeed like to give kisses, when Erika corrected her. "She's *not* a licker," she told her mother. "She only licks you. Not anybody else."

Gracie's life revolved around Linda, no question. Linda was her sun, her moon—her whole galaxy. When Linda was around, Gracie was truly able to let down her guard. She'd never forgotten that it was Linda who had plucked her out of the shelter, driven her away from the cacophonous, hard, cement den, and invited her into her home—a genuine home with a cushiony bed just for her, smells of dinner wafting off the stove, and, best of all, endless shows of affection. Ryan took his cue from Gracie and gave her some distance. The girls showered her with attention, but at times they wanted more from Gracie than she was willing to give. Linda was different: She let Gracie decide for herself how much interaction she wanted—whether to climb up on Linda's shoulders or relax in her lap. Gracie returned the favor with unswerving loyalty.

She slept in Linda's bed, her head on Linda's pillow, her gentle, rhythmic snoring right in Linda's ear. When the alarm clock went off in the morning, the two of them would start the day with a little banter. Linda, still sleepy, would wave her hand obligingly from one side of her body to the other, and Gracie would follow it, jumping back and forth across Linda's torso. She pawed at Linda's face teasingly and licked her ears and face. "Gracie, lie down," Linda would murmur, but she made no move to stop her. Gracie was livelier in the morning than at any other time—as if she had awakened to discover that her wonderful new life wasn't a dream after all. It was *real* and, what's more, a whole promising new day was about to begin.

She glommed on to Linda as much as possible. In the bathroom, while Linda was getting ready for work, Gracie would nose open the door and make a beeline for the freshly applied lotion on Linda's legs. In the evening, while Linda cooked dinner, Gracie parked herself in a corner of the kitchen and watched, fixated. When Linda mowed the grass, Gracie followed behind her, no matter how nonsensical the path. If Linda circled the yard ten times in a row, Gracie tagged behind unquestioningly. Linda laughed out loud at her dedication.

The unwavering attention was intense, but Linda liked it. She'd known other people who'd felt a close attachment to their pets—whose dogs loved them no matter what—but until now she'd never experienced anything close to that feeling. She wasn't looking for it

Linda was drawn to Gracie in ways she could
never have imagined.

when she adopted the Cavalier. She'd wanted a dog for her kids, not
herself. But, inexplicably, a bond had formed between them, a con-
nection that felt both powerful and good.

There was a flip side, of course. If Linda suddenly left the room,
or if someone lifted Gracie out of Linda's arms, the little dog's heart
pounded. She whipped about, frantic, until Linda called to her. Her
separation anxiety operated on high alert.

The first time Linda took Gracie to Karen's Pet Stop to be
groomed, the Cavalier paced back and forth with apprehension.
Linda usually bathed Gracie herself, but she relied on a groomer to
trim the dog's nails, clean her ears, and clip the hair out from
between her paws. Being left at the doggy spa for hours at a time
was nerve-racking for Gracie. The Cavalier seemed convinced that
once Linda walked out of the shop, she would never come back.

The same thing happened the first time Linda took a vacation.
She and Eric planned a trip to Aruba—a romantic getaway for just
the two of them. They left Gracie with Eric's mother, Anna. Gracie,
distraught, spent the first night running from room to room in
Anna's house, searching for Linda. By day two she had calmed

down, but just knowing that Gracie was upset dampened Linda's enjoyment of the trip.

Traveling was the one downside to the new job Linda took after the holidays. She left the YMCA to work for the Team Pennsylvania Foundation, a public-private partnership that fostered economic development. As the director of development, she not only had to commute thirty miles to Harrisburg every day, but she spent an average of two days a week on the road. There was no way to explain her absences to Gracie. The Cavalier lay in her bed, her ear tuned to the back door, waiting for what must have seemed an eternity for Linda to come home.

To make it up to her, Linda began taking Gracie with her as she ran errands around town—to cash a check at the bank, fill the car up with gas, or buy groceries. Lebanon, population 24,000, was a picturesque former steel town divided by railroad tracks. On the north side were blocks of row houses and a historic downtown distinguished by the ornate spire of the century-old Samler Building. The south side of town, where the Jacksons lived, was defined by midcentury shopping centers and neighborhoods with rolling lawns and mature trees.

Gracie had no interest in the scenery. She lay on the center console of Linda's sedan with her head in Linda's lap, her eyes closed blissfully. The sound of wheels on pavement seemed to conjure memories of their first trip together, the day they drove away from the shelter and left Gracie's old life behind for good.

As Linda made her rounds, shopkeepers and service employees began to comment on the strikingly colored Cavalier stretched out next to her. "What a darling little dog!" they would say. Linda would explain that Gracie had been rescued from a puppy mill. She would tell them the story of Michael Wolf's kennel and how Gracie had been used as a breeding dog. And she would point out the vision problems Gracie still suffered as a result of her scratched, scarred eyes.

She'd talked about Gracie with her officemate at the Y, Diane, who had recently gotten her first dog. At Team PA, her colleague Steve wanted to know all about the Cavalier; he had a rescued dog, too. Linda told Gracie's story to her college roommate, Jennifer, who lived near Philadelphia. She commiserated about Gracie's health problems with her friend Bill, owner of Wertz Candies; his rescued Dachshund had to have an eye removed. And before long, the neighbors who watched Gracie trot so faithfully behind Linda knew her story, too.

Linda talked about Gracie so much it surprised her. She'd never been the type to be politically active—she had enough distractions just getting through the day. Suddenly, though, she had a desire to spread the word, to get people to see that puppy mills had to be stopped. The friends and acquaintances she spoke with were disturbed by the details of Gracie's past life. Until then, many of them had known little about puppy mills. Before Gracie, Linda hadn't given puppy mills much thought, either. The town she grew up in had no pet stores. Her grandmother bred Poodles a few times and sold the puppies, but that was a far cry from the large-volume kennels that had given dog breeding such a black eye.

In the fall of 2007, after a reception to celebrate the tenth anniversary of Team PA, Linda had a chance to talk with Governor Rendell about the subject. They were standing near the dessert table when she introduced herself. She thanked Rendell for supporting tougher dog laws, and told him she had adopted one of the dogs from Wolf's kennel. She found she was conversing with a kindred spirit. A couple of months earlier, Rendell and his wife, Marjorie, had taken in their third rescue dog, a Golden Retriever they named Maggie. They found her through Main Line Animal Rescue. A breeding dog in a puppy mill, Maggie had been deemed useless after giving birth to a stillborn litter. Now she was free to roam about the most prominent residence in the state.

Julia played with Gracie when Gracie allowed it, but still yearned for a dog of her own.

Linda's kids, too, had grown to understand how Gracie's past shaped her personality. Ryan no longer took her fear of him personally—her behavior might have something to do with her past experience with men. When Erika's friends made fun of Gracie's "zombie eye," Erika set them straight. "You don't know what she's been through," she'd tell them. "She was abused, and don't make fun of her."

Even Julia, who'd wanted a dog the most, was philosophical about Gracie's need to cling to Linda so closely. Gracie needed an emotional lifeline—just one, apparently—and she'd found it in Julia's mom. A year after the family adopted the Cavalier, "I thought she might become more outgoing and playful," Julia said, "but I know why she's not."

18

The Crackdown Begins

B Y THE FALL OF 2007, Pennsylvania's puppy mill operators were feeling the heat. The year before, the Bureau of Dog Law Enforcement had revoked the licenses of a half dozen kennel operators. Now the bureau was yanking an average of two licenses a month. By year's end, 120 more breeders shut their doors voluntarily.

Among them was John B. Miller of Millcreek Puppy Barn Kennel. He paid a $1,750 fine and gave up his license as part of a plea agreement after a state inspector found his dogs living amid feces and sharp wires, their food and water bowls contaminated with rust and debris.

In West Hempfield Township, the state revoked the license of breeder Elvin High and fined him more than $1,000 for letting eleven of his sixty-five dogs languish with severe ear and leg infections. The suffering dogs were seized.

The state also went after John Esh and his son Daniel of Ronks, Pennsylvania, who between them had more than 750 dogs. Dog wardens found the food bowls were contaminated with feces and dirt, and cages were full of moldy excrement. John Esh was unable to produce paperwork documenting that all of his dogs had been vaccinated against rabies. Daniel Esh was cited for confining dogs to cages too small even by state standards; wardens said they found six dogs crammed into one ten-foot-square cage.

Eight months earlier, the Eshes' kennels had passed inspection with no bad marks.

In January 2008, Governor Rendell replaced the head of the Dog Law Bureau with Sue West, a board member of the Humane League of Lancaster County and a newly appointed member of the new Dog Law Advisory Board. The attorney general's office gave Jeffrey Paladina, special prosecutor for dog law enforcement, the authority to represent dog wardens in court, leveling the playing field with the private attorneys who represented breeders on the other side of the aisle.

For the first time in the state's history, would-be kennel operators were asked whether they had ever been convicted of animal cruelty and whether their proposed business complied with local zoning ordinances. Lying on an application was grounds for rejection.

After responding to 8,000 animal cruelty complaints in 2007, the Pennsylvania SPCA launched a toll-free animal cruelty hotline. And the American Society for the Prevention of Cruelty to Animals joined forces with the Humane Society of the United States to lobby for change at the state capitol. In addition to serving on the governor's ad hoc advisory committee, Bob Baker was now employed by the ASPCA as a senior investigator.

Baker was pleased with the progress the state was making. For the first time in a long time, he felt, the Bureau of Dog Law Enforcement was taking its job seriously.

Bill Smith, though, wasn't convinced. Where Baker was willing to work from inside the system (as well as outside of it), Smith subscribed to the Molotov cocktail approach. He badgered the Dog Law Bureau by e-mail several times a day, demanding to know why problem kennels were still in business. If authorities failed to act on the tips he sent in, he alerted the news media. Publicity, he'd decided, had a magical way of getting the job done.

Smith, 46, was the founder of Main Line Animal Rescue, a nonprofit organization that since 1997 had rescued more than 5,000 dogs, rehabilitated them, and adopted them out to new homes. The work was demanding, and Smith received no salary—he lived on an inheritance and his savings. But he'd found his calling rescuing animals.

Smith dealt with hundreds of breeders looking to get rid of older female dogs worn out from having so many litters, or younger male dogs who simply weren't needed. The dogs frequently emerged in shockingly bad shape—suffering from mange, bladder stones, multiple tumors, and broken jaws or backs. Smith saw dogs who had undergone more than a dozen C-sections, without anesthesia, and more dogs crammed into kennels without food or water than he could count.

"Frightened, malnourished, often without medical attention of any kind, [a mother dog] shivers in the cold days of winter and bakes under the August sun," he wrote on his website. "Never knowing kindness or the slightest affection, she is a prisoner for profit."

At one of the earliest meetings of the new Dog Law Advisory Board, Smith brought with him a balding, skeletal Maltese-Poodle mix he'd rescued two months earlier from a kennel in Lancaster County. He purchased the dog for $100; Main Line subsequently spent $4,300 nursing the dog back from the brink of death. The dog's sadly appropriate new name was Shrimp. This is the cash crop puppy millers refer to when they talk about their dogs, Smith told the advisory board as he cradled Shrimp in his arms.

Main Line was the group responsible for the 2005 billboard that had publicly identified Lancaster County as home to hundreds of puppy mills. The group leased a second billboard in Missouri—a huge puppy mill state—followed by a third sign on the Pennsylvania Turnpike. The billboards resonated with motorists. By the winter of 2008, contributions to Main Line enabled the organization to move into a $2 million headquarters on fifty-eight acres in Chester Springs, with a barn big enough to house one hundred dogs.

Now it was time to take the message nationwide. Smith targeted one of the biggest markets he could think of. His organization leased a billboard in Chicago, four blocks from Oprah Winfrey's studios. "OPRAH—please do a show on puppy mills; the dogs need you!" the sign begged, next to the photo of a sorrowful-looking dog. To Smith's delight, Winfrey took his suggestion. She assigned her own reporter, Lisa Ling, to go undercover with Main Line staff and visit some of the most dreadful kennels in Lancaster County.

Smith and Ling presented their findings on Oprah's April 4, 2008, show. In a half-hour segment, the investigators told the wrenching story of puppy mills, complete with videotape. They traced several puppies for sale in pet stores to kennels where the mother dogs remained crammed into rabbit hutch–style cages that reeked of excrement. The investigators visited a third kennel where dozens of Pomeranians scrambled for attention in outdoor cages exposed to the elements. Smith explained why Pennsylvania breeders, many of them Amish, thought nothing of treating hundreds of dogs so neglectfully. It was a cultural thing—Plain-sect people didn't see dogs as companion animals deserving of humane care. To them, he said on the show, "dogs are like an ear of corn."

He and Ling were able to rescue thirty-nine dogs on their rounds. In the show's most moving segment, Smith helped a Golden Retriever who had spent years in a cage struggle to stand on solid flooring. "It's always amazing to me when I go out to pick up a dog, and they've had the dog eight or nine years, and it doesn't have a name," he told Winfrey. "It's never been out of the hutch, it doesn't know how to walk, and I have to carry it to the car. It's heartbreaking."

For the show's finale, Smith brought out Shrimp who, once emaciated and nearly bald, was now transformed. His snow-white coat was thick and silky. He even wore a red bow. The audience cheered wildly.

Winfrey put her own personal stamp on the issue by vowing to "never, ever adopt another pet now without going to a shelter to do it. I am a changed woman after seeing this show," she declared.

The program struck a nerve. Millions of viewers had gotten a rare and unforgettable glimpse at the underbelly of commercial dog breeding. Puppy mill opponents could not have asked for a bigger publicity jackpot. Back home, even the head of Pennsylvania Dutch Convention and Visitors Bureau of Lancaster County called for a cleanup of puppy mills. "Change can't happen fast enough," the organization's president and CEO, Christopher Barrett, said. "What's happening in these puppy mills is atrocious."

For all the improvements Rendell had imposed, puppy mills still flourished. What was worse, some of the most egregious practices were legal. For example, breeders weren't required to provide water to dogs all the time; if they provided water for just six hours of the day, that was considered adequate. A two-foot-long dog could be kept in a two-by-three-foot cage with no bedding. There were no hard and fast rules governing temperature or ventilation. And it was entirely permissible to confine a dog to a crate for the animal's entire life, not removing the dog even once.

Rendell couldn't change all that on his own. To overhaul the Dog Law, he needed the legislature's help. And it was going to take more than Oprah's disapproving glare to get state lawmakers on board.

The public wasn't the problem. Sixteen thousand people had commented on Rendell's far-reaching recommendations, a clear majority of them in support of change. Aside from the drumbeat of newspaper and television coverage about the horrors of puppy mills, interest in the issue cropped up in unexpected ways. In the summer of 2007, the F.U.E.L. Collection art gallery in Philadelphia's Old City unveiled an exhibit devoted to the evils of large-volume dog breeding. The title of the exhibit, "Puppies Are Biodegradable," came from a comment a dog breeder made at a zoning board hearing in Lancaster County two years earlier. Asked what happened to dogs who were not sold, the breeder had said they were exterminated, their remains spread over the fields as fertilizer. "They are biodegradable," he explained.

The exhibit included forty works of art chosen from several hundred submissions. One, by Philadelphia artist Jillian Kesselman, showed a farmer holding a mother dog upside down, puppies dropping out of her body. The dog was headless. Another painting depicted the menacing shadow of a farmer leaning over a cage where malnourished dogs lay, unmoving, around an empty bowl. A third showed a Pennsylvania Dutch hex sign with two scrawny dogs sitting back-to-back, shedding tears. Hanging over them was the word "money." Gallery director Jennifer Yaron even installed chicken wire throughout the exhibit so visitors would view the artwork as if they, too, were inside a crate.

But Rendell's plan also drew heated criticism from breeders, who said that complying with the proposed changes would cost each kennel anywhere from $5,000 to $20,000. Hobby breeders and sportsmen's groups argued that they shouldn't be held to the same standards because their dogs weren't confined 24/7—they were able to get exercise. The administration responded by rolling out a new plan that exempted smaller kennels but held the largest operators—the 650 or so breeders who sold sixty or more dogs a year—to even tougher standards than first proposed. Cages would need to be more than two times a dog's body length, for example. And each dog would have to have access to an exercise run at least twice the size of the primary enclosure.

All commercial kennel dogs would have to be examined once a year by a veterinarian. Kennel owners would be forbidden from administering rabies vaccinations or euthanizing dogs themselves. Veterinarians alone would be allowed to dock tails or perform C-sections; they could debark dogs only if there was a valid reason for doing so. Crate sizes would not change for puppies, nor would they have to have solid floors, but the crates could be stacked just two high. The temperature inside kennels would have to hover between 50 and 85 degrees Fahrenheit. Kennels would be required to have smoke alarms, fire extinguishers, and possibly sprinkler systems. Dogs could not be tied up, and breeders would have to give them greater access to water.

There were more proposed new rules. Civil penalties could be issued if breeders violated the Dog Law, and breeders would have to pay the costs of caring for their dogs while their cases were being appealed. Breeders convicted of cruelty would automatically lose their licenses. Dog wardens would be allowed to inspect unlicensed kennels, something they currently weren't permitted to do. And instead of relying on humane officers to enforce cruelty laws, the wardens could file charges themselves.

The case of breeder Ervin Zimmerman, a Mennonite breeder in Berks County, was a perfect example of why Pennsylvania needed a new law. The state revoked Zimmerman's license in November 2007 after humane officers rescued eighteen dogs—some of them reported to have broken limbs, open wounds, and infections—and filed cruelty charges. Three months later, three more dogs were taken, including one Chihuahua reportedly with bite wounds and another with an ulcerated eye. Yet even though he no longer had a license, according to newspaper accounts Zimmerman continued to operate with 200 dogs.

Several loopholes were to blame. For starters, dog wardens were forbidden by law to investigate unlicensed kennels. Even though humane officers said they found the kennel littered with feces and dead rats, they were permitted to take only those dogs showing visible signs of cruelty and neglect. And because Zimmerman was appealing his conviction, state officials said they could take no further action against him. But as animal welfare advocates saw it, Zimmerman was thumbing his nose at the system and getting away with it. "Dogs are literally starving to death—in one case, one was pregnant and starving," Baker protested. "The kennel owners have discovered they can surrender their licenses and continue to do business."

THE RENDELL ADMINISTRATION broke the proposed changes into three separate pieces of legislation. House Bill 2525 would impose the laundry list of new standards for dogs kept in commercial kennels. House Bill 2532 would permit medical procedures such as debarking or ear cropping to be performed only by veterinarians. The final measure, House Bill 499, would increase fines and jail terms for breeders convicted of cruelty. Violators could pay up to $1,000 per offense and civil penalties of up to $1,000 a day.

On May 15, 2008, state representative James Casorio, a Democrat from southeast of Pittsburgh, held a press conference to introduce the most far-reaching measure, House Bill 2525. "If you're a breeder that doesn't give a dog adequate water every day, doesn't give it food free from toxins and doesn't take the dog out of the cage to clean the cage," Casorio said, "we're coming after you today."

Advocates fanned out across the state to lobby for support. Main Line Animal Rescue held town hall meetings in districts of lawmakers who were leaning against the overhaul. The organization also continued to gather evidence of abuse and neglect. In the aftermath of the Oprah show, breeders circulated more than 300 photos of Smith and warned colleagues about his undercover tactics. But Main Line had dozens of volunteers willing to pose as would-be customers to document conditions at puppy mills.

Arguing against the overhaul was the Professional Dog Breeders Association, which represented 300 commercial kennels; that was to be expected. More surprising was that the Pennsylvania Veterinary Medical Association came out against it, too. The veterinary group said breeders should not have to provide solid flooring for their dogs because the dogs' waste would just sit there, with nowhere to go. They recommended coated wire flooring or some other permeable surface.

On June 24, House Bill 2525 cleared its first hurdle when the House Agriculture and Rural Affairs Committee passed it by a vote of 17 to 12—almost entirely along party lines, with Democrats supporting it and Republicans voting no. The House Appropriations Committee then passed the bill. A vote by the full House was scheduled for July 4. Of 203 members of the Pennsylvania State House, more than 100 supported puppy mill reform. Desperate to stop the momentum, opponents turned to a time-honored delaying tactic: They weighed the bill down with amendments, dozens of them, each of which could be debated to death as the clock wound down.

Republican representative Bob Bastian of Somerset, a veterinarian and member of the American Veterinary Medical Association, proposed several amendments designed to gut the bill. Republican representative Art Hershey, a dairy farmer, protested that House Bill 2525 would put legitimate breeders out of business. Hershey wasn't above a little sarcasm. He filed one amendment that would have added the word "dishwasher" to the types of housing considered unsuitable for dogs—an apparent reference to a pro-reform billboard that showed a dog staring out from inside an electric dishwasher. "Under the current kennel regulations," the sign said, "an adult Beagle can spend twelve years in a cage the size of your dishwasher and never be let out."

Interestingly, Hershey's district included Chester County, where two years earlier the raid on Michael Wolf's puppy mill had turned klieg lights on the ugly truth behind large-volume dog breeding.

The opposition's strategy succeeded. Heading into recess, lawmakers faced a more pressing issue: the July 1 deadline for passing a state budget had come and gone and the budget was still not in place. There was too little time to resolve the budget and take up a second protracted issue, too, before going home. House leaders postponed the dog law debate until the fall, exactly as opponents of reform had hoped they would do.

Jessie Smith, special deputy secretary for dog law enforcement, lamented the delay. "Every day that goes by without action on House Bill 2525 only prolongs the suffering of dogs kept in commercial breeding kennel cages their entire lives," she said.

THE LEGISLATIVE RECESS didn't stop the Dog Law Bureau from going after abhorrent puppy mills. While they were at it, Smith also decided to take a fresh look at one of the state's most notorious breeders, Joyce Stoltzfus.

From her Puppy Love kennel tucked away off a country road in the remote community of Peach Bottom, Stoltzfus had spent at least twenty years acting as a broker for dozens of breeds of dogs and churning out more of her own. She'd had repeated run-ins with the law. In the mid-1980s, federal inspectors cited Puppy Love for selling puppies to pet stores without a federal license. Twice after that, the attorney general's office fined Stoltzfus for distributing medicine without a veterinary license. In 1997, the attorney general's office sued to close Puppy Love, but a state court denied the request, citing lack of evidence.

Then in 2005, a cloudburst of consumer protests from across seven states landed Stoltzfus back in court on the grounds that she was selling puppies plagued with everything from parasites to parvovirus, distemper, heart defects, hip dysplasia, and pneumonia. Libby Williams's New Jersey Consumers Against Pet Store Abuse alone collected more than seventy complaints against Stoltzfus. The breeder agreed to pay $75,000 in fines and restitution, allow state dog wardens to inspect her kennel four times a year, and reimburse buyers twice the price of a puppy if the dog turned out to have congenital defects. Despite her status as a repeat offender, Stoltzfus remained in business, however. To skirt the bad publicity, she changed the name of her kennel to CC Pets. State inspectors wrote up CC Pets twice for failing to clean cages adequately, yet Stoltzfus continued to rake in the profits. In 2007 alone, she reportedly sold 2,000 dogs.

In the summer of 2008, Jessie Smith met with prosecutors to discuss whether Stoltzfus was violating the earlier agreement. The attorney general's office investigated whether Stoltzfus had also ignored a three-year-old court-ordered consent petition mandating that she identify her kennel in all classified ads so that prospective buyers who did their research could learn of her history of selling sick and defective dogs. Dozens of Stoltzfus's ads failed to identify the business, according to the *Philadelphia Inquirer*.

Meanwhile, animal welfare groups also continued to ferret out problem breeders. On July 17, with a camera crew from the television show *Animal Cops* in tow, the Pennsylvania SPCA seized twenty-one dogs from Amish breeder John Blank in Chester County after volunteers from Main Line Animal Rescue convinced Blank to sell or give them nine dogs who were in terrible shape: The animals had missing eyes, chewed-off ears, and, in one case, teeth so decayed the dog was unable to close his mouth. Blank, who'd been cited for two violations in 2006, also allegedly sold a three-week-old puppy to an undercover agent. State law required that puppies be at least seven weeks old before being sold. The dog died three days later of dehydration, hypothermia, and emaciation.

The deplorable conditions at Blank's Limestone Kennel raised the issue of how the Bureau of Dog Law could have overlooked the problems. The kennel had been inspected six months earlier by Maureen Siddons—the same warden who had visited Wolf's kennel with Cheryl Shaw—along with Siddons's supervisor, Richard Martrich. In a letter to Jessie Smith, Howard Nelson, the CEO of the Pennsylvania SCPA, said the conditions suffered by Blank's dogs had festered for years. Before a week had passed, officials inspected Blank's kennel again and announced that he was no longer licensed to breed dogs. A spokesman for the Dog Law Bureau said Blank gave up his license willingly. Siddons and Martrich were reassigned desk duties while the Dog Law Bureau investigated the matter.

"We wish the department would act this swiftly with all substandard kennels in Pennsylvania," Baker commented.

CRUELTY CHARGES AGAINST other breeders kept the puppy mill debate simmering. Whether the Rendell administration had enough votes to reform the Dog Law when the legislature reconvened wasn't clear, but the foot-dragging was a bad sign. Then, in August, the *Inquirer's* Amy Worden broke an explosive story: Ordered by the state to have their dogs examined by a veterinarian, Berks County kennel operator Elmer Zimmerman and his brother Ammon had abruptly decided that they were finished with dog breeding. In a single afternoon, the Amish farmers shot their dogs to death, one by one—all eighty of them.

His veterinarian had recommended they kill the dogs, Elmer Zimmerman claimed. He said he thought the state was trying to close him down. Dog warden Orlando Aguirre had indeed given Zimmerman a bad inspection report on July 24; he'd cited the breeder for twenty violations, including huge gaps in the wire flooring of the dogs' cages, inadequate bedding, extreme heat, and dogs with skin infections. The warden ordered Zimmerman to have thirty-nine of the dogs checked for fly bites and fleas.

Aguirre learned about the mass killings five days later, when the Zimmermans turned in their licenses. Elmer had shot all seventy of his dogs; Ammon had shot the remaining ten. When Aguirre questioned their story, Elmer Zimmerman fired up a backhoe and scraped away enough soil on his property to show decomposing Poodles, Shih Tzu, and Cocker Spaniels piled in a heap. Since shooting dogs wasn't illegal, the inspector did the only thing he could: He ordered Zimmerman to destroy his dog hutches to make certain they would never be filled with animals again.

The story came to light two weeks later, and Pennsylvanians were stunned. Shooting dogs was both legal and common in puppy mills, but it wasn't something ordinary residents of the state had ever given much thought. The cold-blooded callousness of the slayings was a wake-up call. "For far too long, the state has ignored or tolerated unscrupulous kennel owners who mistreat their animals," the *Inquirer* said in an editorial. "The legislature needs to act on [House Bill 2525] soon. The state can't keep toying with this cruel industry."

Three days later, more than one hundred people held a candlelight vigil just off the Zimmermans' property to honor the memory of the eighty dogs. Advocates from Lancaster County's United Against Puppy Mills, Main Line Animal Rescue, North Penn Puppy Mill Watch, New Jersey Consumers Against Pet Store Abuse, and others sang "Amazing Grace" and placed eighty chrysanthemums and eighty dog biscuits next to the tractor Elmer Zimmerman had parked across his lane to block the crowd. They also read out the names of legislators who had not yet lent their support to puppy mill reform.

"These were dogs with no names," Jenny Stephens of North Penn Puppy Mill Watch told the assemblage. "These were dogs who never knew the kindness a human hand can offer, and these were dogs who died a violent and terror-filled death, with no one to comfort them."

NJCAPSA's Libby Williams said news of the wholesale shootings sucked the wind out of her. "But they did the state a favor," she said. "People are now learning the truth about the 'gentle' Plain people."

As the vigil neared to a close, Elmer Zimmerman stepped out of the darkness and approached the group. He said he was sorry he'd killed his dogs and asked what he could do to stop the harassing phone calls that had been coming in nonstop.

"I just got the impression that I had twenty things wrong on my farm, and I've got to work day and night to get things back to the way they should be," Zimmerman said. One volunteer suggested that he could have surrendered his dogs to a shelter. He didn't know that, Zimmerman said.

"I understand there's a thousand people against me," he told the group. "I want to have peace again."

If anything, Zimmerman had accomplished just the opposite: He had injected the puppy mill campaign with the ammunition it needed to galvanize momentum for change. The day after the candlelight vigil, Rendell held a press conference at a dog park in Philadelphia's Center City, where he decried the "brutal killing" of the Zimmermans' dogs. "Dogs who live in this type of kennel are valued only for the sale price of their offspring," the governor said.

A MONTH LATER, the legislature returned to business. This time the state House was ready to act. On September 17, representatives passed House Bill 2525 by a vote of 181 to 17. They also passed without opposition House Bill 2532, which barred owners and breeders from performing surgery on their dogs.

The bills now needed to pass the Senate.

Two weeks elapsed before the Senate Agriculture and Rural Affairs Committee took up House Bill 2525. Before passing it, the committee watered down the bill. Among other things, they agreed to allow slatted floors in kennels. Breeders would not have to install outdoor exercise runs if local zoning laws forbade them. Kennel operators would have to "make an effort" to lower the temperature of a kennel if the temperature exceeded 85 degrees, but weren't required to do so. And dog crates could be stacked thirty inches high instead of just twelve. Moreover, any kennel that had gone three years without being cited for a violation would be exempt from having to abide by the new standards.

Instead of six months, kennel owners would have a year to comply with regulations. And the Department of Agriculture would appoint a Canine Health Board of veterinarians to review requests for exemptions having to do with ventilation, flooring, and lighting.

Animal welfare advocates were unhappy with the changes. "In two to four years, they could undo all the good this bill does," Nancy Gardener, a member of the Dog Law Advisory Board, said. She pointed out that Pennsylvania had a lot of bad kennels that had not been cited for violations and would now be exempt from the upgrades.

The bill passed the Senate Appropriations Committee and then the full Senate by a vote of 49 to 1. In the course of melding the House and Senate bills, reform advocates were able to win back some of the tougher provisions. Among other things, the final version doubled the minimum floor space for dogs, eliminated wire flooring, and required at the minimum unfettered access to an exercise area twice the size of a dog's enclosure. Dogs kept in large-volume kennels would have to be examined by veterinarians twice a year, and, effective immediately, veterinarians and veterinarians only would be authorized to euthanize dogs. The bills that would have forbidden breeders from performing medical procedures and increased fines and jail terms for cruelty violators failed to make it out of committee. Still, Rendell was satisfied. The most meaningful legislation had passed.

The governor signed Act 119 into law on October 9, 2008. Two weeks later he held a second, ceremonial signing, this time with his rescued Golden Retriever, Maggie, by his side. Most dogs confined to wire hutches suffer not only physical problems but tremendous behavioral problems as well, the governor told the crowd assembled to witness the milestone. His own dog had overcome those issues. "Maggie must have been touched by God," Rendell said, a catch in his voice, "because she is the happiest dog I've ever had in my life."

THE ENACTMENT OF the new dog law wasn't the end of the story. The same week Rendell signed the new law, the Pennsylvania SPCA raided the Almost Heaven kennel in Upper Milford Township, home to more than 800 neglected animals, including 400 dogs found crammed into cages, many of them injured, dehydrated, and ill. The SPCA removed dozens of the dogs and filed cruelty charges against a repeat offender, breeder Derbe "Skip" Eckhart. The state revoked his kennel license almost immediately.

It frustrated advocates that two months earlier, Almost Heaven had passed a state inspection conducted by two dog wardens, their supervisor, and Sue West, the director of the Dog Law Bureau. The conditions discovered in October weren't present the day of the August 7 inspection, bureau spokesman Chris Ryder said. But Pennsylvania SPCA head Howard Nelson said the animals suffered from chronic problems that could not have flared up in as quickly as a couple of months. Undercover investigators for his organization were buying sick and grimy dogs from the kennel months before state officials paid their visit.

Pattie Fontana, a longtime former sales manager for Almost Heaven, was one of the whistleblowers. She told the Allentown *Morning Call* that Eckhart used to feed his dogs raw, frozen chicken he threw onto the ground—a free-for-all that triggered vicious fights and left weaker dogs injured and starving. In rescue circles, the dogs taken from Almost Heaven were long known for their extraordinarily atrocious smell.

In late October, state dog wardens teamed up with the Humane League of Lancaster County to close an unlicensed kennel and seize twenty dogs. And in December, the state shut down the kennel operated by Ervin Zimmerman, the breeder who had remained in business even after his license was revoked. Ninety-six dogs were removed.

By year's end, the newly formed Canine Health Board had approved new standards governing temperature, humidity, ammonia levels, and lighting in large kennels. The regulations weren't perfect, but they were far superior to standards required by the U.S. Department of Agriculture, Baker said. After thirty years of tracking puppy mills, he was finally seeing progress.

19

Elsewhere, Suffering

T HE WEBSITE OF the Pine Bluff Kennel in Lyles, Tennessee, suggested a veritable dog heaven. It was filled with bucolic photographs of rolling farmland and descriptions of how the dogs kept
there were free to romp about on all ninety-two acres. When local
law enforcement raided the kennel in June 2008, they documented
a much harsher reality: Pomeranians, Chihuahuas, German
Shepherds, Great Danes, and other breeds were crowded two and
three to a hutch—nearly 700 dogs in all—and exposed to summer
temperatures and humidity so unrelenting they were at risk of suffering heat stroke. Newborn puppies were kept in a whelping trailer
that was even more suffocating.

Stephanie Shain encounters that sort of deception all too frequently in the dog breeding world. She aches for the dogs bred in
substandard kennels and the people who buy them. "At the end of
this pipeline," she said, "there's a chance they'll end up with a big
bill and a dead puppy."

Shain, 38, is the driving force behind a puppy mill offensive being waged by the Humane Society of the United States (HSUS). Launched in 2006, the HSUS says it's the most comprehensive effort undertaken by an animal welfare organization in the sixty-year history of large-volume dog breeding.

"With Stephanie at the helm, for the first time we have the prospect of addressing this issue in a fundamental way and stopping the abuse of dogs in puppy mills," HSUS CEO Wayne Pacelle said.

An army brat, Shain always had pets growing up. The family's cats slept in her and her sister's beds, and there was always a Labrador Retriever or Lab mix in the house. During visits to her grandfather's farm in Iowa, she would point to a particularly cute animal and beg, "Please, Grandpa, don't kill calf number 257."

The family moved to Doylestown, Pennsylvania, outside Philadelphia, when she was in high school. After college, she got a job at the Bucks County SPCA, where she cleaned kennels, took in stray animals, and adopted out dogs and cats. The shelter work made her realize how often mixed breeds—many of them smart, affectionate animals—wound up on a shelter's death row simply because they were neither puppies nor purebreds, which were the types of dogs most families were looking to adopt.

Shain spent five years working at a veterinary hospital and at the American Anti-Vivisection Society in Jenkintown, Pennsylvania, which lobbied against the use of animals in testing and research. In 2000, she landed her job at the HSUS in Washington, D.C. For the first few years, she helped pet owners solve behavior problems and find housing that permitted dogs or cats—anything to help pets remain in the homes they already had. She promoted adoption and spay/neutering. Her time in Pennsylvania, though, had piqued her awareness about a more urgent issue: Unbeknown to the public, hundreds of thousands of dogs were spending their lives in grimy crates, producing puppies. Puppy mills were a hidden scandal in America, and the problem was getting worse.

She began pestering Pacelle to get involved.

With 11 million members and $120 million in annual revenue, the HSUS was the country's largest animal welfare group, capable of generating headlines with the issues it chose to showcase. Among the hot-button topics on its plate were cockfighting, factory farms, canned hunts of captive exotic animals, and the commercial fur trade.

Pacelle was open to Shain's arguments. He knew that puppy mills affected untold numbers of animals. More than 4,000 large-volume kennels were licensed by the U.S. Department of Agriculture, and many more operated off the radar. Second, while other organizations had addressed large-volume breeding, none had the resources of HSUS.

The biggest question was whether the HSUS could make a difference in curtailing puppy mills by persuading the public not to do business with puppy mills. Shain was confident they could make headway. If dog lovers really knew how many puppies were sold by these unsavory operations, they would do the right thing and not buy dogs who came from puppy mills, she argued. But someone needed to inform them of the terrible truth. "People were supporting this horribly cruel industry and they didn't even know it," she said.

Pacelle agreed to launch the anti-puppy-mill campaign. Shain's first step was to hire Kathleen Summers, a staff person dedicated exclusively to the cause of puppy mill reform. By then, raids of problem kennels had started to escalate. The same month authorities dismantled Michael Wolf's kennel in Pennsylvania, the owners of Pearlie's House of Pomeranians in Orange County, California, pleaded guilty to selling sick and neglected puppies—thirty-nine of their dogs were found stuffed in a closet in their attic. At a kennel near Searcy, Arkansas, officials seized seventy-seven Pugs and Terriers, some of them with chewed ears and missing toes. In Oklahoma, 130 dogs were taken from a breeder who had let the water in their bowls become black and the food moldy. Rescuers found a newly dead puppy being eaten by a rat.

The Dog Law Governor Ed Rendell was working to revamp in Pennsylvania was already more rigorous than the federal law regulating large-volume commercial dog breeding. The USDA's Animal Plant and Health Inspection Service had about 100 inspectors—barely twice as many as Pennsylvania alone—responsible for inspecting 10,000 kennels, zoos, and research labs nationwide. The standards set for high-volume dog kennels were minimal, and pet stores weren't inspected at all; they were exempted on the theory that customers could see for themselves whether the animals were being treated humanely. The USDA's own inspector general concluded in 1992 that federal inspectors could not ensure the humane care and treatment of animals as required by the Animal Welfare Act.

In 2005, U.S. Senator Rick Santorum, a Republican from Pennsylvania, introduced the federal Pet Animal Welfare Statute, which would have required anyone selling more than twenty-five dogs a year to meet the same standards as large-volume wholesalers. The HSUS and the American Veterinary Medical Association supported the legislation, as did the American Kennel Club. Many of the AKC's member clubs fought the bill, however, on the grounds that the extra paperwork and inspections would be too cumbersome. The bill died.

Over the past forty years, the number of dogs in the United States had more than quadrupled, to 77 million. Nearly two-thirds of all American households now had a dog, a cat, a bird, or other companion animal, and nearly half of pet owners considered their pets to be members of the family, according to a 2007 survey by the American Veterinary Medical Association. By 2008, the country's love for animals had exploded into a $43 billion industry, the American Pet Products Manufacturers Association said.

The growing interest in dogs fueled an increase in large-volume breeding. Missouri, Iowa, Kansas, Nebraska, Oklahoma, Arkansas, Ohio, and Pennsylvania were the biggest dog-breeding states. By far, Missouri had the most: It was home to 4,000 kennels, many of them not licensed by the U.S. Department of Agriculture. In Oklahoma, the number of registered breeders had doubled to 702 between 1996 and 2006. A 2007 investigation by the *Tulsa World* estimated that from 2003 to 2006, federal inspectors found 20,000 dogs in Oklahoma living in filthy conditions or suffering health problems—and those were just at the licensed kennels. Meanwhile, Amish and Mennonite breeders unwilling to abide by Pennsylvania's tougher scrutiny had begun moving to Wisconsin and the Finger Lakes region of New York State, where they could buy cheap farmland and resume business under much more lax regulations.

The dog industry was booming. In 2005, the Hunte Corporation, the country's largest puppy broker, bought more than 88,000 dogs from breeders of all types and sold them to pet stores. Thousands more breeders sold directly on the Internet, advertising puppies for sale on sites such as nextdaypets.com, puppyfind.com, and terrific-pets.com. Thanks to a sizable loophole in the federal law, breeders who sold directly to the public didn't have to be licensed or inspected by the federal government. Despite the existence of puppy lemon laws in several states, on-line buyers who wound up with diseased or injured pets were largely out of luck.

By 2007, the HSUS estimated that anywhere from 2 to 4 million puppy mill dogs were being sold each year in the United States, and that the number of puppy mills had swelled to 10,000. The organization defined puppy mills broadly—as any operation that confined dogs to cages, regardless of how clean or well fed the dogs were. "Dogs being bred should be part of the family. They shouldn't be sitting out there in cages and kennels," Shain said.

The HSUS assumed that 80 percent of U.S. Department of Agriculture Class A-licensed breeders were puppy mills. There were 4,228 breeders licensed by the U.S. Department of Agriculture in 2009, and the HSUS calculated that 3,382 were puppy mills. Assuming the average kennel had sixty dogs (which was the case in Pennsylvania; national data is unavailable because federal inspectors aren't required to count dogs), and assuming that 65 percent of the dogs were female (because a smaller number of male dogs can impregnate many more females), that came to 131,914 breeding females. Multiply that number by 4.7 (the average litter size, as provided by the AKC during congressional testimony), and again by two, because the average female dog produces two litters a year, and the total came to 1,239,988 puppies a year. And that was only facilities licensed by the U.S. Department of Agriculture. The HSUS's data suggested that the actual number of breeding kennels in the United States was twice the number of licensed kennels, which meant double the number of puppies. The organization's "very conservative" figure: 2,479,976 puppies born in puppy mills each year.

"They're everywhere," Shain said of puppy mills. "There isn't a state that can say they are immune to this problem. With the Internet being what it is today, it's so easy to sell [puppies]. You can put an ad online and stick that puppy on a plane."

Stephanie Shain of the Humane Society of the United States cradles a Yorkie rescued from a puppy mill in Lyles, Tennessee, in 2008. Nearly 700 dogs were removed from the kennel.

She finds it a sad irony that at the same time breeders are crank-
ing out puppies, animal shelters euthanize as many as 4 million dogs
and cats a year, according to an HSUS estimate.

The HSUS created a website with facts about puppy mills, and in
December 2006 the organization launched a billboard campaign
similar to the one Main Line Animal Rescue was waging in
Pennsylvania. "Find out the true cost of that puppy—www.puppymill
truth.org," the billboards said. The first signs went up in Columbus,
Ohio; Norwalk, Connecticut; and Los Angeles—cities where puppy
mill problems had recently come to light.

The following year, state and local law enforcers and humane
officers raided dozens of substandard kennels. In Bloomer, Arkansas,
114 dogs were found abandoned in the scorching sun. In Buxton,
Maine, 250 Australian Shepherds, French Bulldogs, Brussels
Griffons, and Shetland Sheepdogs were removed from squalid conditions. In Houston, fifty starving American Bulldogs were rescued.
In Van Buren County, Arkansas, 200 dogs covered in feces and
urine were carried to safety. In Burns, Oregon, nearly 200 dogs
were seized. In Jackson County, Missouri, sixty Labrador Retrievers
were taken from a kennel. And in Dyersburg, Tennessee, more than
130 puppies were removed from cages, including one puppy who
had scald marks from lying in its own urine.

IN 2007, AFTER fielding numerous complaints about negligent kennels
in Virginia, the HSUS spent five months investigating that state's
dog-breeding industry. They found that only sixteen of Virginia's
breeders were licensed by the U.S. Department of Agriculture. The
number of unlicensed commercial kennels was far greater: 900 kennels in all. After watching video footage shot by the HSUS, Carroll
County authorities raided the kennel of Hillsville, Virginia, breeder
Junior Horton and rescued 980 Yorkshire Terriers, Poodles,
Maltese, Shih Tzu, Lhasa Apsos, and other small dogs—nearly
twice as many dogs as Horton was licensed to have—from filthy

cages. Volunteers from as far away as Florida and New York descended on the tiny town to help care for the dogs. Pacelle called the kennel "an inevitable consequence of an out-of-control and irresponsible industry."

Horton disputed the use of the term "puppy mill" to describe his operation. He was convicted of animal cruelty and neglect, but his punishment was light. The judge in the case ordered him to pay $4,775 in veterinary costs, suspended his twelve-year prison sentence, and put him on probation, but allowed Horton to continue operating with 250 dogs. An appeals court judge upheld the verdict.

Lenient judgments were all too common. Hoping to minimize the burden of caring for hundreds of rescued dogs, officials frequently cut deals that let breeders off easy so that victimized dogs could be adopted out quickly. The case of Gallatin, Tennessee, breeder Irene Meuser was a good example. In October 2006, acting on a tip, more than 100 local authorities, volunteers, and veterinarians descended on Meuser's property where, in three outbuildings, they found 36 cats and 246 sick and malnourished Poodles, Shih Tzu, Chihuahuas, and other small dogs in cages so cramped some of them were unable to stand. The animals' food and water bowls were dirty, and the smell of ammonia was so pungent that rescuers had to strap on ventilation masks. This wasn't the first time Meuser had been in trouble. Authorities had investigated her eleven years earlier, but hadn't charged her with any crime. She was given guidelines for housing the dogs, but no one had followed up to see whether she was following them.

This time, Meuser was charged with animal cruelty and, like Horton, she lucked out. In exchange for pleading guilty to the charges and agreeing to give up her animals, she was given two years' probation and banned from breeding or selling dogs or cats again. She was allowed to keep five personal pets, however, and the first fifty people to adopt her animals had to pay $100 each to help Meuser offset the loss of future income. The upside was that, as a result of the deal, the case was resolved in four days and the dogs were spared from waiting weeks or months to be adopted out to new homes.

A similar outcome occurred in March 2007, when eighty-three Golden Retrievers with bite and scratch marks, some with chains embedded in their necks, were seized from a puppy mill in Bismarck, North Dakota. The breeder voluntarily forfeited the forty-six adult dogs, but a Minnesota rescue group, Retrieve a Golden, had to pay more than $5,000 for the thirty-seven puppies. Treating the dogs' medical problems was expected to cost the organization another $25,000.

Two months later, 171 dogs were rescued from a puppy mill in south-central Nebraska. Pomeranian mixes, Terrier mixes, Yorkshire Terriers, and other small dogs were confined to small buildings and surrounded by excrement and trash, with little water; they suffered from dehydration, parasites, and skin infections. The owner agreed to give up the animals, and, in turn, the county attorney agreed not to prosecute her so that the dogs could be adopted out to new homes.

The following January, 150 Labradoodles were discovered languishing with no food, water, or bedding in a puppy mill in Lamartine, Wisconsin. The 69-year-old breeder had a track record of neglect, and the Wisconsin Puppy Mill Project, a statewide organization, offered to help rescue the dogs. But the Fond du Lac County Sheriff's office opted against filing charges against the kennel operator—and even permitted her to move the dogs eighty-eight miles away to the town of Kenosha.

DOG AUCTIONS WERE another sordid aspect of the puppy mill trade. Auctions sprang up in the mid-1990s as a way for breeders to either sell off dozens of dogs of a single breed, dump all of their breeding dogs so that they could start fresh, or sell their entire stock and get out of the business.

The format is similar to that of a livestock auction. Dogs are brought into a seller's ring in an auction barn and sold to the highest bidder, usually to other kennel operators looking to augment their breeding stock. The HSUS investigated dog auctions in Ohio, Kansas, Arkansas, and Oklahoma and found hundreds of dogs deprived of food and water while they waited to be sold, housed for hours on end in cages so tiny they could neither sit upright nor lie down comfortably. Depending on their age and ability to produce, the dogs were priced at anywhere from $1 to $1,000. Even animals with obvious genetic defects were auctioned off.

Dog auctions are common in Missouri, Iowa, Nebraska, Ohio, and Wisconsin, too. At a typical auction, roughly 250 dogs change hands. A dog's ability to produce litters is the biggest selling point. Auctioneers think nothing of exposing a pregnant dog's belly to show bidders they'll be getting a whole litter of dogs with their purchase. The *Kansas City Star* described a 2008 auction in Missouri, where a Dachshund sat shivering on a table while the auctioneer talked her up. "She's young. She's an '07 model," he said. "She's ready to work."

In Missouri alone, an estimated 18,000 dogs were sold at auction in 2007. The Buckeye Dog Auction in Ohio, though, is the biggest in the country. Dog auctions are illegal in Pennsylvania, so many of the breeders in that state buy and sell dogs at the roving Buckeye auction. Puppy mills have begun sprouting in Geauga and Holmes Counties, where the auction takes place. By 2007, the two counties, whose combined population is 130,000, had nearly 600 kennels.

PET STORES ALSO came into the crosshairs of puppy mill opponents. A third of America's 11,500 pet stores sell as many as 400,000 puppies a year, all told, and animal welfare groups estimate that 90 percent of them come from puppy mills.

In June 2007, the HSUS filed a class action lawsuit against the Wizard of Claws pet store in Broward County, Florida. The suit claimed the store misled customers into believing the puppies they'd purchased had come from reputable breeders. In fact, the dogs were the products of decrepit kennels, and a number of the animals suffered health problems and genetic flaws. The litigation actually began on a smaller scale four years earlier with a handful of disgruntled customers, but the HSUS helped unearth more than 250 victims. The lawsuit said the store's veterinarian had signed health certificates allowing the sale of sick puppies. When customers confronted store personnel, they refused to reimburse them the purchase price of the dogs or their veterinary bills, which in some cases came to thousands of dollars.

That same year, the HSUS released a video report on a pet boutique in Los Angeles called Pets of Bel Air. Investigators visited five of the twenty-eight commercial breeders in the Midwest that supplied puppies to the store. All five were large-volume operations housing 100 to 300 dogs. Puppies frequently arrived at the stores ill or diseased.

On tape, the manager and employees of the pet shop could be heard openly discussing how to play down a puppy's illness when customers were around. "Never say the dog is sick. Ever, ever, ever, ever," one employee cautioned. "Never say 'sick,' 'parvo,' 'distemper.' Never. I usually say 'sniffles.' It sounds cuter."

Other animal welfare groups pressured pet stores to stop selling dogs from puppy mills. Last Chance for Animals succeeded in shutting down four Posh Puppy stores in Los Angeles that were selling dogs produced in puppy mills. The group persuaded the new owner of another store, OrangeBone, to stop selling puppy mill dogs and offer rescue and shelter dogs instead. Best Friends Animal Society launched a similar campaign against the Pet Love pet store in Beverly Hills. The owners bowed to the criticism and announced they would terminate their lease the following month.

In 2008, the HSUS waged a major campaign against the practices of the Petland chain. The HSUS tracked puppies sold in twenty-one Petland stores across the country to thirty-five breeders who kept their dogs in squalid conditions, with little care or socialization. In contrast to Petland's assurance that it dealt only with kennels that practiced "the highest standards of pet care," state and federal inspection records found that more than 60 percent of the breeders selling to Petland had been cited for failing to provide basic care. Petland denounced the claims as "sensationalism at its best."

It's easy to see why pet stores want to sell dogs and cats. A purebred puppy purchased from a broker for $300 can be sold for three or four times that amount. Pet sales alone often generate 20 percent of a store's revenue. But by the close of 2008, some pet stores began turning to the more politically correct practice of offering homeless animals instead. Customers could adopt a dog or cat and then turn around and buy hundreds of dollars' worth of supplies from the store—a win-win scenario.

RAIDS ON PROBLEM kennels continued into 2008. In eastern Oregon, rescuers seized more than sixty dogs who'd been abandoned three weeks earlier. In Stoughton, Massachusetts, authorities removed ninety Yorkshire Terriers, Cockapoos, and other dogs squeezed into a single house. In Henagar, Alabama, nearly seventy dogs were taken from a kennel so toxic workers were advised to don protective gear. In Jay, Oklahoma, enforcers removed more than 100 dogs who had gone without food for six days. In DeKalb County, Alabama, 131 dogs were seized. In Wenatchee, Washington, forty-seven Husky puppies were rescued; they were being sold on the Internet as part of a "Christian outreach." In the Florida Keys, workers carried out forty-six dogs found locked in a warehouse. In Dexter, Wisconsin, workers removed eighty-four dogs from the kennel of a repeat offender. In Georgia, rescuers found 182 Chihuahuas,

Yorkies, Shih Tzu, Pugs, and Poodles with bald spots, open sores, and severe ear and eye infections.

Communities were often caught off guard when dogs confined to hidden kennels suddenly surfaced in need of care. After Georgia closed a puppy mill, L&D Farm and Kennel in Jackson County, in February 2008, animal control officers seized more than 300 malnourished and mange-ridden dogs and farmed them out to a dozen area shelters. A month later, 750 dogs, mostly Chihuahuas, were removed from a triple-wide trailer in Pima County, Arizona. The Humane Society of Southern Arizona estimated it would cost $400,000 to rescue and treat the dogs. Two months later, fifty-four Dachshunds needed to be placed when authorities closed a puppy mill in Rockport, Texas.

While animal welfare groups were stepping up their vigilance, the country's preeminent dog registry, the American Kennel Club, faced criticism for failing to do more to address problems in puppy mills. The organization rarely suspended breeders for poor standards of care, but instead tried to help them comply with its standards—seldom checking back, critics said, to see if any improvements were actually made.

To its credit, the AKC started a program in 2000 to better ensure the parentage of dogs in its registry. Any male dog who sired seven or more litters in a lifetime or more than three litters in a calendar year had to be DNA-tested, along with the puppies, to verify their parentage. The test involves swabbing the cheeks of the dogs.

A number of commercial breeders resisted the move. Unwilling to go along with the new requirements, members of the sizable Missouri Pet Breeders association boycotted the AKC and began registering their dogs with a little-known group based in Arkansas called the American Pet Registry, Inc. Like the American Canine Association, the American Purebred Registry, the North American Purebred Dog Registry, and two dozen similar groups, the American

Pet Registry offered dog breeders an alternative form of registration that sounded impressive but required no proof of parentage. From 1999 to 2006, AKC registrations fell by nearly 250,000.

The AKC said it inspects annually breeders who produce more than twenty-five litters a year, and kennel operators who produce seven to twenty-four litters a year are inspected every eighteen months. The organization also conducts random inspections of kennels that are subjects of written, signed complaints, spokeswoman Lisa Peterson said. An AKC inspector's main job is to check records and make certain the puppies' parents are purebred and that all record-keeping is accurate. Inspectors also look to make sure dogs have adequate food, water, and shelter and that their kennels are appropriately built and not overcrowded.

The organization lacks regulatory authority, but its board of directors can suspend or revoke a breeder's AKC privileges and forward information about poorly run kennels to officials who do have the power to shut down a kennel. Breeders convicted of animal cruelty are suspended from the AKC for ten years and fined $2,000, or fifteen years and $3,000 if the circumstances warrant it. Breeders like Michael Wolf are suspended permanently, meaning they can never again register a dog with the AKC.

When the AKC formed a High-Volume Breeders Committee in 2001 and invited Gretchen Bernardi to serve on it, she was delighted. Bernardi was steeped in credentials: an Irish Wolfhound breeder, she is an exhibitor, an AKC judge, and an AKC delegate representing the Mississippi Valley Kennel Club, the oldest kennel club west of the Mississippi. She belongs to the Illinois Livestock Commission and writes a column for *Canine Chronicle* magazine. She had long believed something needed to be done to rein in puppy mills.

Over the course of a year, the committee came up with several suggestions. It recommended that the AKC increase inspection and investigation staff and budget more money to inspect all high-volume breeders at least once a year; that it expand pet store inspections; that it develop a rapid-response plan to deal with high-volume kennels whose operators had become ill and were no longer able to take care of their dogs; that it build a closer relationship with regulatory agencies; and that it start a speakers bureau to talk about registration procedures and policies involving care and condition of dogs. The panel suggested setting a five-year goal of having DNA on file for every parent dog in the AKC registry. Finally, it recommended establishing a dialogue with high-volume breeders.

The AKC did expand its presence at pet stores and auctions, and it lowered the number of litters that could prompt a possible inspection. It required that all AKC-registered dogs sold at auction be at least 8 weeks old and microchipped.

But the method by which the AKC established a dialogue with high-volume breeders made Bernardi wince. The organization became a platinum corporate sponsor of an educational conference sponsored by the Montana Pet Breeders, the same group that had boycotted the registry. Gone, suddenly, from the AKC website was its warning to avoid buying puppies from pet stores. The organization offered limited-time-only discount registration coupons, a move critics said was targeted at attracting high-volume breeders. In 2006, the AKC even signed a deal with the Petland chain offering to preregister some of the puppies sold through Petland stores. The AKC quickly backed out of the agreement following an outcry from responsible breeders.

Bernardi was disappointed when the heart of the suggestions put forth by the High-Volume Breeders Committee were ignored. "I always thought that if people like me who go to dog shows and care for dogs only knew how bad conditions were in many puppy mills, they would rise up," she said. "But I have found in the last ten years after registrations have gone down—and told by people at the AKC that we have to have [high-volume breeders] to survive—how quick they were to adjust their values."

Despite AKC policy, Bernardi said, records showed that some of the most problematic kennels went two years without an inspection. Peterson said registration privileges of problem kennels can be put on hold until the deficiencies are corrected. If they're not corrected, the AKC's board of directors may suspend the breeder. The organization's goal is to treat all breeders equally, regardless of the size of their kennel, the spokeswoman said. "We do not believe that intentionally excluding large numbers of purebred dogs from these AKC requirements is doing a service to the dog or to the pet-buying public," Peterson said. She said refusing to register puppies from certain breeders would not discourage breeding, it would only mean fewer breeders were inspected.

ACROSS THE COUNTRY, Americans have reached out to puppy mill survivors, no matter how daunting the odds. Breed rescue groups nurture sick and injured dogs and help them find new homes. Among the twenty dogs the Elmbrook Humane Society rescued from a kennel in western Wisconsin in 2007 was a 3-year-old Poodle they named China who was missing two of her legs. Her mother had chewed them off, a sign of stress commonly manifested in puppy mills. In a matter of months, officials had fashioned a custom-fitted cart that enabled China to scoot around happily, and a local resident stepped forward to adopt her.

At dog auctions, ardent animal lovers show up with enough money to outbid breeders on at least a few of the dogs. The salvaged dogs are taken to rescue groups, which work to find them new homes. Rescuing dogs at auctions is somewhat controversial: Critics say it enables kennel operators to make money off of their worn-out breeding dogs and creates openings in kennels that must be filled by still more breeding dogs. But rescuers feel they are giving deprived dogs a well-deserved chance at a decent life.

At an estate-sale auction of a Georgia breeder in 2006, the Chattanooga-based Humane Educational Society spent $20,000 buying dogs who might otherwise have gone to other puppy mills. The next year, Helen Hamilton, a veterinarian from the San Francisco Bay area, drove to a kennel liquidation auction in Arkansas with $9,000, enough to rescue more than a few breeding dogs. Of the 300 Pugs, Dachshunds, Boston Terriers, Pekingese, Scottish Terriers, Yorkies, and Cairn Terriers for sale, she bought sixty-nine. Two of the dogs were 11 years old and still producing puppies. Awaiting them back home was Loree Levy-Schwartz, chairwoman of the American Shih-Tzu Club and the Golden Gate Shih-Tzu Fanciers, who had offered to help find homes for as many Yorkies as Hamilton could deliver.

"You know, you're never going to save them all," Levy-Schwartz told a newspaper. "But . . . it's one dog at a time. To me, it's worth it."

When Wallace Haven, the owner of Puppy Haven Kennels north of Madison, Wisconsin, decided to go out of business in 2008, the Wisconsin Humane Society swooped in. Haven sold roughly 3,000 designer-breed puppies a year—Puggles, Peekapoos, and dozens more hybrids—and boasted that he had dog breeding down to a science. His animals had food and water and access to small indoor kennels, but no beds to sleep on and no toys.

To keep him from selling off his remaining dogs to other breeders, the Wisconsin group did something unprecedented: It bought the dogs—1,600 of them by the time several litters were born—at a steep discount. The dogs were so unsocialized that to prepare them for adoption, volunteers sat on stools and read to them until they became accustomed to the sound of human voices. The kennels at the rescue shelter automatically dispensed treats any time a person walked by in hopes that the dogs would learn to associate human beings with something good. When the time came to adopt the dogs out, a number of area pet stores allowed rescue groups to display the animals in their shops. Six months later, all of the dogs had new homes.

By mid-2009, the HSUS had a staff of six devoted exclusively to fighting puppy mills. A task force was formed to help law enforcers process cases, especially in communities that found themselves overwhelmed at the prospect of caring for hundreds of rescued animals.

Shain takes part in puppy mill rescues whenever she gets the chance. In the spring of 2009, she helped other rescuers remove more than 350 matted Shetland Sheepdogs, Shih Tzu, Poodles, and other dogs who had been squirreled away in a series of ramshackle buildings in the hilly countryside around Paris, Arkansas. One animal in particular stood out: a dignified-looking Akita who'd been confined alone to a fenced-in outdoor cement pad connecting two of the barns. At the end of the day, after the other dogs had been removed, a worker slipped a leash-collar around the Akita's neck and began to lead him toward safety. The dog did just fine until he reached the edge of the cement. Then he stopped. He refused to go any farther. It finally dawned on rescuers that he was blind. Despite years of deprivation, the dog was afraid to venture into the unknown.

Workers finally coaxed him out and, once he was freed from puppy mill life, the Akita surprised everyone. He was sweet and loving—so much so that the first shelter that cared for him named him Gentle Ben. An Akita rescue group in New York State took him in next, and not long after that, Shain received a photo in the mail of Gentle Ben posing happily alongside his new owner. The mellow countenance of the big dog is what she remembers most about that raid.

"It's so sad to see dogs in those conditions," she said, "but it's so wonderful to be able to take them out."

20

Two Lives Changed

L INDA WAS ACTING nonchalant, but Erika and Julia could tell something was up. She'd told them, "I have to run an errand out to Frystown. Why don't you come with me?" But it was clear the girls didn't really have a choice in the matter. When they quizzed their mother for details, she refused to say anything more.

It was Christmas Eve 2007. The house was decorated, the presents were already under the tree, and the girls couldn't imagine what would necessitate this last-minute trip. For the duration of the thirteen-mile drive, Linda was conspiratorially silent. Gracie was along for the ride, although there was nothing unusual about that. The girls' brother, Ryan, was bagging groceries at Weis Market; if he wasn't, he would have been dragged along, too.

On an isolated stretch of the highway, Linda turned in to a driveway and pulled up next to a car plastered with Cavalier King Charles Spaniel stickers. Erika immediately put two and two together.

"Oh my God, are you serious?" she said. "Are we getting another dog?"

Linda kept up her silence. But just as Erika suspected, the sound of barking dogs from a nearby building greeted them as they walked down a brick path by the side of the house. A woman stepped onto the back porch and invited them into her kitchen, where a handful of Cavaliers were milling about.

Linda finally admitted the obvious: "I was thinking we could get another dog." She seemed to have one in particular in mind, the dog she was kneeling by—a tricolor Cavalier with especially curly hair.

A second dog could work, the girls agreed. The family cat, Kitty, had died of a respiratory infection right after Thanksgiving. Having another Cavalier around might be fun—even more fun if it was the chestnut and white puppy chasing a ball in the corner.

"Why can't we get a puppy?" Erika wanted to know. She thought but didn't say, "instead of an old dog who isn't even potty-trained."

But the decision had already been made. A short time later, Linda and the girls were headed home with Gracie in the front seat and the new dog, Jackie, nestled between Erika and Julia in the back. The irony of the moment wasn't lost on Linda: Here she was, the same woman who two years ago had given away the family's Yorkie and sworn off dogs for good, inviting a new dog into her life—to go with the *other* dog she'd vowed never to get. Yet if she really thought about it, the turn of events made perfect sense.

Ever since she adopted Gracie in the summer of 2006, Linda could not stop thinking about the plight of puppy mill dogs like her. An image would flash through her mind, fleeting but memorable, of thousands of breeding dogs trapped in deplorable cages, destined to produce puppies until their bodies were ravaged and their spirits destroyed. By happenstance, Gracie had escaped her fate. Most puppy mill dogs weren't so fortunate.

A year and a half had passed since Gracie had begun her new life. Emotionally she was transformed, thoroughly acclimated to living with a family. She was loving and sweet-natured, almost serene at times, as if somehow she'd been able to erase the memories of those first six years. Her bond with Linda was closer than ever. The only thing missing was a canine companion—not just for Gracie, but for Julia, too. Julia still yearned for a dog of her own. Gracie clung so steadfastly to Linda that the kids felt a little left out. There was a time when Linda would have preferred a puppy over an older dog. But what better solution than to give another breeding dog the chance to be just a pet?

She began combing Cavalier rescue sites on the Internet, but none of the groups responded to her inquiries. Then a stylist at her hair salon overheard her talking one day and told her about a Cavalier kennel in Frystown. The owner had a breeding dog she was looking to get rid of, the stylist said. She insisted the kennel was not a puppy mill.

Linda contacted the woman. The dog she had for sale was three years old and had produced three litters. The woman did not intend to breed her again. They haggled over a price. The breeder wanted $800; Linda countered with $500. The breeder asked if Linda had a fenced-in yard—her dogs were accustomed to running freely outside, she said. Linda's yard wasn't fenced, but the new dog would have a playmate in Gracie. And she agreed to sign papers promising to have the dog spayed. They agreed on the terms.

Jackie resembled Gracie physically, but she was bigger—twenty-two pounds to Gracie's sixteen. Her coat was a bit whiter and her tail fanned out into a gorgeous plume. And her personality could not have been more different. She was a daredevil, always nosing open the back door and ducking out. More times than Linda liked, she had to chase Jackie down the block in her pajamas. Inside, Jackie scampered through the house, tipping over trash cans. While Gracie liked to plant herself in Linda's lap during car rides, Jackie thrust her head out the window, eager to take in the sights. Gracie had mastered the rules of potty training in a matter of months, but Jackie never did seem to get the hang of it.

Early on, when Gracie growled at Jackie out of jealousy, Linda wondered if she'd made a mistake trying to introduce a second dog. But in a matter of weeks the Cavaliers warmed up to each other. To keep Jackie from marking territory all over the house, Linda crated her whenever she was out. Jackie didn't mind the confinement. She seemed to actually like the den-like feel of the crate.

Before long, to Linda's surprise, Gracie began climbing into the crate with Jackie. The two dogs curled up together and slept side by side. When they weren't napping they were playing. Jackie was more assertive, the ringleader: If she grabbed a mouthful of grass from the yard, so did Gracie. If Jackie lay on her stomach and spread her back legs out as if she was bodysurfing, Gracie imitated her. On Linda's bed, the two dogs would go at each other, jumping back and forth in mock combat. Linda had never seen Gracie act so lively. She was glad to see her focused on something other than herself.

Between the two pets, one thing was understood: Linda belonged to Gracie and no one else. If Jackie slept on Linda's bed, she was relegated to the foot of it. Gracie alone claimed the coveted spot next to Linda's pillow.

Anxious to be with Linda from the start, Gracie grew more so as time passed. Where once she relished going on errands in the car, she now grew frantic if Linda left the car to get a cup of coffee or to run into the grocery store—even if Erika and Julia stayed behind to keep her company. One afternoon when Linda dropped Erika off at a friend's house and got out of the car for just a moment, Gracie panicked and hurled herself out the open window. She wasn't injured by the fall, but Linda decided the car rides were becoming too traumatic. She began leaving Gracie at home.

The Cavalier's eyesight exacerbated matters. Gracie's vision, poor to start with when Linda adopted her, had worsened over time. Now she was practically blind. No longer able to see Linda, she went in search of her constantly. Gracie had committed to memory the floor plan of the family's house, but if she was any-where unfamiliar, she was in trouble. At the family's beach house in

Ocean City, New Jersey, she was completely disoriented; she constantly ran into furniture and doorways. At home, when Linda let Gracie outside to use the bathroom, the dog often had trouble finding her way back—she would run in circles until she heard Linda's voice. One wintry afternoon, when Linda's back was turned, Gracie toppled headfirst into the goldfish pond at the edge of the patio. Linda quickly fished her out, but it disturbed her to see Gracie having so much difficulty.

The Cavalier still suffered from dry eye. At one point her veterinarian, Dr. Kezell, recommended remedying the problem by surgically removing her eyeballs. It seemed too drastic a cure; Linda couldn't bring herself to do it.

Another sign of Gracie's past remained: While Jackie ate her food slowly and patiently, Gracie inhaled hers—as if her kibble would be taken away if she didn't consume it fast enough. She never learned to eat at a leisurely pace.

Although her eyesight worsened, Gracie was still able to enjoy life.

Despite her problems, Gracie was happy, and she had become far more sociable than she once was. Linda noticed this especially with her cycling buddies, the friends she got together with most weekends for long bike rides on country roads outside of town. For months, when her friends pedaled into the driveway on Saturday mornings, Gracie stuck by Linda's side; she wanted nothing to do with the interlopers. In time, though, she let down her guard. If one or another of the cyclists called to Gracie, she would venture toward them. She would even stand still next to them and let them reach down and pet her.

IN JUNE 2007, a fire swept through a dog kennel in a nearby town, killing eighteen Pugs and French Bulldogs, just hours after an official had investigated conditions there. The fire looked suspicious. Upset by the surprise inspection, the breeder had threatened to have the dogs put down rather than clean up the kennel. For the first time in memory, Linda was compelled to go public with her feelings.

"Like many, I was horrified after reading the story about the kennel fire in Bethel Township," she wrote in a letter to the editor of the *Lebanon Daily News*. "The owners should be prosecuted to the fullest extent of the law. Kudos to Gov. Ed Rendell, a true animal lover, for recognizing that the proliferation of exploitation and animal abuse in Pennsylvania requires swift and arduous punishment.

"As an owner of one of the infamous Chester 300 (300 animals rescued last year in Chester County, Pa.)," she wrote, "I have seen the lasting effects of an animal held captive in a puppy mill for her entire first years of life. When I see her stumble into objects because her vision has been greatly impaired from scar tissue and disease, or see her struggling to chew food because her teeth had to be extracted because of neglect, I can't fathom how humans can be so heartless."

She ended the letter with a word of advice.

"When considering pet ownership, please do your homework," Linda wrote. "The Internet is a powerful means of marketing and selling animals bred in puppy mills. These breeders offer below-market prices and will even ship the animal to you. Purchase only from reputable breeders, and better yet, consider adoption.

"Let's put an end to puppy mills in Pennsylvania."

Her cycling friends teased her about her conversion into an animal lover. "They're thinking: Where did this come from?" she said. Linda laughed along with them. "Yeah, I'll be one of those eccentric old women living in a house with fifty dogs. Me and all the dogs."

THE YEAR 2008 was full of change. In February, fourteen months after going to work for Team Pennsylvania, Linda switched jobs again. Her new position was development director for Luther Care, a non-profit continuing care retirement community that operated three nursing home–assisted living centers as well as a couple of large childcare programs. The new job meant a little more money, it was closer to home and, best of all, it involved little to no travel. Still, any work-related change entailed a degree of stress. Linda was just settling into her new position when, after being together for six years, she and Eric split up. They reconciled in April, but by the end of May they were separated again. "I think my life is too complicated for him," Linda said.

She struggled to get over the breakup. At 47, she was blond, blue-eyed, and fit and could easily pass for someone ten years younger. Yet she wondered if she was getting past the point of finding a meaningful relationship. She had the kids, of course; they were talented and good-looking and she was crazy about them. But at 17, 14, and 11, they were also a handful.

For all her challenges, Gracie offered the sense of grounding Linda needed. There was something about the dog's unfailing loyalty, her complete and unreserved focus that Linda found comforting. Did it stem from gratitude? She had no way of knowing. She sometimes wondered if Gracie hadn't survived such hellish conditions whether she would be the devoted dog she had become.

Linda's friend Jennifer was amazed at how faithfully Gracie would sit at Linda's feet, gazing up at her in utter adoration. "Enjoy her while you can," Jennifer told her. "She's your once-in-a-lifetime pet." Jennifer had developed a close bond with her own pet, a Siamese cat named Kirbie. When Kirbie got hit by a car and died, Jennifer was overcome with grief. Linda knew that if something happened to Gracie, she would be equally devastated.

By the end of summer 2008, Linda and Eric were back together and her personal life regained some stability. And on a completely different level, thanks to Gracie she found herself concerned about animals in ways she'd never been before.

She thought twice about the silver fox coat that hung in her closet and the suffering that had taken place needlessly to produce this bit of frivolous luxury. On bike rides outside Lebanon, she fretted over the black-and-white calves who stood, tied outside Dogloos, dotting the farms they passed. The vulnerable-looking calves had been taken from their mothers early; they were isolated and were being fed a diet of milk. In a matter of weeks they would be slaughtered and turned into veal. From a distance they reminded Linda of her Cavaliers, and seeing them began to upset her.

She donated money to the Berks County Animal Rescue League, a small thank-you for having cared for Gracie those first few months after the raid. And she became a dues-paying member of the HSUS. When the organization issued an appeal to stop the practice of dragging ill or injured "downer" cattle to slaughter, Linda wrote her member of Congress asking for his support.

Her concern over puppy mills deepened. She began following the efforts of the Rendell administration to overhaul the state's dog law. She wasn't annoyed when she heard people complain that the Rendell administration was putting animals' rights ahead of humans'; there was a time when she might have agreed with them.

From left to right: Erika, Julia, Ryan, and Linda Jackson with Jackie, Molly, and Gracie. From one Cavalier to three.

But no longer. For the first time in her life, she felt it was important to have compassion for all creatures. "People who care about animals care about all living things, really," she said. "That doesn't diminish the importance of other people."

She wondered why Pennsylvania's dog breeders, even the responsible ones, balked at the proposed reforms instead of joining the effort to weed out the reckless breeders. "They're all worried about it—they're *all* worried about it," she said, "and it makes me wonder if they're not maybe just walking the fine line there."

She cautioned friends and acquaintances who were thinking about buying a dog at a pet store about the perils of doing so. "Maybe you might want to rescue a dog," she suggested.

In January 2009, thirteen months after purchasing Jackie, Linda returned to the breeder in Frystown to buy a third retired breeding dog, a seven-year-old black and tan Cavalier named Molly. The circle was now complete. Julia had Jackie. Erika and Ryan had Molly. And Linda had Gracie.

Blind, needy, now nine years old, Gracie wasn't destined for greatness. She would never capture the top prize at Westminster or save a child who had fallen down a well.

Nevertheless, she had accomplished something. She had survived a puppy mill. She had learned to trust in people, to love and be loved. And in her own humble way, she had helped focus attention on the plight of the hundreds of thousands of dogs like her.

At the end of a workday, when Linda walked through the door and announced, "Hi girls, I'm home," Gracie ran toward her with absolute joy. That alone seemed a small miracle.

Epilogue

PENNSYLVANIA'S ENACTMENT of a tougher dog law had a ripple effect nationwide. Before passing its reform bill, the state had a reputation for lawlessness when it came to dog breeding. "You could break the rules all you wanted and you were not going to get in trouble," Stephanie Shain of the Humane Society of the United States said. The new message was, "If they can do it in Pennsylvania, there's hope."

Overhauling the federal Animal Welfare Act would be the most uniform way to tackle puppy mills, but activists have had better luck at the state level. Nebraska and Rhode Island addressed dog breeding in 2007, the year before Pennsylvania's breakthrough. In 2008, the same year Pennsylvania revamped its dog law, legislators in Louisiana, Virginia, and Maine passed new statutes. In 2009, Arizona, Connecticut, Indiana, Oregon, Tennessee, and Washington voted in new standards for kennel operators. By 2010, fifteen states had passed puppy mill laws.

Before Pennsylvania's law passed, Bob Baker, the dean of puppy mill investigators, had urged animal welfare advocates in Missouri, the country's largest puppy mill state, to lobby for a stronger law there as well. But the activists were so demoralized by their failed attempts in the past that they dismissed his suggestions. In the wake of Pennsylvania's success, they invited Baker back to hear again what he had to say. This time they were galvanized. In the fall of 2010, with help from the Humane Society of the United States, the animal welfare community convinced Missouri voters to pass a ballot initiative designed to limit the size of kennels and curb the abuses that had been so rampant.

Pennsylvania officials continued their cleanup efforts. On June 23, 2009, Pennsylvania's Dog Law bureau seized 216 dogs from Almost Heaven and closed the kennel, pulling the plug on one of the state's worst operators. A year earlier, the Pennsylvania SPCA had found up to 800 dogs and other animals living in squalid conditions just two months after the kennel passed a state inspection. A day after the June 23 raid, the Pennsylvania SPCA removed another 22 sick and injured cats and other animals the state had not been authorized to rescue. (State officials were allowed to remove dogs only.) The Dog Law bureau was able to shut Almost Heaven down permanently after the owner, Derbe "Skip" Eckhart, failed to meet the deadline for appealing the denial of his 2009 kennel license.

The state Department of Agriculture fired Richard Martrich, the dog warden supervisor for the southeast region of the state, where Almost Heaven, Michael Wolf's Mike-Mar Kennel, and a host of other problem breeders were located. The state Board of Veterinary Medicine suspended the license of Tom Stevenson, the veterinarian for Michael Wolf, Joyce Stoltzfus, and a number of other large-volume breeders, after he was charged with animal cruelty. An undercover investigator with the Pennsylvania SPCA said she saw him place the tail of a nine-week-old Poodle-mix puppy under scalding water and amputate it without anesthesia.

In 2009, Governor Ed Rendell signed into law a bill banning tail-docking of dogs five days or older, debarking of dogs, and cesarean sections on dogs unless they are performed by a licensed veterinarian and under anesthesia. Puppy mill operators had been known to practice all three procedures on their own, with nothing to relieve the dogs' pain.

Pennsylvania's crackdown had a chilling effect on breeders. By 2010, two-thirds of the state's large-volume operators had gone out of business.

Following their convictions on animal cruelty charges, Wolf, Gordon Trottier, and Margaret Hills were suspended for life from the American Kennel Club, which also fined them $5,000 each. In December 2006, they were found to be in violation of their probation after SPCA humane society police officer Cheryl Shaw and others conducted a surprise inspection of Wolf's property and found two kittens, a cat, dog food, and dog feces. None of the defendants was jailed as a result of the violation, but all three were forbidden to own or keep animals for fifteen years.

In 2007, Wolf put his Lower Oxford property up for sale and moved to nearby Christiana. He bought land in South Carolina and by 2009 was believed to have relocated there with Trottier. No one knew for certain his whereabouts. The Chester County probation office said only that Wolf was no longer required to report in.

Bill Smith of Main Line Animal Rescue began urging a boycott of organic dairy operations run by farmers who had puppy mills on the side. Several breeders who also supplied milk to Horizon Organics shut down their dog kennels entirely to avoid repercussions for their milk sales.

Smith's puppy mill rescue dog, Shrimp, died in the spring of 2009, and Smith grieved the loss. Shrimp's story had spread across the globe; a week before he died, the dog received a fan letter from a child in Sudan.

Pam Bair pampered Jolie, her adopted Cavalier, for two years until Jolie developed heart problems and had to be euthanized on

June 29, 2008. Pam became involved with a Cavalier King Charles rescue program and has since adopted two more rescued Cavaliers.

In Chester County, Shaw continued her work nabbing suspected animal abusers. Assistant District Attorney Lori Finnegan became the go-to prosecutor when it came to animal cruelty; she handled more than thirty cases before leaving the D.A.'s office in 2009 to practice law privately. She continues to prosecute animal abuse cases pro bono.

Gracie spent four years with Linda Jackson's family until she suffered complications from an inoperable tumor in her throat. She was euthanized at her home on October 21, 2010. The story of her rescue touched the lives of thousands of readers, many of whom were unaware of the atrocities of large-volume commercial dog breeding. "Puppy mills need to be regulated. Puppy mills need to be overseen. But more than that, puppy mills need to be closed down and done away with," one reader, Jeannie Rogers, wrote.

Acknowledgments

Saving Gracie is more than a book about a dog. It's the story of a cast of characters who stepped up to help rescue a damaged dog—and of the people who rescue thousands of dogs like Gracie.

Topping the list is Linda Jackson, a woman who had not sought publicity but who graciously allowed me into her life to chronicle Gracie's transformation as well as her own change in attitude. She opened her home and her heart, and her children, Ryan, Erika, and Julia, cooperated, too. That was priceless.

Humane society police officer Cheryl Shaw and the rest of the staff of the Chester County Society for the Prevention of Cruelty to Animals were more than willing to dredge up the minute details necessary to describe the raid of Michael Wolf's kennel and the aftermath. Susie Spackman, Chuck McDevitt, Jill Green Roxbury, Mike Beswick, Craig Baxter, and Becky Turnbull were enormously helpful.

At the Berks County Animal Rescue League, CEO Harry Brown took time from his crowded schedule to talk about his work. Pam Bair was a delight to spend time with; her compassion for animals spilled over into every conversation we had.

Chester County assistant District Attorneys Lori Finnegan and Kate Wright provided me a transcript of the court proceedings against Michael Wolf, which was hugely helpful, and patiently answered round after round of questions.

Puppy mill experts Bob Baker and Libby Williams shared a wealth of historical background on large-volume dog breeding. Bob has more firsthand experience than anyone when it comes to investigating reckless breeders, and Libby is a one-woman clearinghouse of information. They provided much-needed perspective about the epidemic growth of the industry.

I thank Laura and Mike Hewitt, Alycia Meldon, and Susan Krewatch for sharing the stories of their Cavalier King Charles Spaniels; they are consummate animal lovers, all. Gretchen Bernardi and Lisa Peterson helped me understand the American Kennel Club's role in the debate over large-volume breeders. The Humane Society of the United States' Stephanie Shain was most cooperative in sharing information and photos.

None of this would have been necessary, of course, if my agent, Jeff Kleinman, hadn't seen the potential in a book about a puppy mill rescue. His unbridled enthusiasm kept me stoked, and his unerring eye helped mold the framework of the book. I couldn't have asked for a better guide through the byzantine world of book publishing.

My editor at Howell Book House, Pam Mourouzis, had the foresight to recognize a story that needed to be told. She was a pleasure to work with. Development editor Beth Adelman brought a broad base of knowledge and a surgeon's skill to bear with her questions, suggestions, and gentle carving of my words. Her bedside manner was superb. Wiley & Son's Amy Sell, Malati Chavali, and Adrienne Fontaine worked behind the scenes to market and publicize the book.

I counted on a stable of writer friends for commiseration and support as I struggled to make the transition from newspaper reporting to tackling an entire book. Rochelle Sharpe was there from the beginning; she helped me examine every tea leaf along the way. Deb Pines helped me resurrect the beat-notes system we'd used many moons ago at the Gannett Westchester Newspapers in New York. Roni Rabin edited the manuscript with care and expertise. My parents, George and Irene Bradley, were there for me, and my brother, Jeff, and sister, Brooke, cheered me on all the way.

In Great Falls, I thank a host of other friends who knew when to ask how the book was going and when to change the subject. Their support meant more than they realize. I'm grateful to Ralph Beltrone and Brad Opheim for transforming the slope-ceilinged attic of our 1916 house into a cozy writer's loft—the perfect place to hole up on a wintry Montana afternoon. (The pups like it, too.)

The biggest shout-out goes to my husband, Steve L'Heureux, whose steadfast love and encouragement enabled me to keep my eye on the prize. He was there for me all the way, and I can't thank him enough.

Appendix

Finding the Right Dog

You can avoid doing business with a puppy mill. Here are a few tips to keep in mind.

- Good breeders have nothing to hide. Don't let one talk you into meeting at some halfway point to sell you a puppy. Breeders should be happy to show you their kennel, where both the adults and the puppies are kept. Ask to stand in the doorway if the kennel operator doesn't want you inside the building. All of the dogs should be clean and healthy looking and protected from the elements.

- Good breeders will test the parent dogs for hereditary diseases before breeding them. They will advise you on the health issues particular to the breed.

- Good breeders will have a dog's registration papers ready when you pick up the dog. Their records will be complete and well organized.

- Good breeders will provide documents outlining the vaccinations and any deworming the puppy has been given and what further shots or medicine the puppy needs.

- Make sure you understand the health guarantee and return policy. Breeders should offer a two- or three-week guarantee on contagious diseases, longer for congenital or other defects. Breeders whose guarantees expire after a few days are bad news. Be sure to have your puppy checked out by a veterinarian within forty-eight hours after you take the dog home.

- Good breeders know a great deal about the breed, are willing to share that information, and encourage you to ask questions.

- Good breeders will want to check *you* out before selling you a puppy. They will ask how long you're home during the day, whether you have a fenced-in yard for the puppy to play in, and what if any experience you've had with dogs. They'll insist that if for any reason you have to give up the dog, you'll bring it back to them.

- Good breeders don't work with a multitude of different breeds, nor do they advertise puppies for Christmas or other holidays.

- If you buy a puppy, charge the purchase to a credit card. If problems surface later, you can ask your credit card company to withhold payment.

- Avoid buying dogs at pet stores that do business with large-volume breeders, where dogs are kept in crates and are given almost no socialization and sometimes very little veterinary care.

- Beware of wonderful-looking websites filled with photos of adorable puppies. Some of the worst puppy mills have professional-looking sites full of false reassurances about their dogs. Breeders who sell animals on the Internet do not have to comply with the federal Animal Welfare Act and don't have to be inspected by the U.S. Department of Agriculture. Check the breeder's name on the Internet to see if any complaints pop up.

- Consider adopting a dog from an animal shelter or a breed rescue group. One in four dogs in shelters is a purebred. Regardless of whether they are purebred or mixed, many dogs housed in shelters are healthy, loving animals just waiting for the right family to take them home.

If You Do Buy a Dog on the Internet

There are numerous websites that advertise dogs for sale. Before you buy:

- Ask for references and follow up with them.
- Find out if the puppy pictured on the website is the same puppy you are buying. If not, have the breeder e-mail you a photo of the puppy and photos of the facility where the dogs are kept.
- Ask the person you're dealing with if he or she is the breeder or is working for a commission. If other people are breeding the dogs, get their names and contact them.
- Never buy a puppy until he or she is at least 8 weeks old.
- If the puppy is being flown to you, ask the breeder if the puppy has been given supplements recommended by a veterinarian to better withstand the flight.
- Find out whether the breeder is a member of an AKC-affiliated club and, if so, contact the club to make certain the breeder is in good standing.

- Beware of breeders who register their pups with registries that offer no means of verifying parentage or weeding out bad apples.
- Have an online escrow service withhold part of the fee until your puppy arrives and can be examined by a veterinarian.

Adopting a Puppy Mill Dog

All dogs deserve a good life, but dogs who have spent years in puppy mills come with special issues you may or may not be prepared to handle. Many of these dogs have never lived inside and are difficult, if not impossible, to housetrain. A lack of socialization may prevent them from bonding well with a new family, and they will need time to overcome their fear of ordinary noises and activities that normal dogs take for granted.

A rescued puppy mill dog may suffer tremendous separation anxiety from his or her rescuer and become destructive when the owner leaves. Puppy mill dogs are also more apt to have medical problems that may not become apparent until they have settled in to their new lives. Before adopting a puppy mill dog, have a clear understanding of the challenges that may lie ahead.

Reporting Bad Breeders

Here's what to do if you suspect or know for a fact that dogs in a particular kennel are being abused or neglected.

- Write a first-person account of your findings and send them to:

  Your county dog warden or humane society

  Your state consumer affairs office or Better Business Bureau

  Your county's department of health and your state department of agriculture

- Check online to see whether the breeder is licensed with the federal government and, if so, get a report of the latest inspection. At www.aphis.usda.gov, click on "FOIA Reading Room," "inspections reports," "inspection reports" again, and finally "breeder" to find a state-by-state list of licensed kennel operators.

- Contact the AKC's Investigations and Inspections division at:

  AKC Compliance Department

  8051 Arco Corporate Drive

  Suite 100

  Raleigh, NC 27617-3390

  (919) 233-9767

- Contact your state legislators and ask them to crack down on puppy mills in your state. The USDA website (www.usda.gov/wps/portal/usdahome) can provide you with a list of federally licensed breeders in your state, but be aware that many breeders are not licensed.

Notes

The primary sources for this book were interviews and correspondence with the author.

Several dozen on-the-record interviews and a number of off-the-record interviews and background conversations were conducted. Many of the on-the-record interviews were recorded, and most sources were interviewed more than once. Some of the principal characters were interviewed more than half a dozen times. Much of the book's dialogue and direct quotes are the result of multiple interviews and recordings. Participants and witnesses to conversations were asked to provide their best recollection of what was said. Photographs were used to convey conditions and background scenery.

The secondary sources for the book include articles, court records and transcripts, legal opinions and court decisions, press releases, and other reference materials. The Humane Society of the

United States, the American Society for the Prevention of Cruelty to Animals, and the American Kennel Club were among the sources of information used. Biographical information on Michael Wolf came, in part, from *The Pekingese* by Anna Katherine Nicholas (TFH, 1990). Some of the advice on working with puppy mill survivors came from Kim Townsend (NoPuppyMills.com) and Michelle Bender's (ANewStartOnLife.com) paper "Rehabilitation of a Puppy Mill Dog" (2009).

Several news organizations covered the raid of Michael Wolf's kennel as well as the court hearing, and many more covered various aspects of the campaign to overhaul Pennsylvania's dog law. The *Philadelphia Inquirer* and the *Allentown Morning Call* deserve special mention for their comprehensive coverage of the puppy mill issue. Facts and events were verified where possible; otherwise, the author relied on the newspapers' accuracy and on multiple accounts of events.

Photo Credits

Index

Aguirre, Orlando, 183
Alice, John, 74, 90–91, 98
Almost Heaven kennel, 186–187, 217
American Anti-Vivisection Society, 189
American Kennel Club (AKC)
  DNA testing, 200, 202
  High-Volume Breeders Committee,
    201–202
  inspection of Mike-Mar Kennel, 21
  Menaker's comments on breeders, 75
  Pennsylvania puppy mills and, 148
  registration certification, 20–21
  registration of dogs by, 20–21, 147,
    200–203
  support for Pet Animal Welfare
    Statute, 191
  suspension of breeders, 21–22, 201,
    203, 218
  suspension of Michael Wolf, 21–22
  volume of registrations, 21, 201
American Pet Registry, 200–201
American Society for the Prevention of
    Cruelty to Animals (ASPCA), 149,
    156, 173, 218
Amish farmers, puppy mills and, 139,
    148, 150, 153–154, 158, 175, 182
animal cruelty
  charges as summary offenses, 70
  convictions, 92, 195, 201, 218
  enforcement in Pennsylvania, 154,
    156, 157, 159
  guilty plea by Wolf, 97
  hotline, 173
Animal Rescue League of Berks County,
    49, 54–67, 101, 213
Animal Welfare Act, 191, 216, 218

Applebrook Inn Pet Resort, 43, 45, 49, 89

Arkansas, puppy mills in, 148, 190–191, 194, 204–205

auctions, dog, 196–197, 202, 203–204

Bair, Pam
  adoption of Jolie, 129–132, 219
  adoption of Paulie, 219
  care of dogs at Animal Rescue League, 54–61, 63–66, 102–104
  photograph, 108

Baker, Robert O.
  Canine Health Board regulations, 187
  on Dog Law Bureau, 173, 183
  investigations of puppy mills, 145–151, 155, 173, 217–218
  on legal loopholes, 178–179
  photograph, 152
  on Rendell's ad hoc committee, 149–151, 155, 159

Barrett, Christopher, 176

Bastian, Bob, 180

Baxter, Craig, 30, 32, 39–42, 44–45

Bear Track Acres, 160–161

Bender, Michelle, 135

Bernardi, Gretchen, 201–203

Beswick, Michele, 38
  raid of Mike-Mar Kennel, 30–31, 33–36, 38–39, 43–44
  at Rendell's press conference, 156
  at Wolf's trial, 87–88

Blank, John, 182

Brandt, Ken, 158–159

breeders. *See also* puppy mills; *specific individuals*
  AKC registrations, 20–22
  AKC suspension of, 21–22, 201, 203
  auction sales by, 196–197

Internet sales by, 192, 212
  license revocation, 172, 178, 187
  relationships with dog wardens, 154, 160–161
  response to regulations in Pennsylvania, 157–159
  use of brokers by, 155, 192

breeding stock, fate of dogs selected as, 4–6

broker, 155, 192

Brooks, Gene, 32

Brown, Harry D. III, 59, 101

Buckeye Dog Auction, 197

Bucks County SPCA, 49, 189

Burkholder, Aaron, 160

California, puppy mills in, 190, 194

Canine Health Board, 185, 187

Carroll, Jennifer, 73

Carroll, Joe, 71, 95

Casorio, James, 179

CC Pets, 181

cesarian sections, 218

Charlie, James, 36

Chester County Society for the Prevention of Cruelty to Animals
  adoption of rescued dogs, 100–102
  care of rescued dogs, 99–100
  cost of Mike-Mar case to, 101
  investigation of Mike-Mar Kennel (2000), 20
  Mike-Mar Kennel reported to, 7–8
  planning for raid of Mike-Mar Kennel, 25–30
  raid of Mike-Mar Kennel, 30–36
  restitution payment to, 92, 97

Coates, Eric, 74, 77–79, 83–86, 90–91, 93, 141

Companion Animal Protection
    Society, 149

Danby, Jennifer, 89
debarking, 129–130, 177–178, 218
Delaware County SPCA, 43, 44, 49
Delaware Humane Society, 49
Delaware State SPCA, 43, 49, 89
Dieter, Larry, 52–53, 72, 85
Dluhy, Amy, 156, 157
DNA testing, 200, 202
Docktors Pet Center, 149
Dog 132. *See* Gracie (Dog 132, Wilma)
Dog Law, Pennsylvania
  Almost Heaven kennel and, 187
  enforcement of, 159–160
  original (1982), 148, 154, 159
  reform of, 150–151, 158–160,
      176–181, 183, 185–186, 216–217
Dog Law Advisory Board, 151,
    155–156, 158, 173–174, 186
Dog Law Bureau, 19–20, 52, 151,
    154–155, 160, 172–174, 181–182
dog shows, Michael Wolf and, 14–17, 19
dog wardens, Pennsylvania, 154, 156,
    157, 159–160, 173, 178, 187
Donwen Kennel, 19

Eckhart, Derbe "Skip," 187, 217
Elmbrook Humane Society, 203
Engler, Gwen, 61–64, 66
Esh, Daniel and John, 173
euthanasia, 186, 194

factory farming, 3
Farmer, Harry, Jr., 30, 76, 80, 83, 91–93
Federation of Humane Societies, 148
Finnegan, Ed, 69

Finnegan, Lorraine Marie Belfiglio, 70
  appeal by defendants, 92–98
  career history, 69
  current activities, 219
  preparation for trial, 70–74, 74–75
  search warrant for Mike-Mar Kennel,
      28–29, 36
  visits to SPCA, 68–70, 73
  Wolf's trial, 77–79, 80–90
Fontana, Pattie, 187
F.U.E.L. Collection art gallery, 176–177

Gardener, Nancy, 186
Georgia, puppy mills in, 199–200, 204
Gracie (Dog 132, Wilma)
  adoption of, 110–114
  bathing of, 62–64
  at Berks County Animal Rescue
      League, 55–56, 59–67, 102–104
  health problems of, 61, 119, 125–126,
      209–210
  Humane Society of Berks County, 49
  introduction to new home, 115–118
  Jackie and, 209
  life with the Jacksons, 120–128,
      162–171, 207–213, 215
  medical care of, 102–103
  naming as Gracie, 117
  naming as Wilma, 65
  rescue from Mike-Mar Kennel, 41–42
Green, Jill
  meeting with Wolf after raid, 47–48
  planning for raid of Mike-Mar
      Kennel, 25
  raid of Mike-Mar Kennel, 39, 40, 42–43
  on Wolf's personality, 51
  at Wolf's trial, 88–89
Greenlaw, David, 160–161

Griffith, Edward, 94–97
grooming, of dogs from Mike-Mar
    Kennel, 61–64

Hamilton, Helen, 204
Harper, Dave, 32
Harrisburg Area Humane Society, 156
Haven, Wallace, 204
health problems, of dogs from Mike-
    Mar Kennel, 39, 52–53, 61, 72,
    82–86, 142–144
Hershey, Art, 180
Hewitt, Mike and Laura, 129, 137–143
Hickory Springs Farm Boarding
    Kennels, 49
High, Elvin, 172
Hill, Lisa, 64–65
Hills, Margaret
    animal cruelty charges against, 52
    appeal of case and settlement, 93–97
    defense of, 90, 91
    initial verdict against, 92
    during kennel inspection (2006), 12
    partnership with Wolf, 19
    at Shaw's visit to kennel (2000), 20
    SPCA raid of kennel, 33–35
    suspension and fines by AKC, 218
hoarder, 51
Horton, Junior, 194–195
housetraining, 66, 125, 132, 135, 166, 208
Humane Educational Society, 204
Humane Farming Association, 149
Humane League of Lancaster County,
    49, 72, 84, 160, 173, 187
Humane Society of Berks County, 49
Humane Society of Southern
    Arizona, 200

Humane Society of the United States
    (HSUS)
    campaign against Docktors Pet
        Center, 149
    dog auction investigations, 197
    Linda Jackson and, 213
    pet store investigations, 198–199, 218
    puppy mill investigations, 145–149,
        189–190, 205
Hunte Corporation, 192

Iannuzzi, Charles, 74, 76, 78, 90
Internet, sale of dogs on, 4, 22–24,
    51–52, 192–193, 199, 212
Iowa, puppy mills in, 148, 191

Jackson, Erika, 214
    Gracie and, 116–118, 120, 122, 124,
        126, 162–164, 166, 171
    Jackie and, 206–207
    Molly and, 213
    Spike and, 105
Jackson, Julia, 171, 214
    desire for a dog, 106, 171
    Gracie and, 116–118, 120, 124, 126,
        162–163, 171
    Jackie and, 206–208, 215
    Spike and, 105
Jackson, Linda, 127, 168, 214
    adoption and life with Jackie, 206–210
    adoption of Dog 132 (Gracie), 110–114
    adoption of Molly, 214–215
    animal advocacy and, 211–214
    decision to adopt a dog, 106–114
    introducing dog to home and
        children, 115–119
    letter in *Lebanon Daily News*, 211–212

life with Gracie, 120–128, 162–171,
207–213, 215, 219
Yorkshire Terrier puppy and, 105
Jackson, Ryan, 214
Gracie and, 116, 118, 120, 126,
162–163, 165, 167, 171
Jackie and, 206
Molly and, 213
Spike and, 105
Jeffords, Kay, 15–17
Jeffords, Walter, 15

Kansas, puppy mills in, 147, 149, 191
Karen's Pet Shop, 168
Keith, Dotsie, 148
Kesselman, Jillian, 177
Kessler, Kim, 165
Kezell, Robert, 118–119, 126, 210
Krewatch, Susan, 129, 138, 143–144

Lambert, Sandy, 61, 64, 103
Lancaster County's United Against
Puppy Mills, 184
L&D Farm and Kennel, 200
Langlois, Bryan, 72, 84–85
Last Chance for Animals, 198
Levy-Schwartz, Loree, 204
Limestone Kennel, 182
Ling, Lisa, 175
Long Lane Kennel, 160

Main Line Animal Rescue, 170,
174–175, 179, 182, 184, 194
mange, 142–143
Martrich, Richard, 182, 217
McDevitt, Chuck
on adoption of dogs, 100
on deal possibility with Wolf, 93

raid of Mike-Mar Kennel, 25, 27,
30–31, 35, 43–44
on verdict against Mike-Mar Kennel, 93
McGlory, Katie, 54–56
McMichael, Dennis
meeting with Finnegan, 69
raid of Mike-Mar Kennel, 25, 28, 30,
35, 44
Meldon, Alycia, 129, 132–137
Menaker, Ron, 75
Menkin, Cori, 161
Mennonite farmers, puppy mills and,
148, 150, 158, 178
Messaros, Crystal, 22, 50
Meuser, Irene, 195–196
Mickelson, Margaret "Peggy," 75–76
Mike-Mar Kennel
AKC inspection (2004), 21
case preparation for trial by prosecu-
tion, 70–74
citation of (2002), 20
complaints from neighbors, 22
establishment of, 17–18
inspection of February 8, 2006, 8–13
Internet sites for sale of dogs, 22–24
investigation by SPCA (2000), 20
license revocation (2002), 20
Rendell's response to raid, 155–157
SPCA raid on, 30–36
trial, 76–79, 80–91
Millcreek Puppy Barn Kennel, 172
Miller, Cynthia, 159
Miller, John B., 172
Missouri, puppy mills and auctions in,
146–147, 175, 191–192, 194, 197
Missouri Pet Breeders, 200
Montana Pet Breeders, 202
Montgomery County SPCA, 49

Murarka, Ravinda, 72, 82–84
Murray, Liz, 30

Nebraska, puppy mills in, 191, 196
Nelson, Howard, 182, 187
New Jersey Consumers Against Pet
    Shop Abuse, 149, 151, 181, 184
Nicolini, Suzette, 89
North, Verna, 160–161
North Penn Puppy Mill Watch, 184

Ohio, puppy mills and auctions in, 191,
    194, 197
Oklahoma, puppy mills in, 148,
    190–192, 199
OrangeBone pet store, 198
Oregon, puppy mills in, 194, 199

Pacelle, Wayne, 189–190, 195
Paladina, Jeffery, 157, 173
Parkman, Amy, 72
Pearlie's House of Pomeranians, 190
Pennsylvania
    puppy lemon law, 150–151,
        154–155, 158
    puppy mills in, 139, 146, 148–161,
        172–185, 191, 217–218
Pennsylvania Federation of Dog Clubs,
    148, 158
Pennsylvania Professional Dog Breeders
    Association, 148
Pennsylvania SPCA, 43, 44, 49, 72,
    82–84, 173, 182, 186–187, 217–218
Pennsylvania Veterinary Medical
    Association, 179
Perelmen, Marsha, 151, 152
Pet Animal Welfare Statute, 191
Peterson, Lisa, 201, 203

Petland pet stores, 199, 202, 218
Pet Love pet store, 198
Pets of Bel Air, 198
pet stores
    adoption of animals from, 199
    AKC inspections, 201–202
    dog sales by, 3, 147, 151, 197–199
    HSUS investigations, 149, 198–199
Pine Bluff Kennel, 188
Posh Puppy pet store, 198
Professional Dog Breeders
    Association, 179
puppy lemon law, Pennsylvania,
    150–151, 154–155, 158, 192
Puppy Love Kennel, 29–30, 181
puppy mills
    dog auctions, 196–197
    exposure on Oprah Winfrey show,
        175–176
    growth in number of, 191–193
    HSUS campaign against, 189–194
    life of a caged dog, 1–6
    Midwest, 146–148
    number of puppies born in, 193
    Pennsylvania, 139, 146, 148–161,
        172–185, 217–218
    pet stores and, 197–199
    prosecution of, 172–173, 178, 179, 181
    raids on, 182, 186–187, 190, 194–196,
        199–200, 217
    Richard, 145–151, 155
    shooting of dogs by, 183–184
    William's investigations of, 151–154
    registration of dogs, 20–21, 200–203
Rendell, Ed
    appointments, 150–151, 156–158, 173
    dog law reform, 149–150, 155–159,
        161, 176–177, 179, 186, 213

Dog Law signing ceremony, 186
Linda Jackson and, 170
press conference on dog killings, 185
press conference on dog law, 156–157
Rendell, Marjorie, 150, 170
rescue groups, 203–205
Retrieve a Golden, 196
Rickards, Tom, 51
Robers, Rebecca, 156
Rudy, Alison, 54–55
Ryder, Chris, 187

Santorum, Rick, 191
search warrant, 28–30, 35–36, 76–77, 79
separation anxiety, 168
Shain, Stephanie, 188–190, 192–194,
    205, 216
Shaw, Bobby, 26, 37–38, 45, 100
Shaw, Chauna, 26
Shaw, Cheryl, 27
  agreement with Wolf, 79, 85–86
  care of rescued dogs, 99–100
  current activities, 219
  evidence against Wolf, 51–52
  inspection of Mike-Mar Kennel
      (February 8, 2006), 8–13
  inspection of Wolf's property
      (December 2006), 218
  meeting with Finnegan, 69
  meeting with Wolf after raid, 47–48
  personal history, 12–13
  planning for kennel raid, 25–30
  preparation for trial, 73–74
  raid of Mike-Mar Kennel, 30–36
  at Rendell's press conference, 156
  videotape of kennel, 71, 81–82
  visit to Mike-Mar Kennel (2000), 20
  at Wolf's trial, 78–79, 81–82, 85–86, 97

Shaw, Kevin, 26
Siddons, Maureen, 8–13, 29–30, 77–78,
    80–81, 182
Smith, Bill, 174–176, 179, 219
Smith, Jessie, 156–157, 181, 182
Spackman, Susie
  meeting with Finnegan, 69
  raid of Mike-Mar Kennel, 25–26, 44
  settlement with Mike-Mar, 95, 96
Stephan, Robert, 149
Stephens, Jenny, 184
Stevenson, Tom, 12, 78, 86, 217
Stidham, Harvey, 51
Stoltzfus, Joyce, 29–30, 181
summary offense, 70
Summers, Kathleen, 190

tail-docking, 218
Tennessee, puppy mills in, 188, 194,
    195–196
Texas, puppy mills in, 194, 200
Thielz, Sandra, 156
Townsend, Kim, 135
trial, of Mike-Mar Kennel defendants
  appeal and settlement, 93–98
  day one, 76–79, 80–86
  day two, 87–91
  preparation by defense, 74
  preparation by prosecution, 70–74
  verdict, 92–93
Trottier, Gordon
  appeal of case and settlement, 93–97
  charges against, 52
  initial verdict against, 92
  during inspection of kennel, 12
  Internet sale of dogs by, 22–24
  partnership with Wolf, 19
  SPCA raid of kennel, 35

Trottier, Gordon *(continued)*
  suspension and fines by AKC, 218
  threatening behavior after raid, 48
Trottier, Wendy, 19, 50, 76
Turnbull, Becky, 8, 13, 25, 51, 69,
  141–142
Twin Valley Veterinary Clinic, 12

U.S. Department of Agriculture
  (USDA), 147, 190–194

Veltri, Carl, 61, 67, 102
Virginia, puppy mills in, 194–195

Walter, Eric, 118, 122, 165–166, 168,
  212, 213
West, Sue, 173
West Chester Veterinary Center, 44, 72
Williams, Kimberly, 89–90
Williams, Libby, 149, 151–154, 181, 184
Winfrey, Oprah, 175–176
Wisconsin, puppy mills in, 196, 199, 204
Wisconsin Humane Society, 204
Wisconsin Puppy Mill Project, 196
Wizard of Claws pet store, 198
Wolf, Chad, 19
Wolf, Michael. *See also* Mike-Mar Kennel
  appeal of case and settlement, 93–98
  appearance at dog shows in 1980s, 19
  charges against, 52
  comments after hearing, 91
  defense strategy, 74
  dog show successes of, 14–17, 19

establishment of Mike-Mar Kennel,
  17–18
Hewitts' dealings with, 137–141
initial verdict against, 92
inspection of kennel (2006), 8–13
Internet sale of dogs by, 22–24
interview in *Kennel Review*, 18–19
kennel license revocation (2002), 20
Krewatch's dealings with, 143–144
meeting with Shaw and Green, 47–48
partnership with Kay Jeffords, 16–17
Pekingese show dogs and, 14–17
post-trial comments by, 97–98
public relations statements by, 49–50
relocation to South Carolina, 218
SPCA raid of kennel, 31–34, 42–43
suspension by AKC (2004), 21–22,
  201, 218
Wolf, Michael, Jr., 19
Wood, Sandy, 136
Worden, Amy, 160, 183
Wright, Kate
  appeal by Mike-Mar 94–96
  personal experiences with dogs, 71–72
  preparation for trial, 72–75
  Wolf's trial, 80, 84, 87, 91

Yaron, Jennifer, 177

Zevnik, Ann, 50
Zimmerman, Ammon, 183
Zimmerman, Elmer, 183, 184
Zimmerman, Ervin, 178, 187

About the Author

Carol Bradley grew up in Kingsport, Tennessee. She spent twenty-six years as a newspaper reporter, covering state legislatures in Tennessee and New York and the U.S. Congress in Washington D.C., and writing features and investigative stories in Montana. She studied animal law as a 2004 Nieman Fellow at Harvard University and became interested in puppy mills after covering a case involving 180 Collies crammed inside a tractor trailer.

She now lives in Great Falls, Montana, where she is married to an architect, Steve L'Heureux, and has three grown stepchildren. She is a member of the Institutional Animal Care and Use Committee of McLaughin Research Institute in Great Falls, serves on the local Historic Preservation Advisory Commission, and sings in the Great Falls Symphonic Choir. When she's not writing, she's scoping out old houses, checking out the local blues scene, cheering on Pat Summitt and her University of Tennessee Lady Vols, and playing with her two dogs.